News, Crime and Culture

Maggie Wykes

Pluto  Press

LONDON • STERLING, VIRGINIA

First published 2001 by Pluto Press
345 Archway Road, London N6 5AA
and 22883 Quicksilver Drive,
Sterling, VA 20166–2012, USA

www.plutobooks.com

British Library Cataloguing in Publication Data
A catalogue record for this book is available from
the British Library

Library of Congress Cataloging in Publication Data
Wykes, Maggie, 1951–
    News, crime and culture / Maggie Wykes.
        p.   cm.
    Includes bibliographical references (p.).
    ISBN 0–7453–1331–0
    1. Crime and the press. 2. Journalism—Social aspects.
    I. Title.
    PN4784.C88W95   2000
    070.4'49364—dc21   99–37924
                                                                 CIP

ISBN 0 7453 1331 0 hardback
ISBN 0 7453 1326 4 paperback

10 09 08 07 06 05 04 03 02 01
10 9 8 7 6 5 4 3 2 1

Designed and produced for Pluto Press by
Chase Publishing Services, Sidmouth, EX10 9QG
Typeset from disk by Stanford DTP Services, Northampton
Printed in the European Union by Antony Rowe, Chippenham, England

Contents

Introduction

Crime news mobilises the extremes of value judgements: it is about good and bad, innocent and guilty, heroes and villains, victims and abusers. It is the site of our national conscience and moral codes. *News, Crime and Culture* examines accounts of crime in relation to broader societal relations and the norms and values that reproduce and sustain them; relations and values which for most of the last twenty years of the twentieth century have existed in a culture of political conservatism. The continuum of criminality is explored as a measure, mediated through the news, which informs our view of our world, of others and of ourselves.

Content

News, Crime and Culture is based on research in a range of areas, which took place over ten years. For the most part data was collected contemporaneous with the actual events; sometimes analysis was also immediate, at other times I went back to my cuttings and tapes at a later date to produce a lecture or write a conference paper. Crime news was collected neither systematically nor with any intention of ever producing a book so my collection is eclectic, sometimes haphazard and very specific to my own interests. In spring of 1996 parts of the various components were brought together as a module on the MPhil in Criminology at the University of Cambridge; in spring 1998 a revised version was taught to MA students in the Department of Criminology at Keele. Aspects are currently used on undergraduate and postgraduate modules in the Department of Journalism at the University of Sheffield but its grounding in contemporary politics and social relations place the content comfortably also in the disciplines of politics and sociology, particularly in areas focusing on class, gender or race.

The methods used reflect changes in my own perspective but always focus closely on language: the earlier work is more structured, quantified and formal; the later more discursive and interpretative. Some analysis was done systematically at the time of the reported events, other analysis was originally (as I found when I started this

1

book) not much more than a collection of notes and thoughts and is therefore more retrospective.

I have drawn from a wide range of academic work but several texts in particular have been inspiring and invaluable. *Policing the Crisis: Mugging, the State, Law and Order* (1978) by S. Hall, C. Critcher, T. Jefferson and J. Clarke (a collection of contributions discussing the mugging phenomenon of the late 1970s) and *Law and Order News* (1977) by S. Chibnall (a single-authored close study of crime journalism). More recently, Alison Young's *Femininity in Dissent* (1990) and *Imagining Crime* (1996) offered feminist, subjective and post-modern accounts of the media and deviance, in both instances in order to critique criminology. Various texts focus on news language, incidentally considering crime or conflict: R. Fowler *Language in the News* (1991); R. Fowler, G. Kress, R. Hodge and T. Trew *Language and Control* (1979); N. Fairclough *Media Discourse* (1995). For support for discourse theory Foucault remains indispensable and I greatly value Stuart Hall's *Representation: Cultural Representations and Signifying Practices* (1997). But some of these texts pre-date Thatcherism and others only tangentially acknowledge the importance of crime news, so I wrote this book simply because I was surprised that no one else had. Despite the consistent references to the role of the media and a glut of theoretical books, particularly recently around issues of media globalisation and new technology, there is real lack of topic-focused or empirically-supported analyses. Nor as far as I know has anyone overviewed retrospectively the content of any topic/genre of mass media during Thatcherism.

Organisation

The chapters are organised as chronologically accurately as possible and I have tried to let original analysis stand the test of time, but in some cases retrospective review has tempted me to interject some updated comments and references. Each chapter could be read and was written as a discreet piece. Only in post-Thatcherism did I begin to see the patterns and consistencies between what were in many ways very different topics of crime news. So this is a loose collection and incomplete, linked by my interest in language, journalism and crime, but finally, this a political book.

Chapter 1 reviews contemporary crime and explains my focus on crime news. It investigates criminal statistics, fear of crime, popular culture, issues of criminal justice, moral panics and policy. It argues that criminology has systematically failed in the project of understanding and explaining crime in any way that might reduce it – in fact much evidence suggests that crime has grown alongside the academic discipline of criminology. The chapter calls for a transgression of criminology in work on crime and argues that such a transgression must consider issues of discourse and power as normalising and legitimating norms and values, which concurrently render abnormal and illegitimate 'other' actions and attitudes. Such a focus necessarily mobilises research on news as the source of information about issues that audiences may not experience personally.

Chapter 2 relates to Stuart Hall's reference to black communities in the inner cities of Britain as evidencing a 'criminalised protopolitical consciousness'. Largely excluded from the working-class politics of the post-war period by racism, and then by racism and unemployment during the late 1970s and 1980s, black British communities struggled to 'find a voice'. During the street violence of the early 1980s the British press provided an account on their behalf – an account which dredged up the old racist stereotypes and subtly reshaped them for the 1980s with embellishments of terrorism and crime. This chapter explores that construction of criminalised black consciousness as the institutionalisation of freelance racism through the media and the police.

Chapter 3 addresses the role of the press in deconstructing the British working class. It looks at the representation during the 1980s and 1990s of two examples of activity traditionally associated with the working class – industrial strikes and football. It argues that the law and language were invoked to control the miners in 1984 and 1985 whilst commercial pressures and the construction of the hooligan have begun to move the support base of football from working-class men standing on the open terraces to families and couples seated at much expense in new covered stands, and global audiences watching from home or pub/club on subscription television. In both instances the media directly and/or indirectly has served a wider agenda of political-economic activity directed towards the control through degradation, dissipation and exploitation of a politically resistant, cohesive working class and the concurrent promotion of new marketplaces for capital in the leisure and media industries of the twenty-first century.

Chapter 4 explores the panic about undisciplined youth. The chapter focuses on areas of popular youth culture that border on the illegal/deviant. It includes discussions of new age travellers, environmental protests, raves, joy-riding and drugs. The chapter revisits some of the seminal work on subcultures undertaken by analysts like Cohen (1973) on Mods and Rockers in order to interrogate more recent 'post' approaches to youth culture which tend to focus on consumption and pleasure and leave unaddressed the continuing and consistent criminalisation of young people in Britain – a process readily mediated through the news media. The chapter argues that most public domain youth-crime discourses are complicit with the reinstatement of traditional models of family and community.

Chapter 5 uses the topic of homelessness to raise issues about representations of difference/deviance. Again, youth, were foregrounded in the media accounts during the Conservative period. An Englishman's home may be his castle but how is the concept of home used to discriminate between valuable and invalid models of living? How has home-ownership become the marker of respectability and what are the implications of being homeless? The chapter looks at media images of the homeless which prefer explanations linked to crime and deviant behaviour to those linked to poverty or lack of decent affordable housing. It asks why journalists so systematically label homeless people as at best feckless, sometimes immoral and often criminal, and suggests that such news reports are effectively constructing a new criminal collective. The chapter shows how the process holds discussion around homelessness within a criminological accounting agenda effectively precluding the kinds of debates around the economics of homelessness that campaigning groups like Shelter would prefer.

Chapter 6 focuses on violence between men and women and its depiction in relation to broader gender norms and values, with particular reference to issues of justice for women and the broad impact of media representations of women criminals. It offers a systematic analysis of news about intimate killing to try to redress the constant references to the role of representation in the construction of gender roles and the commensurate lack of empirical evidence for those references. It argues that for the Conservatives the reconstruction of gender was central to their moral and political project.

Chapter 7 addresses the fact that the conservatism of the last two decades of the twentieth century has been evident not only in news about public life and collective behaviour but also in debates about private issues around sexuality and family. This chapter argues that sex has been a site of reconstructive discourses where anything 'outside' of traditional, respectable, monogamous, familial hetero-sexuality was subject to a back-to-basics critique. The news about gay sexuality has been dominated by AIDS and in the UK gay parenting, sado-masochism and the age of consent debates also provided a forum for journalists to promote sexual conservatism often against a backdrop not of morality but of health and welfare. That conserv-ative effort consistently reproduced arguments about the effect of representations of sexuality, especially anything other than 'normal' sexuality in the ongoing panic about pornography. The chapter argues that many of these issues link to the increasing reification of the traditional family during Thatcherism and beyond against an ever more revealing backdrop of realised violence which is very often in some sense familial – domestic violence, battered wives who kill, child sexual abuse, infanticide, violent children and rape. It argues that the media systematically reinforces conservative family models by diverting the blame for family violence on to other areas such as feminism, the media and homosexuality. Missing from the discourses is a critique of family life and most specifically any critique of the role of husbands and fathers in the enactment of family violence.

Chapter 8 draws together the analysis and theory presented in the book and seeks to relate the issues of news, crime and culture to the broader discourse of politics, specifically to the shifts generated by Thatcherism informing consensus, centralisation and conservatism. It suggests that news-making through its affiliation to crime has contributed to the creation of a criminalising culture, often presenting information in a crimino-legal context which might be more appropriate to debates on economics and politics.

Like others, I think 'news accounts of matters which are of intense concern in contemporary life: inequality, discrimination, inhumanity' (Fowler 1991: 9) are important whether they merely reflect and publicise existing perspectives and attitudes or actively create them. Studying the press retrospectively in the context of a well documented and analysed political climate and in relation to the development of a society increasingly oriented around crime, fear of crime and law and order has not only confirmed for me the significance of the role of journalism, it has made me realise just how extensively, subtly and systematically representation works on behalf of the already powerful.

Newspapers were my primary data, partly because when I began to collect material it seemed a rather neglected medium; much attention was being paid to broadcast news, for example, by the Glasgow University Media Group, but I also recall being told that there was more information just on the front page of a broadsheet than on the 9 pm BBC1 News. Even today, it seems to me that the press dictates what is to be news: beginning with BBC2's *Newsnight* briefly looking at the next day's front pages and continuing with BBC Radio 4 building their news agenda on the basis of the papers at the start of the day.

I prioritise news texts over audience reception, partly because the whole area of effects seems to be over-hyped, over-researched and yet unresolved but also because it seems more useful, politically, to encourage critical reading than to seek to provide evidence that might support further censorship and regulation. My analysis is retrospective and culturally specific, otherwise it would be prediction and guesswork. I am a British academic and the topics in the book are local topics; the types of news I refer to are created within British journalism; the politics are those which shaped the end of the twentieth century in the UK. Yet, the issues for theory and method cross national and media boundaries and will do so long as the relationship between language, ideology and power remains a site for research.

Nonetheless, towards the end of the 1990s it is clear that any further work on news will have to cross national and media boundaries as we are, increasingly if not equally, integrated into a global journalism electronic network. Only five years ago even the most advanced American intellectual would have been unlikely to have come across the Internet: 'back then the Internet didn't exist as a consumer experience ... You needed serious computer skills to get on to it and then you found a nerd-scape, baffling and dull' (Andrew Marr, *Observer* 2.8.98). By 2000, most major news producers use on-line digests and many journalists depend on the WWW for research and for publication.

A millennial version of this book, considering the first twenty years of the twenty-first century rather than the last twenty of the twentieth, would have to focus on Web journalism sites and stories and offer an account of Net news and the construction (or not) of global culture and global markets. As technology expands access, and standard English becomes the lingua franca of international communication, it may become impossibly difficult to isolate the traditional press from interactive cyber forms, British culture from European, American or Chinese, and nation states from transglobal corporations. Culture is changing as rapidly as electronic technology is binding nations, institutions and individuals into a single (however unstable, exclusive and fragmented) cyber-communications system. The work that is constitutive of this book, the systematic analysis of the news in relation to identifiable power, norms and values, is rapidly becoming both more urgent and less possible for anyone concerned about the role of the media.

1
Criminological Crises

Criminology has systematically failed in the project of understanding and explaining crime in any way that might reduce it – rather the level of popular[1] anxiety about crime seems to suggest that crime has grown alongside the academic discipline of criminology – and for most people the major source of information about crime is mass media news. This chapter traces the argument that for criminology to develop it must move beyond its traditional boundaries of investigation and consider not just how crime is realised but how it is represented in our culture, why and with what possible consequences.

Criminology

At the end of the twentieth century, crime occupies a central space in popular culture, policy, politics, news and morality. It is the trope about which much of everyday life is lived in either reality or representation (Stanko 1990). It symbolises good and evil, normal and deviant, moral and immoral, saint and witch, insider and outsider, self and other. In academic terms, the initial project of any research should be to define the terms of the investigation. Yet, crime eludes definition. Young (1991) takes particular issue with the paucity of definitions offered by criminologists such as Downes and Rock (1988) who defined crime as 'the breaking of legal rules' and deviance as 'the breaking of any rules'. For Young: 'After the tantalising brevity of this definition, the text plunges into theoretical pluralism and diversity without a backward glance at the addressed problem of naming' (1991: 2).

These apparently simplistic definitions actually open complex issues for understanding crime. Defining crime and deviance clearly depends on interrogating models of 'normal' rules of social interaction in either the legal or the moral order, in order to arrive at what is not normal. This is not a common academic undertaking. Young points out a lack of willingness in what she dubs the cosy world of criminology to engage in self-criticism of its own project that such an investigative impetus would require. Arguably, lack of reflection on the origins of definitions of crime has led to a proliferating body of knowledge on the empirical evidence of crime that has never properly reflected on the substance about which it is exercised. Young explains this lack as relating to a theoretical gap within the modernism and patriarchy that constitute the mainstream/malestream of the discipline.

Mainstream criminological theory remains largely embedded in modernism, dependent on a concept of crime as empirically knowable and objectively mappable. The discipline grew by the process of observing, counting, labelling and theorising, yet all this intellectual and financial effort over the twentieth century appears to have had little impact on resolving the problem at its heart, crime. If anything, public knowledge about crime, popular narratives about crime and the prevalence of fear of crime[2] suggest it is an increasing not decreasing area of activity. Criminology's vague terms of reference, combined uncomfortably with a fascination with cause and effect, has generated both widely disparate agenda and great effort toward totalising explanations. Such broad and complete explanations are popular with both media and public, and with the funding bodies that sustain the research community, because our history of knowledge is highly influenced by scientism and the effort toward establishing proof. Similarly, criminological commitment to empiricism and determinism has injected a synthesis of apparent rationality and objective truth into the crimino-legal discourse that in turn informs both lay and legal publics about the incidence and causes of deviance as if a truth were known. However, of course, if a truth was known the criminological *raison d'être* would cease to exist. As Young argues, 'if criminology were ever to answer its own questions' (1991: 4) about why people commit crime and how they might be stopped, it would signal the end of criminology itself.

Critical Shifts

So, criminology itself is a part of the problem in the understanding of crime, partly because the discipline has a vested interest in maintaining the problem it seeks to resolve but also due to an adherence to mythic modernist narratives wherein a golden crime-free, community-based past has given way to the rampant violence of the contemporary inner city (Young 1991). Interpretations of crime figures perpetuate such myths, encouraging much research into both violence and the city, which then feeds into the cycle of representation. The news systematically reports Home Office crime data, as in:

> Death list grows as violence increases ... there were 728 unlawful killings – murders, manslaughters, infanticides – in England and Wales last year, up by nearly 10% on the previous year. Ten years ago the figure stood at 556. In the last year, there were 12 victims of homicide for every million people. (*Guardian* 4.8.92)

Such journalistic 'news about crime' informs the public, who vote for the politicians. Politicians adopt the policies that prescribe the funding of criminological research that informs the process of law-making and enforcement. Such laws are used to prevent criminal acts, castigate offences and offenders, punish wrongdoers and legitimate the public censure of 'rule-breaking'. Public censure is informed by news about crime.

Media, state and academy have tended to construct crime-narratives interactively around taken-for-granted models of social rules and norms. This is unsurprising in Foucault's (1975) terms, because the history of knowledge about crime is embedded in the construction of discourses of social control. Further, as Nietzsche (1887) implied, those with power and influence judge themselves and their actions to be good, so the values they have the authority to disseminate will be commensurate with their own. In the process those who are different from the dominant group are readily made invisible, lesser or deviant. So, difference, once recognised, becomes the object of study, the problem. Hence there exists a historical lack of criminological attention to white-collar crime and to masculinity – even though this latter variable is apparently, statistically, crim-inogenic[3] – and a tendency for traditional criminological practice to reproduce broader social power relations in its own ideologies.

Victorian criminology marked difference from the dominant norm as the problem, and indicators of difference readily became the object of criminological investigation. Frequently, the focus was on visible, physical indicators of difference that could be linked to the atavism of Darwinian biologism, so influential at the turn of the nineteenth century. White, heterosexual, mature, middle-class masculinity became the unquestioned standard, the evolutionary peak, against which any other human manifestation was measured as always, though variably, more primitive. Lombroso and Ferrero's (1895) focus on forms of biological degeneration as criminogenic created a set of practices and theories that preferred to explain crime as linked to individual pathology. Although technically no longer influential, this approach to crime remains popular with both professionals and the public. For example, explanations in the 1980s and 1990s for the sexual brutality of two serial killers of women, Peter Sutcliffe and Fred West, referred to traumatic head injury as causal of violence but offered little account of why this type of damage might manifest itself specifically in violence against women.

In the later twentieth century, traditional criminology has been consistently criticised for its adherence to biologism and its reluctance to explore social and cultural factors. During the 1970s, Marxist scholars argued that some criminology was effectively replicating and reproducing the interests of dominance. Critical initiatives, informed by the less reductionist Marxism of Gramsci (1971b) and Althusser (1977), argued that social roles and relations are not directly imposed according to economic power but mediated via institutions such as the mass media, law and religion which have relative autonomy from the material base. The exponential growth of the mass media as a source of ideas, the relation of that cultural institution to power and the inherent implications for cultural and political formations were a substantial focus for academic research. Knowledge about deviance, it was argued, depended on the representations of dominant institutions wherein a mutuality of powerful interests ensured that the preferred and legitimated behaviours and views were likely to be conducive with their own. In these terms, breaking the law or flouting social codes and rules could alternatively be seen as an act of political resistance, an assertion of self and difference. Kidd-Hewitt (1995) described this 'new' criminology as based around an agenda concerned with political and sociological issues, within which the mediation of definitions of deviance and its implications for the political subject were foregrounded. The concept of deviancy as constructed, not natural, led to a range of influential work on the media and crime (Taylor, Walton and Young 1973; Cohen 1971, 1973; Cohen and Young 1973; Chibnall 1977; Hall *et al.* 1978). Pre-war models were challenged as bourgeois – middle-class, middle-aged and white – but that challenge in many ways seemed to seek to invert the deviancy model, favouring the values of those previously classified deviant. Although they admirably drew attention to the media as complicit with dominance in the construction of social values, the new criminologists were partially guilty of the same fault as their predecessors. The old school took for granted the class values at the heart of their project;[4] the new school challenged these but left patriarchy in place, so crime was studied as a human phenomenon rather than as an over-whelmingly male behaviour. The effort towards a single explanatory paradigm was shifted from analysing biological propensities to analysing political relations.

Women's low crime profile[5] and criminology's traditional empiricism still supported a dominant focus on the most pervasive and problematic crimes, which were/are overwhelmingly male.[6] Yet, failure to account for gender difference meant that the masculinity at the heart of most of that crime was not problematised, nor was the academic, criminological sexism underwriting these lacks recognised. Consequently, women's offending was ignored, under-researched or subsumed within the grander criminological project – but ironically so was men's.

Feminist Criminology

During the later 1970s, as part of their larger, political project, feminists began to query the position of women in the criminal justice system. Until then, deviant women had tended to be explained by a crude biological reductionism, as either not 'normal' women or not 'men', with both these standards taken for granted as objective truth. The natural state of womanhood was, according to Lombroso and Ferrero (1895), likely to be directed biologically towards passivity, conformity and caring, hence their lesser tendency towards criminality. The inference of such a model was that non-conforming women are subject to conditions, or place themselves in conditions, which are abnormal hence confounding the natural tendency of femininity and unleashing disturbing consequences. Respectable, normal, Victorian womanhood included a range of acceptable roles – virgin, wife, mother, heterosexual. Deviance from these traditional (but still culturally current a century later) expec-tations of femininity inevitably meant women's crime was (and still is) linked to feminine non-conformity – promiscuity, infidelity, childlessness, lesbianism.[7] Alternatively, the nature of femininity itself was seen as sometimes promoting offending behaviour in women (Adler 1981), albeit beyond their control. Women have been (and continue to be) depicted as hysterical, illogical, emotional and often at the mercy of their hormones.[8] There is a kind of double bind in models of traditional femininity in that the sexual and social are often blurred, contradictory and yet mutually dependent definers of deviance. Women who break the rules are often theorised as doing so either because they are 'normal' and therefore 'hysterical' women. Yet, alternatively, their deviance may be explained by their social/sexual 'abnormal' femininity, implied by terms such as careerist, feminist, lesbian or promiscuous, which imply non-traditional female roles and values.

Carol Smart's *Women, Crime and Criminology* (1976) was one of the earliest interrogations of these issues in the still expanding body of critical work broadly constituting feminist criminology. The critique of biologism central to this intervention was complex, not least because some feminists argued that women's biology should allow a special case to be made on their behalf in terms of certain kinds of crime. A range of legal defences and academic arguments has consistently focused on premenstrual syndrome, menopausal crisis and post-partum depression, in many ways continuing Otto Pollak's belief that, for women, the reproductive phases of menstruation, pregnancy and menopause:

> Are frequently accompanied by psychological disturbances, which may upset the need and satisfaction balance of the individual or weaken her internal ambitions, and thus become causative factors in crime. Particularly because of the social meaning attached to them in our culture, the generative phases of women are bound to present many stumbling blocks for the law-abiding behaviour of women. (1950: 157)

Gibbens points out that research in the 1970s apparently showed that 'crimes of violence by women (but not of theft) are significantly concentrated in the paramenstruum' (1981: 117), the time immediately preceding and during menstruation. Wilczynski (1991) found the 'hormone' plea was often brought into arguments for leniency in cases of neonaticide. The argument was that for some women the drama of their experience of their own body chemistry was such as to render them out of control and therefore not responsible for subsequent crime. Diminished responsibility on these grounds has been used to defend women within what was perceived as a criminal justice system unsympathetic to the feminine condition.

The price paid for that defence was the continuation of depictions of women as 'mad' rather than bad, continuing and reinforcing a model of women as frail, fickle and illogical. Biological approaches tended to construct criminal women as victims of their hormones, so reinforcing a model of femininity as subordinate and weak.

Other feminist work also addressed women in the criminal justice system as victims not of their hormones but of crimes, especially sexual crimes. Efforts to gain empathy for women in cases of assault or rape often focused on feminine instability, vulnerability or passive, fearful collusion. Although laudably pro-woman, a negative effect of this politico-academic turn was that focusing on the victim deflected attention from the, usually male, perpetrator. Added to the paucity of studies on male abusers and rapists this created a kind of blaming of women, who became the focus for investigation in the courts in the effort to explain male violence. Detailed sexual and mental histories made such women appear as either frigid (so driving men to rape) or over-provocative (so driving men to rape) or apparently compliant (so driving men to rape). Occasional blame was directed toward men but it accompanied a patholigisation of individual men[9] rather than a critique of the kind of social arrangement where men have so much power that some will inevitably abuse it (Cain 1990).

A powerful, and for feminists disturbing, sideline to the biology debate was that if women went against the grain of their passive, subordinate 'nature', in Lombroso and Ferrero's terms, they would be as likely as men to commit crime. This was taken up with enthusiasm by those anxious about the increasing struggles for women's emancipation. Adler (1975) argued in *Sisters in Crime: The Rise of the New Female Criminal* that the fight for liberation had insidious social implications. 'In the same way as women are demanding equal opportunity in the fields of legitimate endeavour, a similar number of determined women are forcing their way into the world of major crimes' (Adler 1975: 13). It was this kind of assertion that impelled the major feminist initiatives into criminology. It informed the disquiet both with biologism per se and with efforts toward single causal explanations in general. Neither approach was seen as any kind of useful epistemological or methodo-logical tool in work on crime and deviance. Carol Smart's (1976, 1979) critical interjections were twofold: feminism had not signifi-cantly changed most women's lives, and variables, other than reproductive biology – such as class, age, culture, religion – may well significantly affect all kinds of behaviour.

Smart saw the focus on biology as unproductive for understanding women in relation to the criminal justice system, when crime was, and remains, overwhelmingly male. Biologism also failed in any adequate sense to account for all those women who obey the rules, i.e. whose biology is unproblematic in legal terms. Moreover, it depended on and appeared to legitimise the objective, determinist empiricism, traditional to the criminological project, which had appeared not to be working to solve the problem of crime. A double initiative seemed necessary which would redress the lack of work on crime as largely male and query theory which had steadfastly failed to solve the problem of crime. For criminologist Maureen Cain (1990), such a project necessitated a shift into not only feminism and post-modernism but beyond criminology, which she argued was steeped in terminal masculinism. Such a project would be premised on the idea that to explore the differences in criminality, as between male and female offending or offenders and non-offenders, might be more productive of useful knowledge than to continue to seek patterns of similarity. It represented a move towards work on deviance external to criminological epistemology, and cogniscent of gender as a vital variable in terms of knowledge about, and the performance of, crime.

Transgressing Criminology: Towards Inter-disciplinary Research

By focusing on women's crime as qualitatively and quantitatively different to men's, feminists posited crime as varying relative to gender difference. By unhitching women's crime from their sexual biology, feminist post-modernists simultaneously unhitched criminology from totalling and determining explanations. This double, critical shift began to undo the consensus that crime was something universal, objectively recognisable and in reality preventable and controllable. Instead, crime could be seen as relative (not only to gender but to other variables[10]), complex to define and perhaps even impossible to prevent and control in any real sense. Crime's taken for granted status as something out there, that 'we all know about and agree should be censured was drawn', quite profoundly, into question.

Traditional criminology had failed twice in its project, in terms of justice and in terms of knowledge: in terms of justice it doubly castigated the offending woman by measuring her against norms of both maleness and legality; in terms of knowledge its failure to recognise, and critically engage with, such issues promoted false models of crime, methods of investigation and theories of control. Moreover, the arguments put forward by Young about crime and gender could apply equally to other oppressed social groups. Black deviance is arguably also a double crime, against whiteness and against the law. Similarly, gay deviance offends heterosexuality and legal statutes; youth crime simultaneously counters mature culture, and working-class law-breaking is criminal and conflicts with middle-class values. Being different from the dominant profile in Britain, which at its most powerful is white, middle-class, hetero-sexual, mature and male, makes such a citizen already deviant.

Criminological accounts had tended to allow blame to be doubled on an offender from a socially subordinate group whilst leaving the majority of crime under-theorised due to the failure to reflect on masculinity in particular, but also on the relation of dominance, more broadly, to deviance. Impelled by feminism, 'post' critiques that questioned both modernism and structuralism could expose criminology as peddling as truth a biased account of crime. Young argued:

> The position of Woman, and all characteristics feminine, as the subjugated terms within criminology's binary oppositions, means that Woman is always criminal, always deviant, always censured. This condition is utterly normal. Any feminist criminology has to begin at this point. (1991: 24)

Such a starting point should perhaps apply to all work on crime because the process of defining the deviant allows for the control of deviancy. It underwrites legislation, the criminal justice system, punishment and the exclusion of the offender, through actual or symbolic incarceration from the society of normal, legitimate citizens.

Whereas the main body of criminology has been reluctant to take on this task of critical self-reflection and transgression in the search for knowledge, academics in other disciplines have seen the phenomenon of deviance as relevant to their own areas of concern. From the 1970s to the 1990s, sociologists (Hall 1978, 1982a, 1997;

Willis 1977, 1978) social psychologists (Griffin 1993), psychologists (Gunter 1987b), socio-linguists (Fairclough 1995), cultural analysts (Dyer 1993) and political economists (Murdock 1973) are amongst those who, like feminist scholars, have become interested in deviancy as having potential to inform their own projects.

In addition, alliances have formed amongst social groups to challenge the perceived injustices meted out in the context of criminal justice but also in public perceptions of deviance. Some of these have been formal and organised, as in the struggle for gay rights epitomised by Stonewall, Southall Black Sisters' campaigns for black women, imprisoned for defending themselves against abusive husbands, and the successful fight to free the Birmingham Six and Guildford Four, wrongly convicted of IRA bomb attacks on mainland Britain. Other alliances have been less structured but powerful nonetheless. Inhabitants of Liverpool refused to buy the *Sun* newspaper after their football fans were labelled drunken hooligans and blamed for the Hillsborough stadium disaster. Groups of young people continued to defy the 1994 Criminal Justice Act by organising rave parties without prior permission, so risking possible criminal charges.

Such resistance indicates strong sensibilities. First, that the law is not in any sense given, true and right, and second, that it is particularly not so in relation to those specific experiences and identities which are outside of, or other than, the majority and the normal in British society. The values and interests of the criminological master narrative can be recognised as a dominating narrative not a truth. Once both law and deviance can be seen as constructed within, and therefore relative too, cultures then it becomes vital that such construction is scrutinised in any attempt at understanding crimino-legal issues. Who constructs, what, how and with what potential effect become key questions, relating not to criminology but to language, ideas, communication, the media and the politics of representation.

Normalisation

In order to define the deviant, reference must be made to the norm in our social order, so criminological knowledge depends heavily on assumptions of accepted models of 'normality'. Criminology has not readily engaged with these critically because of its reliance on the fixity and objectivity of empiricism and the modernistic assumption that increased 'knowledge' of that kind will enable progress and human improvement. Those who have crossed over the boundaries of criminology in order to peer within to try to explain its lacks and failings have looked increasingly to discourse and power as conventionalising and legitimating norms and values. (Such conventions also, concurrently, render abnormal and illegitimate 'other' actions and attitudes.) The critical turn in criminology engaged epistemology as patriarchal and modernist, by resisting the truth of what is in effect masculine-dominated meaning. As such, it blended feminism with post-modernism, particularly with the post-structural philosophical aspects of post-modernism. This is an important distinction as it makes serious the challenge to criminology whereas much of post-modern critique merely celebrates a frivolous kind of dismissal of all attempts to account for and change the world – without of course recognising, or acknowledging, or perhaps caring that such a perspective actually works to reinforce the status quo, rendering post-modernism critically impotent at best or simply another incarnation of dominant hegemony at worst.

Post-structuralism challenged the role of history and objective truth whilst acknowledging a relationship between power and ideology, albeit a relationship more subtle and variable than envisaged by even the softest models of political economic determinism. Post-structuralism detaches meanings from forms and places them in the spaces between text, cultural context and the interpreting audience. The potential for meaning becomes not unitary but multiplicit, not given but negotiated, not fixed, true and knowable but struggled over and challengeable. That which we have known as truth is theorised as an exercise of power over meaning. Post-structuralism theorised the construction of meanings as always the result of the 'will to power' – epitomised by the work of Michel Foucault. Foucault applied his ideas to the understanding of a range of socially disruptive behaviours – madness, criminality and sexual non-conformity. Inevitably, his ideas in the late 1970s and early 1980s attracted the interest of those concerned with deviance.[11]

Foucault 'in rejecting the category of totality in general and the Marxist version of it in particular, refuses to limit himself to an analysis of the working class' (Poster 1984: 39). In discussing sexuality he pointed out that although behaviours and social relations can be attributed to the deployment of political power, 'one has to admit that this deployment does not operate in symmetrical fashion with respect to the social classes, and consequently, that it does not produce the same effects in them' (Foucault 1979: 127). Foucault challenged a uni-dimensional theory of deterministic power as directing social subjects from above with the concept of knowledge discourses. Knowledge for Foucault was always the result of the will to power and so it can never be disinterested. Knowledge about social life – sexuality, health, childhood, madness, violence, spirituality – has been gathered, conserved and disseminated since the Enlightenment period of the late eighteenth century, in the belief that intellectual progress will deliver a secure and stable future. This knowledge has been accumulated into disciplines such as law, religion, medicine and education. Inglis explained how Foucault saw the perspectives of dominance become the norm for all, not through force but through discourse:

> Each discipline marks out an area of body and mind for control. First the mad and the sick, then the children and the criminals, domestic life and its great untameable, sex. Each is brought under the terrible domination of language – the discourse of power. (Inglis 1990: 107)

The ideas of the powerful become the everyday understanding of how things are through the processes of communication, over which the powerful have authority. Yet, these ideas are not objective but informed by the interests of those seeking to have power over the social world. In Foucault's terms, the order of things is not a fact but a construct. Nor is that construct the necessary result of the struggle for economic power, as Marx's dictum that the ideas of the ruling class are the ruling ideas suggests. Rather, a range of powerful voices and interests – white, heterosexual, masculine, Western, adult – inform knowledge, albeit each linked to social dominance in the context of the discursive act. Seeking power, these voices necessarily prefer their own interest and values, inevitably denigrating, negating or ignoring others, so by default legitimating dominance as normal.

Foucault's theory of discourse offered an explanation for that normalisation and by default a definition of deviance. In his work, behaviours and values are theorised as made normal through language as it 'penetrates each subject in cultural intercourse'. Language-use is arguably an exercise of ideological power over the subject's psyche making unnecessary the exercise of real force over the physical body. The individual 'body' – self, identity, sexuality –

is central to this thesis. The body is both the object of knowledge and the site of social/sexual control. As subjects come into language during childhood so language enters the subject (Lacan 1976)[12] and social beings are informed by a particular model of the proper, normal order of things in their language community. Holway (1989) viewed that process not as closed once language skills are accomplished by the child, but constantly reviewed/renewed through communal/cultural language use over the life course. She suggested subjectivity is a constant process of negotiation of power relations according to the various discourses encountered during human life, in order to arrive at a sense of self that is appropriate to the context. Language is the means through which we understand what it means to be good and bad. So efforts to understand the criminal or deviant must necessarily consider language and the meanings it imparts to behaviour and beliefs. Once such a consideration can be argued, the sites that collate, process and disseminate meanings should clearly become objects of study.

Reportage and Representation

A focus on language, as reproducing values and interests, norms and deviancies, highlights the mass media as a source of knowledge about ourselves and our world. News is especially salient here in that it informs about events, which audiences may not experience personally[13] and it claims to give us the facts.[14] Indeed, central to the role of the journalist is the act of witnessing. Journalists have been said to write 'the first draft of history' and journalism is a 'window on the world' because at:

> The simplest level journalism presents us with an ongoing narrative about the world beyond our immediate experience. This narrative is asserted to be true. The stories told us by journalists are factual rather than fictional. For this reason, journalism performs a unique and essential social function. For most of us, most of the time, journalists are the main source of our information about the world beyond our immediate environment. (McNair 1994: 17)

Central to the concept of journalism is the idea of objectivity. Journalists claim to seek the truth, to present audiences with the facts, to eschew bias and to resist any effort to curtail their independence. The concept of a free press has a long history within democracies and is a powerful motif both in the Western media and in public consciousness. A free press signifies impartiality and truth-telling linked to the struggles to separate British news from the monarchy and state throughout the late eighteenth and early nineteenth centuries (Keane 1991) in the fight for universal enfranchisement. The ideal of objectivity arose from the effort of opposing the singular perspectives offered by the heavily, state/monarchy, censored and controlled early press.

In theory and in practice there are deep and dangerous flaws in this ideal because, simply and crucially, 'representing events changes them' (Fowler 1991: 207). The flaws are evident in an inherent contradiction in the concepts associated with objectivity – impartiality and truth – because if journalism is to strive to offer impartially, the full range of experiences, views and perspectives in world events, it will necessarily not be able to offer one, single true picture. So even if such impartiality were theoretically possible the result would not be one universal truth but a range of relatively different truths. For many media critics even that idealistic possibility is 'nothing more than a mystification, a legitimating ritual with no real validity' (McNair 1994: 32) because 'journalism, regardless of the integrity of individual journalists and editors, is always a selective, partial account of reality' (McNair 1994: 34). Yet, the accurate representation of real events remains the pursued business of journalism.

The factual media present to audiences the most prolific account of reality beyond our own experience but at best those reports will offer only some of the facts; often they may be prejudicially factual and at worst they may be partial, prejudicial 'faction'. Franklin (1997) asserted that journalism, in its quest for the commercial promise of audience, has largely abandoned the Reithian ideals of information, education and entertainment.[15] In its place is mere entertainment with fiction often replacing or blending with facts, in 'newszak' and 'infotainment'. In terms of its democratic role of informing the public, journalism seems often to have exchanged the political bias of its early history with just as worrisome profitable fantasy.

Unpacking the reasons and evidence for asserting that news is unlikely to be truth, whole truth and nothing but truth is important in a project focusing on the role of the media in the late twentieth century. In Britain, reportage is doubly constrained: once by art in the practices of the profession and once by politics in the cultural context of production and consumption. Representation is the art and craft of the journalist but, to reiterate, 'representing events changes them' (Fowler 1991: 207) because only some real events are reported, those reports are always evaluated and edited, and their dissemination involves technologies and design, which also add to or detract from meanings. Each level of the process of news-making removes the account a step further from the reality, but there are also cultural limits on news. Both journalists and audiences have particular knowledges and expectations, which frame what can possibly be 'news' within a specific politics of representation.

News Values

The gathering of news immediately excludes all but a very few events that can be considered newsworthy. News is a selection of history made by journalists. The selection of stories is not arbitrary but highly systemised and conventionalised by conditions external to the story, as well as integral. External controls may include time, cost, access, expertise, publication space and news agenda. A story that cannot be delivered by the deadline, is too expensive, is too inaccessible or problematic, requires too much journalistic or audience expert knowledge, is too big or too small for the available print or broadcast slot, does not comply with the editor's or owner's long- or short-term agenda,[16] is unlikely to make the news.

Potential news events have to be, practically, reportable but they also have to have particular internal features. These features regulate further the events that are likely to be reported in the news and are identifiable characteristics. Fowler pointed out that 'news is not simply that which happens, but that which can be regarded and presented as newsworthy' (1991: 13). He adheres to the Galtung and Ruge (1965) model of news attributes and points out that these are mainly cultural not natural. These criteria were systematically elicited from news stories. The original twelve features (with my bracketed interpretation) were as shown in Table 1.1.[17]

Fowler stressed that adherence to news values is not part of some journalistic conspiracy but an unconscious function of being a member of a professional collective with a long ideological and commercial history. Journalists themselves find it difficult to explain why a story is chosen as news. Some will talk of having a feel for a story or a nose for one. In essence, journalists share the same concepts and values as their audiences and, of course, they are audiences too.

The relationship is reciprocal, an implicit agreement about what matters based on convention, interdependence and repetition.

Table 1.1: News Criteria from Galtung and Ruge (1965)

frequency	(repetition/speed/quantity)
threshold	(importance/drama/level of action)
unambiguity	(simplicity/straightforwardness)
meaningfulness	(cultural fit/relevance to audience)
consonance	(expected/desired/anticipated)
unexpectedness	(rarity/suddenness)
continuity	(sustainability/durability)
composition	(fit with other news events/fit with news product)
elite nations	(superpowers/authoritative sources)
elite people	(stars/royalty/politicians)
personification	(individual causality/identification)
negativity	(damaging/deviant/sad)

The boundaries between the art of reportage and the politics of representation blur pragmatics and ideologies. Much of what is viewed from within journalism as art or craft is little more than the accreditation of practices that are largely determined by commercial, legislative and technical pressures. Such pressures structure practice, formally via law and capital and informally through a normalising of newsworthiness around particular interests and values, integrating almost seamlessly the party politics of government and the broader political organisation and normalisation of everyday life and relationships. Chibnall (1977) detailed these for the period 1945–75 as epitomised by a sense of Britishness, which provided the common sense shared understanding of what was valuable. Conducive to the critical thinking of the mid-1970s he saw these values as relating in the main to areas such as the national interest, the democratic process, the rule of law, majority values, public and private rights, free enterprise and the state. His table of values related closely to political, legal and economic practices. He acknowledged a 'handful of others such as family life' (Chibnall 1977: 21) but did not expand on these although many of his listed values clearly apply not only to family life but also to sexuality generally and broader cultural relations around gender, ethnicity and age. Briefly, Chibnall suggested the legitimate column is the standard against which 'other' or 'new' forms and practices of social life are evaluated. Chibnall's Table (1.2) is appended with some additional values, which seemed to me to be particularly salient to news, crime and culture in the 1980s and 1990s.[18]

Table 1.2: British Values from Chibnall (1977)

Positive legitimating values	Negative illegitimate values
legality	illegality
moderation	extremism
compromise	dogmatism
co-operation	confrontation
order	chaos
peacefulness	violence
tolerance	intolerance
constructiveness	destructiveness
openness	secrecy
honesty	corruption
realism	ideology
rationality	irrationality[19]
impartiality	bias
responsibility	irresponsibility
fairness	unfairness
firmness	weakness
industriousness	idleness
freedom of choice	monopoly/uniformity
equality	inequality

1980s and 1990s	
conformity	non-conformity
cleanliness	dirtiness
commitment	non-commitment
safety	danger
puritanism	pleasure
natural	cultural

It is easy to see from Table 1.2 how minority, different or subordinate experience and values might be negated on a whole range of value criteria, particularly if that 'other' group actively challenges the standard. Moreover, if an innovation can be labelled in any sense as illegitimate it immediately takes on the important news value of negativity. So, when these criteria are added to the news values of journalistic practice it becomes possible to develop a grid of newsworthiness, which integrates ideology and practice into a measuring scale.

Events which do not score highly enough are not reported. Aspects of stories which make them most newsworthy are highlighted. A simple example would be the routine reporting as news of aspects of feminism that can be described as extreme, intolerant, ideological and unfair, as in the most radical demands for political correctness in the USA, rather than those aspects of feminism that are about equality, co-operation, fairness and freedom of choice. These latter tend to feature only in the women's section. Negativity as a news value makes anti-British norms most commensurate with newsworthiness.

Journalism

The premise of this book is that the media actively, routinely but not exclusively constructed discourses of legitimacy empathic with the interests of conservatism during the period of the Tory governments of Margaret Thatcher (1979–92) and John Major (1992–97). However, I would not want to claim that the journalism of the late twentieth century was free to do otherwise, despite its vision of its role and ideals. For all its ideological protestations, arguably journalism, as industry and practice, has never been nor could be free, doubly constrained, as it is, by the machinations and restrictions of the profession and the sensibilities dominant in any cultural context.

Herman and Chomsky went so far as to claim that even in democracies such as the USA journalism is engaged in propagandising the interests of the powerful:

> Money and power are able to filter out the news fit to print, marginalise dissent and allow the government and other dominant interests to get their message across ... the operation of these news filters occurs so naturally that media news people, frequently operating with complete integrity and good will, are

able to convince themselves that they choose and interpret the news 'objectively' and on the basis of professional news values. (1988: 2)

Raymond Williams's very different model of culture suggested that in each epoch the 'structure of feeling' of a generation which is a 'very deep and wide possession in all actual communities precisely because it is on it that communication depends' (1961: 65) will be left evident in its recorded culture. So even if journalists were unconstrained in Chomsky's terms they would remain during the period of neo-conservatism from 1979 to 1997, in Williams's terms, part of the organism reacting to the changing organisation that was Thatcherism.

Journalists are not external analysts reflecting retrospectively on the past but diarists of the culture of the period in which they live and, in the case of news about British events, the community in which they live. To go against the political grain is rare if a journalist wants to be published or broadcast and stay out of court. Yet, few journalists admit to the limitations under which they work and most continue to claim, and probably believe, that they are in the pursuit of the truth. With the burgeoning of media outlets and audiences in the late twentieth century, enabled by computerisation, publicity has become increasingly the oxygen of power. Journalists can access that publicity and they are consequently sought out, feted and aggrandised. Courting the media has become the business of politicians and pop stars alike. Media management, public relations, press releases, press conferences, spinning and sound bites are the everyday effort of the powerful to tempt journalists to report their activities and interests. Yet, journalists continue to try to convince fellow practitioners, policy-makers and the public that they are in the business of truth-telling.

One reason for this persistence is that although our culture is dominated by the mass media, we remain ill-educated about the processes and relations that shape them. Media education in the early twenty-first century is probably paid even sparser attention on British school curricula than politics or law. In consequence, the ideas many hold about journalism have barely changed since we learnt in classes on English literature that the gentleman journalist was interchangeable with the gentleman novelist, spanning epochs from Dickens to Orwell. Few members of any news media audience have a clear idea of what journalists actually do. Few journalists seem willing or able to reflect on their work and account for themselves. Yet, journalism is for adults their source of information about the world. Even those who doubt the news and distrust journalists are dependent on them and the information they provide.

Certainly it is relatively easy for even a minimally critical reader to take issue with some of the overtly wild accounts of the popular press. However, the way news is selected and presented makes it difficult to uncover the covert messages in the news. The value judgements, repeated themes and exclusions that link, bind and underwrite meaningfulness are inaccessible to the casual daily reader and viewer. Chibnall suggested 'it is much easier for most readers to reject the open, substantive (factual) content of newspaper accounts than the more latent and implicit interpretative schema in which the content is embedded' (1977: 45). He offered a comment, which helps explain the aim of this book:

> The news media are our central repositories and disseminators of knowledge ... They have the power to create issues and define the boundaries of debates and while they may not manipulate our opinions in any direct sense – creating attitudes by changing old ones – they can organise opinion and develop world views by providing structures and understandings into which isolated and unarticulated attitudes and beliefs may be fitted. They provide interpretations, symbols of identification, collective values and myths which are able to transcend the cultural boundaries within a society like Britain. (1977: 226)

In the 1970s, Chibnall examined the role of the press in the period of rapid social change after the Second World War – a period that witnessed burgeoning youth power (economic and political), welfarism, increasing moral liberalism, high employment and the refinement of Western capitalism.

Thatcherism

This book also covers a particular epoch of significant political and cultural change; change involving the deconstruction of welfarism, massive technological growth, the contraction of traditional industry with commensurate high unemployment, the growth of global capitalism and the clawing back of the liberalism of the 1960s and

1970s. The changes wrought by Thatcherism were profound. Margaret Thatcher came to power in 1979 prepared for the end of the industrial age and the beginning of the information age. In Britain, in the pre- and post-Thatcher epochs, particular 'structures of feeling' evidently related to significant social and political shifts. It is a sensibility clearly articulated in the British newspapers of both periods. During the later period, particular characteristics were evident in both media and political language, which made it possible to describe a discourse of Thatcherism (Fairclough 1989).

Fowler identified three political factors as having 'important and analysable implications for a reader's experience of newspaper language' (1991: 6) during the 1980s. First was the adoption of a conflict paradigm 'to segregate and marginalise threatening and undesirable elements' (Fowler 1991: 6). This usefully provided high news value events from the streets of the inner cities to the raves on Britain's common land, and therefore guaranteed exposure of, and legitimated, the struggle for law and order. Fowler also noted that these conflicts were recounted within a consensual framework of British 'national unity of interest and common purpose' (1991: 6). This was achieved partly by the second change, which was the increase of power to the centre through new legislation and a reduction in public spending, so disabling organisations like trades unions and eroding authority from local councils. Third, and essential to the effectiveness of the first two political interventions, was what Fowler called 'the propaganda of individual responsibility or self-reliance' (1991: 7). This was the time of the entrepreneur, young and upwardly mobile. The 'Nanny State' was deconstructed in favour of personal freedom and Margaret Thatcher told us that there was no such thing as society – just a collection of individuals. This radical populism invested ordinary people with authority over their own lives and families and simultaneously justified the deconstruction of the nationalised industries, welfare state, trades unions and local government that had previously provided some collective security and political lobby.

These three shifts were connected and symbiotic but their impact was neither universal nor uniform. Rather, as different areas of social and cultural life came to be seen as 'anti-establishment', the Thatcherite ideological triumvirate of conflict, legal authority and individualisation, worked integratively to facilitate the renewal of conservatism. Much of that work was articulated, legitimated and disseminated by the news media, which found many parallels with news values in the values of this political discourse.

> For a new political tendency like Thatcherism to achieve power, it has to carve out a political base, a sufficiently powerful constituency of supporters. Such a political base is partly 'talked' into existence – politicians construct and reconstruct the people, the political public, in their discourse, and a measure of their success is the degree to which people accept, and so make real these (often wildly imaginary) constructions. (Fairclough 1995: 179)

Fairclough refers to Bourdieu's concept of political discourse as doubly determined, from within the political field and by the relation between politics and the broader context. This latter determining factor clearly includes communications between politicians and the public, increasingly concentrated in the mass media. However, I would argue that political discourse in the media is not limited to those articles referring precisely to the decision-making processes of the House of Commons, or the proclamations of some senior minister, but seeps through news more broadly. Politics is especially evident in news about conflict – whether international, collective or personal – because news about conflict invokes the law, which is the authority of the state.

Erickson, Banacek and Chan (1991) described an affinity between the institutions of the law and the news media based on their authority, articulation of norms and values and claim to represent the public interest. So, when the news is about dissent, deviance, crime or conflict there is a doubling of powerful discourses. Media news values publicise, often personalise, denigrate, explain, dramatise and negate the deviant citizen(s), so legitimating their punishment by law, and maybe the introduction of further law to pre-empt recurrence. Politically what is achieved is a 'publicity of control' without all the problems associated with outright state propagandising in a democracy with a supposedly free media. I have focused on conflict ideology during the period of conservative government in Britain from 1979 to 1997, because it seemed to be the mechanism through which the second and third shifts that Fowler identified could be mobilised popularly around consensus to law and order, rather than through political coercion.

2
Disorderly Publics:
Race in the Inner Cities

While twenty-first century media analysts may find themselves concerned with issues of the global McDonaldisation of national and ethnic cultures, retrospectively my account of the later twentieth century begins with the internal reconstruction of British national culture in relation to whiteness. Largely excluded from the working-class politics of the immediate post-war period by racism, and then by racism and unemployment during the late 1970s and 1980s, black British communities struggled to 'find a voice' through which to express their experiences of alienation, impoverishment, oppression, harassment and cultural disenfranchisement.

During the street violence of the early 1980s the British press provided an account on their behalf – an account which dredged up the old racist stereotypes and subtly reshaped them for the 1980s with embellishments of terrorism and crime. This chapter explores that construction of criminalised black identity as the institutionalisation of previously popular but relatively freelance, informal racism.

Roots of Disorder

Crowd disturbances are by no means a modern phenomena. Kettle and Hodge described a riotous history to the turbulent early 1980s, traceable back 600 years to the 'massive outbreak of popular anger' (1982: 11) that was the Peasants' Revolt. They traced a pattern of violence in defence of perceived rights to work, territory, food, belief, vote and leisure until the growth of the industrial bourgeoisie during the Victorian period underwrote a containment of much outright revolt through hegemony via enfranchisement. Trades unions acted as negotiators on behalf of the newly urbanised working classes whilst social institutions such as education, welfare, the law and the press represented the interests and culture of the middle classes as for the good of all. The radicalism of the late eighteenth century, which in France led to revolution, was in Britain reconstituted as reformism by the late nineteenth century. In the first half of the twentieth century two world wars further decimated not only working-class political and cultural consciousness but also numbers. The Second World War left 'widespread euphoria, a release of collectively experienced tensions, and a raising of expectations' (Chibnall 1977: 54) which generated the affluent 1950s but also a much more material and hedonistic youth. The transformation of the British working class from 'one of the most unruly and violent into one of the most orderly and law abiding' (Shils and Young, 1953 in Chibnall, 1977: 61) was seen to be far from complete as groups of working-class youths[1] – 'Teds' – went on vandalising rampages during the 1950s.

During the 1960s youth was at the centre stage of deviance challenging the state over the bomb and middle-class values over sexual freedom and drugs (Cohen and Young 1973). Radical student groups formed to protest in dramatic ways against the war in Vietnam and British involvement in Northern Ireland. Demonstrations led to clashes with the police and the interests and values of the establishment. Such events were reported as conflict, commensurate with news values criteria of drama and negativity, rather than youthful, and the press began to reflect on the 'violent society'. This shift was also political in that, for the first time, the Conservative Party added a law and order mandate to their successful election manifesto for 1970.

According to politicians and press alike, consensus was giving way to anarchy fuelled and informed by foreign terrorists, an opinion that grew rapidly during the 1970s and was used to explain a range of discontentment, including the build up of resistance to the government's new wage policy. Chibnall refers to the *Sun* in August 1972 as appealing to trades unionists to resist the Trots and Communists. The dangerous outsider was to blame for the deepening social and economic crisis and the government was seen to fail to restore normalcy despite extensive new legislation. The succeeding Labour government oversaw a collapse from bad to worse as unemployment rose during the mid-1970s, accompanied by deepening social unrest. By the first year of Margaret Thatcher's government, the collapse of consensus and the beginnings of a return to revolt were evident amongst the new urban communities of black immigrants and workers in the major industries.

Race in Britain

Before 1948, colonial labour was evident in Britain particularly in the seaports, where Chinese and black workers undertook some of the dirtiest tasks such as stoking the boilers of steam ships. Such labour was often cheaper than equivalent work done by whites – a differential legitimised by the Aliens Restriction Immigration Act. It was also used to strike break – for example during the Seamens' strike in Cardiff in 1911 and in Liverpool in 1919 and 1948 (Fryer 1984). This potential, alongside the nature of the work allocated to immigrants, marked out space for ethnic workers outside of the mainstream of working-class labour.

The allocation of dirty work to the dark skinned is unsurprising in the wake of the Victorian effort to control and convert its empire. Stuart Hall (1997) traced three major influences on perceptions of race in the UK. First, he pointed out that advertising and commodification relayed endless images of the role of British products in the process of civilising the colonies (and the great unwashed white workers of the city slums):

> Soap symbolised this 'racialising' of the domestic world and 'domestication' of the colonial world ... It apparently had the power to wash black skin white as well as being capable of washing off the soot, grime and dirt of the industrial slums and their inhabitants ... (Hall 1997: 241)

Second, slavery reinforced oppositional differences between black and white to justify the trade: white/black, intellect/emotion, culture/nature, civilised/savage, pure/polluted became the bases for characterising human beings merely according to their skin colour. The colour of the body became what Hall terms the discursive site for a range of cultural reference points on racialised knowledge: the darker the skin the more profound the difference. Third, the process of representation of race over time effectively naturalised these knowledges so black biology became black destiny. 'Not only were blacks represented in terms of their essential characteristics. They were reduced to their essence' (Hall 1997: 245). This categorisation underwrote both the nature of paid work available to blacks and their exclusion from white working-class politics in the first half of the twentieth century; it also informed the processes of post-war reconstruction.

By 1948 economic expansion had led to labour shortages as whites were unwilling to take on dirty social jobs in public transport and the health service. The British government funded an advertising campaign to encourage Afro-Caribbeans to return to the 'mother country' from the colonies, where their families had often been enslaved on plantations. On 22 June 1948 MV *Empire Windrush* docked at Tilbury with 492 Jamaican ex-servicemen

> [w]ho had been encouraged to come and help Britain rebuild after a painful and destructive second European war. By the same token these men could be expected to share in the rewards of a regenerated Britain. Needless to say this did not materialise. (Cumberbatch 1998: 12)

It did not happen because of the 'morass of racial discrimination' which led to claims that 'over half the West Indian population were employed at levels below those for which their skills and experience qualified them' and were placed in 'cramped, overcrowded accommodation' (Cumberbatch 1998: 13). Whereas the ports of Cardiff, Liverpool and Bristol had long established black communities, the immigrants of the 1950s and 1960s settled in London and Birmingham.

Work was key to these new communities but from the outset discrimination was rife, not only amongst employers but from the trades unions as well. Cumberbatch reported that in 1955 'the TGWU negotiated with the Wolverhampton bus company that a quota of only 52 out of its 900 bus workers could be black' (1998: 19). Such practices, at a time of relative prosperity and high employment, were destructive enough for the new urban black communities but during the slump of the 1970s, as second generation black workers entered the job market, jobs disappeared and even blacks with high qualifications were 'three times more likely to be on the dole than similarly qualified European counterparts' (Clough and Drew, 1985 in Cumberbatch 1998: 200). The employment situation became even more difficult as British Asians, fleeing violence in Kenya and Uganda, sought refuge, housing and work in Britain's major cities.

Race and the Media

Frequently, news about race focused on immigrant numbers, both in terms of the recent arrivals to the country, which informed a perceived rise in illegal entry, and in relation to the birth rate amongst the now established black communities. In April 1968 Conservative MP Enoch Powell predicted the overwhelming of British culture by immigrants in his infamous speech predicting 'rivers of blood'. It cost him his place in the shadow cabinet but set the scene for an increasing focus on, and panic about,[2] numbers and violence. Despite the fact that Home Office figures for May 1970 showed a decrease in immigration rates, the press still reported '40 immigrants invade' (*Daily Mail* 2.7.70) and news reports preferred the results from the Registrar General in the same year that indicated 'the birth rate amongst immigrant communities was higher than average' (Hartman and Husband 1971: 296).

Hartman and Husband pointed out that the British situation was quickly linked to racial issues in the USA with the *Birmingham Evening Mail* asking, 'Must Harlem come to Birmingham?' The Americanisation of explanations for race relations in Britain rapidly infiltrated journalism and became linked to what the British media termed our 'Violent Society'. Halloran, Elliot and Murdock (1970) argued that the use of violence as a definer of news type led to a particular structuring of news events at anti-Vietnam demonstrations in 1968, which neglected both the issues and the predominantly peaceful nature of the march (Hartman and Husband 1971: 294). This violence paradigm informed future news about social relations generally but the early 1970s also saw a shifting news agenda from a focus on the threat of political violence to the threat of racial violence.

It was a shift informed initially by the Civil Rights demonstrations in the USA, although this was an 'inappropriate framework for reporting the British situation' (Hartman and Husband 1971: 295)[3] and was fuelled by racist stereotypes from the time of slavery and empire. Hall *et al.* (1978) chose to focus on the crime of mugging as the pivot about which the media turned towards the race/violence paradigm. Mugging marks the introduction of a new racial stereotype, which added the potential of the exercise of containment of black people by law to the freelance racism of the workplace, social community and housing market.

British readers were familiar with reports of USA Civil Rights issues, making the introduction of a new American term into race news straightforward. The term mugging was first used to report the killing of an elderly man on Waterloo Bridge during a street robbery in August 1972. British readers had already been told of the dangers on the streets of American cities in the context of racial unrest and violence. Although British papers rarely stated that black violence was on the increase in the UK, the use of the term mugging and the focus on it as linked to the street culture of (predominantly black) inner city localities, such as Brixton, soon placed the West Indian community in the dock, as did some thinly veiled references in crime journalism, for example to 'black spots' (Chibnall 1977).

Anxiety about social change was readily mobilised around the call for a strong law and order response to the problem of mugging. In effect that response was directed towards the black community as the link between mugging and black youth became increasingly publicised leading to a 'strong and vigorous official reaction' (Hall *et al.*, 1978: 17) often apparently led by the press. The *Sun* called for the 'Taming of the Muggers' (13.10.72); *The Times* agreed stating 'Police May Seek More Powers in Mugging' (5.10.72) and six months later the *Sun* was pleased to report the result in '20 Years for Mugger Aged 16' (20.3.73).

By the mid-1970s the rights of blacks whose families had effectively been enticed to this country were under question. The tightened Immigration Act of 1971 was regularly invoked to check on the legitimacy of colonials as the criminal label became an excuse for the further exclusion of blacks, especially young men, from work and housing (Cumberbatch 1998). Race and crime were linked, justifying the police saturation of black communities and leading to the kind of friction pre-empting self-fulfilling prophecy, as black youth felt increasingly closely suspect and surveyed. The mugging phenomenon firmly linked legal institutions of control with media institutions of expression in an ideological symbiosis that was to become obvious again a decade in the future.

Race and the Media during Thatcherism

There was an increasing sense, paralleling the United States again, that the liberalism of the 1960s was somehow to blame for all the ills of the 1970s. A hardening to the right and traditional, even Victorian, values led to the election of Margaret Thatcher's Conservative government in 1979 on a clear law and order mandate. Part of that election campaign included the rally by the racist National Front in Southall at which the anti-racist campaigner, Blair Peach, was bludgeoned to death. Aggressive policing by the Special Patrol

Group of the Metropolitan Police was denied at the time, 'despite the discovery of numerous unauthorised weapons in lockers belonging to the SPG' (*Guardian* 21.3.99). Contextually, the mood in Britain was close to xenophobic and although the links between race issues and economic factors are complex there was something of an acceptance that the crisis in capital in the UK was linked to external threats – political, criminal and racial. This 'supported the view of blacks being an outside force, an alien malaise afflicting British society' (CCCS 1982: 26). The effect of this reconstruction of black as 'other' alongside the increasing media and political focus on black crime, and the still current legacy of colonial stereotypes, is difficult to assess but the period saw the coming of age of second generation Afro-Caribbeans, British born and bred, and it seems no coincidence that black youths were central to the inner-city disturbances that characterised the early years of Thatcherism.

Street disorder in Birmingham, Brixton, Liverpool and Bristol between 1980 and 1985 was immediately reported in conflict terms involving lexical choices connoting tribalism, warfare, crime and violence. This process mobilised already existing and familiar labels for racial issues, some ancient and some barely a decade old, recycling them to make sense of the current conflicts. Myths, stereotypes, journalistic practices and state values seemed seamlessly integrated, producing a 'magic circle, with such effect that it is no longer possible to tell who began the process, each legitimates the other in turn' (Hall and Jefferson 1983: 76).

In 1980, police raided the Black and White Café in the St Paul's area of Bristol with the claimed intent of preventing illicit drinking and the use of cannabis. This overturned the 'blind-eye' police practices of the previous decade, which had largely ignored the Rastafarian use of ganja and taken a laissez faire approach to black street culture, but the press played down this aspect and immediately turned to the 'violent society' paradigm of explanation. The *Bristol Evening Post* referred to the 'Battle of Bristol' (3.4.80) and the *Guardian* preferred a 'mob out of control' (2.4.80) to describe a fracas which ended as police withdrew and left Rastafarians directing traffic and singing 'Beat down Babylon' in celebration of their community. However positive an experience for community members in terms of black identity, the media reports largely re-enforced the notion that Britain was being threatened by 'tribal unrest', reaffirming the rightness of both the immediate raid and the long term 'power relations between the socially defined groups' (Husband 1984: 27) of black and white. In the port of Bristol, those relations between black and white had been built on the misery and profit of the slave trade. Nearly 20 years after the St Paul's incident Supt. David Warren, a mere bobby on the beat during the 'riot', was still actively engaged in the struggle to 'root out racist attitudes' amongst the police in the city (*Channel 4 News* 15.3.99).

The same kind of pre-emptive police action evident in St Paul's could be identified as escalating racial tension in Brixton in 1981. It is worth noting the name of Operation 'Swamp 81' under which initiative the police brought in hundreds of plain clothes police on a stop and search campaign, ostensibly to counteract street crime, mugging and drugs offences. Long existing norms of blue–black interaction were swept aside resulting in conflict that was later identified as justifying the operation in the first place. Lord Scarman, commissioned to consider issues of police, race and community after the Brixton disorders, described the police action at Brixton as 'reminiscent of ancient warriors going into battle' (Kettle and Hodge 1982: 113). Lea and Young argued that:

> The 'Swamp 81' operation serves as a tailor-made example of how to antagonise the greatest possible number of people while at the same time achieving the minimum efficiency in the direct control of a particular type of crime, in this case footpad robbery. (1982: 12–13)

After the troubles in Toxteth, Liverpool during the summer of the same year, the *Financial Times* described the disturbances as 'like an epidemic of some alien disease ... (involving) ... forces, which are capable of sending hundreds of youths onto the rampage' (11.7.81). *The Times* managed in one sentence to denigrate both the black community, and the liberalism it claimed engendered social disorder, by arguing that 'mindless mobs can set out and in one night destroy a community and then find everyone in authority bending over backwards to apologise to them' (13.11.81 in Scraton, 1985: 37).

The Scarman Report (1981) only tangentially took issue with the changes in policing involved in these troubles but did focus on social issues as causal of riot – unemployment, bad housing, racism, educational deprivation. Yet, in contrast, the press virtually ignored the alienation of young blacks in the city ghettos. There was no 'news' about the way that exclusion from work denied black communities the capital necessary to participate in mainstream socio-economic relations; that racism also denied them access to the traditional Labour politics of trades unions (even those in work, Cumberbatch 1998) and thereby the potential for a legitimate political voice. Black Britons in the early 1980s were disenfranchised, doubly – excluded from both capital power and political power. Stuart Hall saw the turn to crime as a response to and a perpetuation of those exclusions. He called it a 'quasi-rebellion', the result of 'proto-political criminalised consciousness' in need of 'a critical transformation into something more sustained and thoroughgoing in a political sense' (Hall *et al*. 1978: 397).

In 1985, that rebellion erupted again and now the press was ready with a repertoire of explanations. The term copycat crept into reporting, relating new events both to the previous British troubles but also to increasing inter-racial friction in South Africa. It was as if black violence was somehow self-perpetuating or natural. The *Sun* headlined its account of Handsworth in Birmingham '*BARBARIANS!*' (11.9.85) and included the sub-headings 'Carnival of Death', 'Blitz of Handsworth' and 'Battle in the Streets'. The *Sun*'s comment included:

In no time, the sociologists will be picking among the debris of Handsworth for evidence of social protest. They will be eager to find signs of resentment over deprivation and unemployment ... The looting of shops is born of greed not social despair.

The same edition quotes Labour Party leader Neil Kinnock high-lighting 'the idleness and poverty, the desire for thrills and tribal attitudes which grow up on the football terraces and the streets', so neatly linking the left and right of Britain in the preservation of middle-class 'civilisation'. Similarly, usually liberal and critical of the Conservatives, the *Guardian* (30.9.85) denigrated the black community with 'Drug Fraternity Blame End of Police Blind-eye Strategy', rather than engage directly with the strong-arm law enforcement tactics that were the flashpoint for trouble.

It may be that the media concentrated on the violence due to news values, or as a result of their white vantage point on the streets behind police lines, literally and metaphorically, but the net effect of the language used was to reinforce both cultural racism and legitimate interventionist policing. This policing completed the magic circle of blame identified by Hall and Jefferson (1983). Cumberbatch suggested that police use of 'stop and search on suspicion' or 'SUS had the effect of defining the entire African diaspora as criminal. Its use meant all blacks could be arrested on suspicion of being about to commit a crime' (1998: 17). This discourse of blame appeared to make violence part of blackness and made alternative accounts almost impossible to articulate. Even the black community struggled for explanations for the inner city disturbances. The Rastafarian poet, Lynton Kwesi Johnson, could only suggest that people do not riot if they have food in the belly, good housing and individual freedom.

The newspapers overwhelmingly reported Handsworth in conflict terms: the tabloids opting for dramatic war metaphors and images and the qualities reiterating the Thatcherite call for law and order. Even the papers on the left, politically, found it difficult to offer any overt criticism of Tory policy in relation to the violence on the streets and only the *Guardian* attempted a critical account of the social situation for the black community. The front pages of the *Guardian* and the *Mirror* for 11 September 1985 are included on the following two pages.

The *Guardian* had a quarter-page photograph showing a street scene of houses with burning cars in the background. Police in riot gear in the foreground are apparently 'looking out' on the scene. The Handsworth story dominated the front page and most information was verbal. The *Mirror* offered a three-quarter page account of Handsworth with a half-page image of a black youth staring forward and holding a bottle. The quarter-page image showed a burning vehicle plus the rear view of one police officer. There was very little verbal information, in fact as many words were included about the death of a football manager.

The headlines for the *Guardian* were focused on the threat to the state but included a resolution in the subheading 'Police Van Rescues Home Secretary', whilst the *Mirror* shifted that threat into a provocative, war scenario with 'Frontline Britain' but had a larger headline referring to the popular football manager's death.

The selection for the layout was such that the *Guardian* foregrounded the community at risk and the *Mirror* personalised the dangerous individual as black (see Kress and Van Leeuwen 1998 on layout and meaning); the *Guardian* indicated a situation now under control thanks to the police, the *Mirror* confronted the reader with a black rioter.

The writing style of the *Guardian* was quite complex with multi-clausal sentences, a lot of passivisation, much description and considerable explanatory detail whereas the minimal writing in the tabloid account was simple, metaphoric and in the active voice.

THE GUARDIAN

Printed in London and Manchester   Wednesday September 11 1985   25p

Two killed and others feared dead as more violence breaks out in Handsworth

Besieged Hurd pledges riot crackdown

Police van rescues Home Secretary from fury of crowd

How the trouble started and flared

By Martin Wainwright

6 PM MONDAY: a fight began outside the Villa Cross pub when police officers approached an Asian man about suspected motoring offences. West Indian youths came to the man's aid — after he appealed to them, according to one version; after they were outraged by police treatment of him, according to another. The man drove off in the melee.

8 30 PM: firemen were called to the Villa Cross hall, opposite the pub. On arrival, they were warned by youths that there would be trouble if they tried to put out the fire.

8 40 PM: bricks, bottles and petrol bombs were hurled at the firemen, forcing them to withdraw. Police arrived and chased youths through back alleys as stone-throwing incidents spread.

9 PM: fires were started in lower Lozells Road, initially

By Gareth Parry and David Rose

The Home Secretary, Mr Douglas Hurd, who was stoned by an angry crowd when he visited riot-devastated Handsworth, Birmingham, yesterday, said later that the rioting was "not a social phenomenon but crimes."

Mr Hurd said he would meet riots by maintaining the rule of law with an effective number of police and "pursuing and arresting those who commit breaches of the law."

His remarks, shortly after he escaped in a police van from a hail of bricks, stones and bottles in Lozells Road, are a clear statement of Government determination to deal with any riot as a law-and-order issue.

That was seen by community leaders in Handsworth as a profound misunderstanding of the causes of the rioting on Monday, which left two people

Flashpoint was challenge to driver; Drugs fraternity blames raids and Carnival bid tensions, page 3; Leader comment, page 14; The view on television, page 11; The bleeding heart of England, page 11

burnt alive and another two feared dead in the worst incident of its kind on mainland Britain for four years.

Sporadic trouble broke out again in Handsworth early today after about 1,000 mainly West Indian youths and a similar number of police officers spent a tense evening watching each other. At least 1,000 offi-

He arrived at Handsworth in a chauffeur-driven Daimler accompanied by only two police cars and got out in Lozells Road almost opposite the post office where at least two people were hurt to death.

Mr Hurd denied later that security arrangements for his visit had been inadequate, but on leaving his car he was immediately surrounded by a crowd of several hundred youths, who jabbed outstretched arms at him, pushing at his guard of no more than four or five policemen and baying at him with rhythmic, orchestrated booing.

Swept along bodily by the crowd, Mr Hurd almost lost his footing, until he was guided to the apparent safety of an area cordoned off behind a metal crash barrier.

There, his public-relations advisers and police tried to set up a staged interview between the Home Secretary and an Asian shopkeeper. Ignoring questions from journalists and the crowd, still baying for his blood, Mr Hurd smiled weakly and said he was there to listen.

The interview was cut short by a hail of bricks, stones and bottles from the crowd behind the barrier. A police officer shouted "Get them out" and Mr Hurd and his entourage broke into a run, diving for cover round the corner of Lozells Road and a residential side street.

Still the public relations team refused to give up, leading Mr Hurd to the home of a white family, who told him that they wanted to have nothing to do with his visit or the television cameras behind him. Shouts from Lozells Road in-

Police wearing riot gear keep a lookout for trouble while cars burn in a street off Lozells Road.   Picture by Don McPhee

Appalled Thatcher ready to back inquiry

Figure 1 *Guardian* 11.9.85

Figure 2 *Mirror* 11.9.85

The *Guardian* used sources, who had been witnesses (an Asian community leader and journalists at the scene), the *Mirror* quoted absentee senior police officers and academics.

The explanations for the riots were very different. The *Guardian* did refer to unemployment, drugs, poor housing and new police strategies (but not on the front page) whilst the *Mirror* offered only criminality, drugs, terrorism and black youth. Although both papers were ostensibly left-wing, neither saw right-wing government policy as causal of the disturbances: the *Mirror* quoted the Home Secretary as saying, 'I'm here to listen' whilst the *Guardian* described, but didn't question, interventionist policing and reported that Douglas Hurd, the Home Secretary, was 'besieged'.

Both papers appeared to be appealing to their specific audiences around racial issues. The *Guardian* offered the kind of sympathetic account of the social conditions faced by black Britons that comfortable, middle-class liberal readers would have approved of but did not raise the issue of racist policing or policies, which would have necessitated a critique of Thatcherism. The *Mirror* repeated the worst of racist stereotyping, which would have been familiar to its working-class readers and focused heavily on the criminality of the violence, so avoiding any need to consider political issues. Although this was only intuitive analytical work on news about race, it seemed clear to me that in the 1980s the British mainstream press was either not acknowledging racism as a problem or was reproducing racist stereotypes. It also seemed clear that when it came to racial issues newspapers normally associated with left-wing politics were unable or unwilling to criticise a right-wing government. Also, all the press accounts were about black issues from a white perspective.

The month after Handsworth, trouble broke out at the Broadwater Farm estate in Tottenham, London. The spark for this was 'the death of Cynthia Jarrett during a police raid on her home' (*News on Sunday* 13.10.85). In the ensuing disturbances, PC Blakelock was killed. In 1987 three black youths were convicted of PC Blakelock's murder and as a newly graduated Communications Researcher I produced an analysis of some of the press coverage of Broadwater Farm.[4]

Media and Method: Broadwater Farm

The impetus for this small study was both concern for the apparent racism in the successive coverage of the inner-city riots and its broader socio-political implications, and my interest in a project to produce a radical independent, investigative tabloid Sunday newspaper. This new newspaper was to be relatively free of obligations to profit and editorial/ownership political intervention. It would be run collectively by a committee responsible to a board, including worker members, who in turn would be responsible to a Founder's Trust committed to independence and the ideals of 'The Campaign for Press and Broadcasting Freedom'. Early trial editions coincided with events at Broadwater Farm and my interest was in whether or not this new radical 'Sun' could offer any different account of events. John Pilger,[5] one of the original founders, had hoped to 'turn stereotypes inside out, to question newspaper language and all the assumptions loaded in the old clichés' (*New Statesman and Society* 2.1.87).

My project was to evaluate how successful the new paper could be in achieving that aim, particularly in relation to the racial issues, which were so high on the newsworthy agenda during its inception. In the event, that research process raised issues of meaning, method and media theory, which were to inform my research and teaching for the next decade.

Language study shifted, during the turbulent 1970s, from a focus on language as an abstract rule-based ideal towards the study of language in use, or discourse analysis. Critical linguistics was a radical new branch of this shift in emphasis, committed to the political potential of the science and to revealing the relationship of language to the social world. For Kress and Hodge language forms and syntactical processes were systematic options from sets of alternatives, which 'code a world view without any conscious choice on the part of the writer or speaker' (1979: 185). Patterns of language were theorised as relating to the 'institutions and socio-economic structure' so for Kress and Hodge a critical approach should investigate the 'underlying causes of the phenomena studied and the nature of the society whose language it is' (1979: 185).

In 1979, Fowler *et al.*, accepting that the pervasiveness of the press plays a part in the formulations of perceptions of social matters, chose to investigate the role of news reports in perpetrating racism. The work of Hartman and Husband (1971) had indicated that there was a correlation between reports of rising immigrant birth rates and the opinions of residents about black people in areas of low immigrant density. Trew (1979) sought to reveal the linguistic mechanisms operating in the popular press which might account for such a correlation, and further to link those mechanisms to the ideology of specific newspapers. He chose to compare news reports of the 1977 Notting Hill 'race riots' in the *Sun* and the *Morning Star* in order to show that the differing ideology of the papers would be reproduced in different syntax.

Beginning with a content analysis of types of syntax, Trew discovered that the *Sun* featured some 31 transactive[6] clauses (50 per cent of all clauses), compared to the *Morning Star*, which tended toward clauses describing relations and used only 16 transactive clauses (38 per cent of all clauses) to report the same event. The two reports occupied a similar number of column inches and were published on the same day. Terms for black youth, such as mob, gang, thugs, dominated the agent noun position in the *Sun* whilst the *Morning Star* described processes more literally, such as 'groups of youngsters started running down the street'. Trew suggested that through the selection of particular terms for agents in transaction the *Sun* was in 'explicit engagement in ideological conflict' (Fowler *et al.* 1979: 134).

Trew argued that the use of the transactive set up a conflict framework of agent/acting on/patient whilst transformation of the term 'groups of youngsters' into mob, gangs and thugs effectively removed them from the white/people category of the dominant group: black youth was identified as the enemy, legitimating oppressive retaliatory measures. He suggested that transactive syntax and agent transformation resulted in a dispute paradigm wherein the way 'people are categorised may involve attributing causally significant causal powers to them and a place in social relations' (Trew 1979: 135). Oppositional groups were denigrated through racist terminology and blamed through attributional syntax to ensure it 'is not society which is on trial' (the *Sun* quoted in Trew 1979), in a continuous process in the popular press.

Using Trew's assumption that the conservative and communist ideologies of the *Sun* and *Morning Star* were reproduced through their style as a model, I aimed to investigate whether the desired radical perspective of *News on Sunday* could also be elicited through linguistic analysis. To test the potential of the new tabloid I matched an article from the new *News on Sunday* with one produced on the same day in the long-established, conservative and populist *News of the World*. The two pieces covered the disturbances at Broadwater Farm in Tottenham and were published on 13 October 1985.

Pictures of the violence in Tottenham had been accompanied by captions such as 'Hooded Animals out for Blood' (*Daily Star*) and 'Face of Monster' (*Sun*). The result was that 'black and white residents accused journalists of systematic racism, lies and misrepresentation' (*Guardian* 30.3.87), evidenced by the use of the kind of emotive terminology Trew had identified some ten years earlier. In this context, I anticipated that the *News of the World,* as a Sunday from Murdoch's press stable, would have been likely to perpetrate similar racist, right-wing ideology whilst *News on Sunday,* aiming for populism with a similar style had declared its radical and anti-racist intentions.

As with the *Sun,* both samples showed a high percentage of transactive clauses and I decided to retain Trew's focus on these as likely purveyors of ideological material because of the support for this contention from social psychological studies of blame attribution. Tajfel and Fraser (1978) argued that in any situation where the actor perceives a problem, the cause of that dilemma will be attributed elsewhere, because actors seek to exclude themselves from responsibility but need to do so in ways that maintain their individual identity. Therefore, in crisis, blame is placed outside the self and preferably, according to psychological needs to sustain belief in a stable identity and secure world, outside of the social group of the perceiver. Syntactical transaction is the linguistic representation of this theorised cognitive structure. With its agent/action/patient structure it presents the framework for the expression of attribution.

The inner-city disorders of the early 1980s were an 'acid test of hegemony' (Bennett 1981a: 311). The economic downswing impinged heavily on the ethnic groups in the major cities leading to their vocalisation of the injustices suffered in terms of work and housing. The response of the mainstream media was a 'further denigration of the inferior group in order that their subordinate position may be deserved' (Husband 1984: 34) eventually including the use of force and changes in legislation to maintain control. My analysis aimed to show how the *News of the World* was part of that denigratory account of the disaffected black groups and to access the extent to which the new radical tabloid managed to present an ideological alternative. The following are sample quotes from the actual newspaper reports:

News on Sunday (3.10.85) 'Aftermath to an Uprising'

Special Patrol Group police yesterday began questioning all residents of Tottenham's riot-torn Broadwater Farm estate. Armed members of the Diplomatic Protection squad have been conducting stop and search operations in the area since last Sunday's riot, sparked by the death of Cynthia Jarrett during a police raid on her home. Rumours are everywhere and tension is high. Today Broadwater Farm is under siege. Hundreds of police patrol the area and most residents are too frightened even to venture onto the walkways, dominated by seven or eight strong groups of police. The estate is overflowing with bitterness. 'They kill a black woman and they get away with it,' said a young black woman, who did not want to be named. 'We see pictures of PC Blakelock's grieving family, but where are the pictures of the Jarrett family's tragedy? We have to defend ourselves. Next time a policeman knocks on my door, how do I know he is not going to shoot me, my mother or my babies?'

News of the World (13.10.85) 'Now It's War on Gunmen'

Demoralised Scotland Yard officers have been given the go-ahead to flush out the gunmen and petrol bombers. And the all-clear from Commissioner Sir Kenneth Newman is expected to signal a new drive to bring the riot ringleaders to justice. A series of raids on the homes of the mob organisers is planned. In one of the most intensive detection operations ever, 50 leaders of the Tottenham riot have been identified. They include gunmen and petrol bombers who led the attack in which P.C. Blakelock died. Among those earmarked for raids are the quartermasters, thought to have been stocking up with petrol bombs and other offensive weapons. For weeks before the flare up, police had constructed a detailed picture of the Broadwater Farm estate's most dangerous criminals. But local police would not let crime squads raid the suspects homes for fear of sparking off a riot. The Yard's elite Serious Crimes squad has been put in charge of the new offensive, a complete about turn by Sir Kenneth.

The first part of the analysis followed Trew's methodology by identifying and extracting transactive clauses from the samples. *News on Sunday* had 60 per cent transactive clauses and *News of the World* 83 per cent, paralleling the new paper with the attributive style of the *Sun* in Trew's study, whilst its purported aim was to produce dissimilar ideology. Following Trew the lexes (word choices) for participants were mapped on a matrix to indicate which selections were being made for agent and patient to try to isolate attribution of responsibility in the texts. Participants in both samples included police, people, state, community and others. Both articles preferred to focus on the police, in *News on Sunday* 68 per cent and in *News of the World* 63 per cent of nouns in the agent role. In *News on Sunday* the people of Broadwater were in the agent role more than twice as frequently (25 per cent) as in *News of the World* (10 per cent). The other frequently occurring agent group in the *News of the World* was the government/state at 27 per cent.

It appeared that the accounts of the disorder at Broadwater Farm were structurally similar in that each preferred the transactive form and the same selections for agency predominated. Yet, my expectation, from cultural knowledge about the political orientation of each paper, was to find ideological difference. Either the new paper was failing entirely in its ideological project or critical linguistic theory was over-concretising the relation between language form and ideology. In other words, the relation between the different syntax of the *Morning Star* and the *Sun* and their different ideologies was not perhaps as directly causal as appeared. Methodologically, I had to find a way of not merely typing and counting syntactic forms and selections made for agency but of clarifying the way in which these might elicit an evaluation in the reading. Whereas Trew had assumed that the ideology of the production context was largely determining of style, and thereby ideology, it seemed to me that in my samples very different production contexts were using broadly similar text-types to deliver different perspectives on the same event.

Language forms are fixed and familiar but their relationship to meaning is a matter of convention rather than natural. Consistent association of a word shape/sound to an item, act or experience welds arbitrarily assigned forms to meanings, apparently immutably. Hall likens this confusion of form and meaning as the 'same' to our ready acceptance of the photograph as a 'meta-message ... this event really happened and this photograph is proof of it' (1982b: 241). The photograph belies the selecting, transforming and reproducing and offers only the apparent evidence of an event. The history of the event and process of production are superseded by actuality and immediacy. The apparent reality of the news photo is the visual equivalent of the apparent meaning of language. Once it is possible to see that only the form of language is *fixed*, the meaning becomes potentially polysemous, with use determining the accent or preferred meaning. It follows that normally the preferred or con-ventionalised meaning will concur with the point of view of those who control the most pervasive means of language-use. Dominance will by convention predominate meaning interpretations of the word-form.

Given this model of language I re-examined the transactive clauses in my newspaper articles in terms of their connotated rather than denotated meaning using the evaluative grid devised by Chibnall (1977) and discussed in Chapter 1. In other words, I tried to evaluate systematically the culturally shared meanings associated with the language in my samples that were not obvious from dictionary definitions or grammatical structures. Chibnall's list related to his own opinion of dominant British values between the Second World War and the mid-1970s but remains relevant to Thatcherism and could also be extended to include other categories with value con-notations, such as racial values and gender values.[7] By interpreting the connoted meaning of agent/process in the transactive clauses in relation to my cultural knowledge of value judgements relating to the groups in agent positions – blacks, police, state – I found significant differences in the meanings either text could make available.

Whereas both reports had used selections for the police most frequently in the agent role, that action was reproduced in the text to connote different evaluations. In each clause featuring the group *police* as agent, *News on Sunday* used selections for noun and process which led to a negative evaluation of agency from the reader whilst *News of the World* chose words that offered a positive evaluative reading of the police agency. Such interpretations were subjective but the evaluation process does identify the whereabouts of a preferred reading for each text as lying beyond the text in shared cultural experience between producer/context and reader/context, rather than in linguistic structures. The value judgement difference between *SPG* and *local police*, for example, was not identifiable merely from the selection of those language forms but required cultural knowledge of the different roles of the aggressive Special Patrol Groups and the more benign 'bobbies on the beat'. The metaphoric transformations in 'Now It's War on Gunmen' would be another example. The construction and connotations placed Broadwater residents in the enemy role in a war scenario and reproduced familiar, and oft repeated, stereotypes. In particular this kind of language connoted Northern Ireland and the IRA with its talk of *quartermasters, gunmen and petrol bombers*. The *News of the World* ignored the flashpoint death of Mrs Jarrett whereas *News on Sunday* emphasised both that event and earlier problems with over-policing as causal of the conflict. The difference in ideology between the accounts lay somewhere amidst selections of events for inclusion and selections of terms for description and explanation.

Yet, to what extent did such evaluative differences support *News on Sunday*'s aim to be radical and alternative? Any attempt to reproduce subordinate and/or oppositional perspectives in terms of race would have required taking a position that positively evaluated ethnic groups, stressed long-term structural causes of racism rather than single events and perhaps inverted attributions of causality from natural black characteristics to white cultural domination. There were marked differences in the two news reports: *News on Sunday* referred to black people as family, residents or community in contrast with the war metaphor and crime allusions of *News of the World*. In terms of social relations, the former were normal descrip-tions whilst the latter nominalisations made black people seem to be deviant or criminal, by aligning violence with ethnicity. But this was only a partial inversion in that 'Aftermath to an Uprising' only minimally presented the Broadwater Farm community as positive and active. Most of the text attributed action to the police, albeit negatively, but did not extend that to a critique of the state or broader structures. The effect was to neutralise the event, which made it somewhat incredible – the inference was how could so much disruption occur for no reason? There was an implied acceptance of the police presence, because there was no critical exploration of norms of police–black relations, just a negative evaluation of the type of policing on this occasion. There was only one account of blacks as active and positive in building a community centre; seven years of tension goes unexplained and the racist media practices of the other tabloids were not addressed.

Yet, the minimal shift did refute the theory that ideology lies straightforwardly in syntax; both samples were dominated by the transactive form and both placed lexical selections for police in the agent role and people in the patient role. However, the connotative evaluations were dissimilar, with *News on Sunday* differently accenting causality than the conservative and consensual *News of the World*. Syntactic form directed the reader towards attribution in

both texts and so provided an ideological predisposition for interpretation, but ideological differentiation between similar forms
depended on cultural knowledge and the evaluation of the text sub-
jectively according to experience.

News on Sunday offered a critique of white authority behaviour in
a specific instance but not of white authority per se. It did not negate
black character or action but neither did it confirm the positive
values of black culture or identity. The crux of understanding
linguistic realisations of racism seems to be that even radical
attempts to select and mediate meanings can only minimally dilute
preferred interpretations because the lived culture constrains the
reader's ability to differently evaluate and accent. The struggle for
radicalism in *News on Sunday* at production level was limited first by
the reduced but still tangential relations with media and capital but
second by the shared linguistic conventions and categorisations
which bind the social – journalists and audiences. The norms and
values of communication structure thinking to the extent that even
if radical alternatives could be verbalised it is doubtful if they would
make sense to an audience steeped in dominance. It would require
different predispositions to generate different understanding (Curran
1990) with an audience able to bring alternate beliefs about their
world to the process of making sense of the text.

Even if *News on Sunday* had managed to install 'radical' control,
organisational and journalistic practices, linguistic ideology would
have still impeded the production of an alternative news because
language meaning is conventionally dominant meaning. In order
to be truly innovative the new tabloid would have had to make
sensible to its designated readership a new meaning potential. Such
a potential would have both upheld the paper's charter and
redressed some of problems of journalistic norms and news values.
Further, it would have had to begin to address the ideological bias
of the media by offering a voice to hitherto unrepresented or
denigrated social groups.

Even subordinate groups themselves, in a shared language
community, lack access to a means of expression that does not
denigrate or negate their experience. Salman Rushdie criticised the
black film-makers of *Song of Handsworth* for merely reworking the
white view of black action. He commented, 'if you want to give voice
to the voiceless you've got to find a language' (*Guardian* January
1987) not rearrange standard English stereotypes with all their
cultural connotations about ethnicity. *News on Sunday* gave even less

column inches to black issues in the UK than did the corresponding copy of *News of the World*. Its best achievement was to present images of blacks as passive and oppressed so negating rather than denigrating. It did not, could not, give voice to the voiceless.

Racial Stereotypes

News on Sunday was not only unable to shift race news into a new representational potential, it was also unable to maintain its ambitions to challenge both traditional journalistic practices and the dependence of the industry on advertising. Resistant to denigratory stereotyping and conventional, commercial journalism, the newspaper had some difficulty in even producing recognisable news about the racial disturbances of the 1980s. It seemed as if racial issues were only newsworthy if they could be represented within particular accounting frameworks, which meant they made sense to readers and matched journalistic processes and ideologies. In relation to the first of these, as Galtung and Ruge (1965) found, news must be consonant with cultural expectations; it must fit existing categories in order to be meaningful. In Britain, in the early 1980s, the familiar categories for black people were almost entirely denigratory stereotypes.

Stereotype, curiously, has a journalistic denotation as it refers to a metal casting of a printing plate from a mould of movable type. In the days of the 'hot metal' press it was a way of fixing type for printing. As a popular figure of speech, it connotes an established, unchangeable association of meaning with a term or phrase. Sometimes that meaning can be very far indeed from the dictionary definition of the term but it becomes moulded to it through use.[8] Stereotypes are a kind of meta-language, depending on the shared community language forms but meaningful only in the specific cultural and communication context. Only occasionally and later might these meanings become part of a dictionary definition.

At one level stereotypes are merely a way for human beings to label objects and processes manageably. Subjective 'shorthand' representations simply become conventionalised through communication. But, commonly, stratified societies mark out categories between people 'which typically point to those who do not fully belong' (Glover 1984: 27). Those highest in the hierarchy will tend to view themselves as normal, will see 'others' who are different as lesser or deviant and will have the authority to disseminate their views as truth or common sense. The 'others' will be denigrated, labelled as deviant or sometimes be negated and made 'invisible' in language. Such categorising naturalises and reproduces existing social stratification and becomes a 'source and support for ideas, which legitimate powerful vested interests in society' (Glover 1984: 27). Although the process is cognitive, relating to norms of group interaction, the content of stereotypes is drawn from experience in the real world.

In the case of racial stereotypes that experience can be traced historically 'back to the pre-colonial world' (Walvin 1982: 63) of trade and exploration. Early anthropology was permeated with Christian norms and values and, by comparison, newly discovered societies were readily perceived as tribal, amoral, savage and idle. Deemed in need of training and control, any black resistance to the new moral and labour regimes was taken as evidence of their inferiority and a justification for slavery. By the late Victorian period, the Negro stereotype had permeated British culture. Tribalism, promiscuity, idleness, savagery, simpleness and slavery featured regularly in education and popular culture throughout the nineteenth century and continued well into the twentieth with 'Little Black Sambo' and 'Uncle Tom' stories for children and films such as *Birth of a Nation*, *Mandingo*, *Zulu*, *Island in the Sun*, *Gone with the Wind* and *Sanders of the River*. Black stereotypes became deeply embedded in white-dominated societies, justifying all manner of exclusion, oppression and exploitation but also corrupting black self-perception to such an extent that some of the most lucrative cosmetic sales to black consumers have been (are) skin lightening creams. In Stuart Hall's terms it became insufficient to merely 'soap' black skin clean, as in the Pear's advertisements of the nineteenth century, it had to be bleached. Richard Dyer in *White* wrote about the glow of white women and to highlight his discussion of whiteness offered an advertisement from *Ebony* (July 1973) which featured *Ultra Bleach and Glow* 'skin lighteners for women of African descent' (1997: 122).

Stereotypical associations are powerful and pervasive but also fluid. New ones can be added and old ones recycled but eradication seems rare however strong the contestation. During the 1960s Civil Rights struggles the phrases 'black is beautiful' and 'black power' signified some of the most profound resistances to black stereotyping, yet by the early 1980s all the old denigratory terms filled the British newspapers, alongside the newly imported criminalising labels.

Stereotyping works alongside violence. Sometimes it justifies the use of real violence, as in exercises like Swamp 81; sometimes the symbolism is violent enough to effectively control or exclude those outside the norm; sometimes so violent that the 'outsiders' abject themselves from the society or adopt dominant norms to seek inclusion. Black stereotyping establishes knowledge in the interest of white power across a range of discourses. It is part of the process of hegemony that naturalises one set of cultural norms, through repetition and mass dissemination, as if they were true and therefore right for all.

Hall argued that any attempt to 'dismantle or subvert a racialised regime of representation is an extremely difficult exercise, about which – like so much else in representation – there can be no guarantees' (1997: 276). He suggested three strategies, each with its own pitfall: first, reversing stereotypes by creating black heroes in, for example, popular film, which does not necessarily reduce the potency of the image of the black villain; second, responding to the negativity of most media accounts of race with positive representa-tions, which does little to shift those negative images off the mainstream and may add to the 'repertoire' of readily denigratable, race labels; last, Hall considered the possibility of changing the form rather than the content of racial representation to 'de-familiarise' by eliciting shock or desire in the audience and so provoking a new reading. This last 'aesthetic strategy' may, ironically (and irony is often part of this project) only work with an audience already sensitive to the politics of racial representation.

News Values

Such theoretical accounts of stereotypifying racial representation help explain *News on Sunday*'s difficulty in finding a voice for the black people of Broadwater Farm but do not really explain why, for the remainder of the press in the first five years of the 1980s, race was such a salient source of news.

Too strong an emphasis on racism as culturally endemic in a sense lets news organisations off the hook in that they can claim to be merely reflecting society and responding to their audiences. Yet news is not just reflection it is selection. Galtung and Ruge (1965) suggested that in fact it is the process of selection that makes an event newsworthy not something inherent in the event itself. Race events are only newsworthy if they can be made to conform to the criteria for news. Those criteria are filters on reality, which allow only certain events, aspects of events or angles on events to be reported. Events with negative, serious, unambiguous or unpredictable implications are preferred, especially if these involve elite groups or individuals and are culturally familiar. Such news is then tailored to fit available space, time, composition, expertise and cost and transformed to be unambiguous, meaningful and personal.

Race becomes newsworthy when some aspect of an event allows journalists to draw on the pool of racial stereotypes pervading British culture because these stereotypes fit the requirement of news for negative, unpredictable and possibly serious connotations. Moreover, race has a long history – it is a familiar and continuous issue – and when race can be linked to crime and violence, authoritative institutions and elite spokespeople from the law courts, police and government can be drawn in as expert sources in news reports. Race events are newsworthy because the shared cultural stereotypes fit the needs of the newsroom. News values ensure that the most damaging racial stereotypes are reproduced not through any conspiracy but in accordance with institutional and professional practices. These ensured that ethnic minorities featured in the news of the early 1980s as scapegoats for the ills of the decade; familiar stereotypes added potency to such constructions because, in Stuart Hall's terms, ideologies work most effectively when our formulations seem to be descriptive statements of how things are. The news media 'map out for us the contours of our culture and society' (Glover 1984: 26), perpetuating racial stereotypes as taken for granted reality.

The criteria of news values inherent in news-making during Thatcherism in essence confirmed the most negative black stereotypes and defined race relations in terms of inter-group conflict which delineated the potential 'categories people use when thinking about race-related matters' (Hartman and Husband 1971: 292). People assume that the news informs us of the 'pressing issues of the day' (Hall *et al.* 1978: 62). In Britain, news about race built increasingly into a crescendo during the 1970s when 'mugger', 'entrammelled in the whole American panic about race, crime, riot and lawlessness' (Hall *et al.* 1978: 28), was added to the fund of racial stereotypes. The increased ghettoisation, unemployment, immigration restrictions, crises in black identity and heavy-handed policing, which underwrote the inner-city disturbances of the 1980s, were readily explained as caused by black crime and violence because news values and racism are ideologically integrated.

Comment

The nature of such accounts of conflict and blame are commensurate with Fowler's (1991) theory of three ideological political shifts being central to the Thatcherite project. The conflict paradigm of explanation for race legitimated a consolidation of authority and escalation of police power and legislative control, consonant with Fowler's claim that there was a shift towards centralisation. Second, any potential for the construction of a politicised black collective was diminished not just by criminalising the black community as a whole but by the wholesale deconstruction of local political potential and trades unionism, which, alongside exclusionary racist mechanisms, meant black presence in these areas was often minimal. 'There was a concerted campaign in the early 1980s to set up black Sections in the Labour Party. These requests were met with alarming hostility' (Cumberbatch 1998: 26). Last, without representation, the rampant individualism of the 1980s meant that if blacks were not succeeding they had no one to blame but themselves. The legacy of the early 1980s has been profound and ongoing for black Britons but it also informed changes with implications for all citizens.

Changes in the law followed the 1981 Scarman Report, yet seemed barely to recognise or respond to that report's largely positive and reformist recommendations. Scarman suggested more aid to improve living conditions in the inner cities, positive discrimination in education and employment, reform within the police, especially in relation to riot tactics but also legal changes linked to powers of arrest, police complaints and political demonstration.

Retrospectively, it is possible to see little evidence of the first three points and a significant development of the fourth, which informed the 1984 Police and Criminal Evidence Act (PACE). This act gave significant new powers to the police in relation to the investigation of 'serious arrestable offences' (yet did not define these). Police gained more authority to gather information both from people at home and on the street, where individuals could be asked to 'justify their presence'. Reasonable force was allowed in stop and search procedures, as were road blocks (these were used throughout the 1984–85 Miners' Strike, discussed in the next chapter). Suspects could be held in custody for four days without questioning, for 36 hours without a solicitor and police were given more power to use 'intimate body searches'. This act established race as a major problem for the Criminal Justice System and arguably institutionalised what had largely been rampant but 'freelance' racism.

In 1986 the Public Order Act had consolidated the aspect of PACE relating to confrontational behaviour by adding new offences of riot, violent disorder and affray to the statute. Each related to any gathering of twelve people or more and varied according to the actual or threatened use of violence, causing fear for personal safety or one person acting violently on behalf of the group. The act was applicable not only to black street culture but to football crowds, political gatherings and youth culture. It included requirements of notice to the police for processions and assemblies and more authority to the police to evict groups deemed to be committing aggravated trespass (this was used regularly to clear young 'ravers' and 'new age' travellers from rural sites as discussed in Chapter 4). This act also appeared to recognise the racism suffered by the urban black communities in that it prohibited incitement to racial hatred or the possession of racially inflammatory material in an upgrade of the 1976 Race Relations Act. But, the effect of this recognition was more about limiting and controlling racial conflict on the streets than about improving conditions more generally for the black communities – in other words, its goal was law and order not anti-racism.

The conflict model of race relations supported by the Conservative government legitimated cultural prejudice and constructed the resources to abject the other. The link between public discourses and state policy was mutually affirmative. Pitts argued that the new police powers and strategies effectively designated any black person a criminal suspect and so transformed 'all police officers into racists irrespective of the intentions of those involved' (1986: 112). People entering the police force trailing behind them clouds of archaic racial stereotypes were rapidly socialised into a culture that constructed those stereotypes as causal of crime – and the job of a police officer is to prevent crime and capture criminals.

In 1999, there was another report into race relations in Britain, the Stephen Lawrence Inquiry conducted by Sir William Macpherson. It recognised and emphasised precisely this institutionalised racism and prompted an immediate debate around what this phrase meant and whether or not it was appropriate. The report was commissioned by the Labour government soon after its landslide victory in May 1997. Four years previously 18-year-old Stephen Lawrence had been knifed to death as he waited at a bus stop in

London. Stephen's parents set up a campaign for justice after Metropolitan police were slow in making arrests of three white teenagers, against whom charges were dropped in September 1995. The family's subsequent effort at a private prosecution against five white youths collapsed yet the following inquest found that Stephen had been unlawfully killed. British law prevents the double jeopardy of suspects being re-tried for the same crime yet the *Daily Mail* named the five, under the huge headline 'MURDERERS' after the coroner's decision in February 1997. (The same paper called the black youths of Birmingham the 'worst elements of society' under the headline 'BLOODLUST' in September 1981.) The Lawrences' claimed that racism was both the motive for the crime and the reason for the failure to prosecute successfully. Although they had to wait for a Labour government to be elected for an inquiry to be instigated, the Macpherson report broadly agreed with their claims.[9]

Macpherson made 70 recommendations including applying the Race Relations Act to the police, dismissal of officers for racist behaviour, anti-racist training and higher levels of freedom of information on policing processes. Not all have been equally welcomed by the government but those that have seem to apply directly to racism in the police. The Home Secretary, Jack Straw, said reforms 'must be implemented within the mainstream of the service at every level, not seen as some "bolt-on extra"' (*Guardian* 24.3.99), which he identified as the impotence of the 1981 Scarman Report.

The Lawrence case was racism in a different context to the disorders of the early 1980s. A cynic might explain the levels of sympathy in the media and in politics as more to do with the apparent middle-classness of the Lawrences than any profound multi-cultural sensibility, particularly as the white suspects came from a London council estate teeming with unemployment, vandalism and racist graffiti (with the exception of one whose father the media readily linked to London's criminal underworld). There has been little evidence to suggest news values have dramatically changed – if anything commercial pressures may well have hardened the commitment to negativity, drama and titillation (Franklin 1997); nor is there much change in the overall profile of journalists themselves (Tunstall 1996; Christmas 1997). My suspicion is that given a different context the old racist stereotypes, which still thrive in the collective cultural subconscious,[10] might readily reappear, albeit perhaps somewhat more covertly, due to the legal constraints on incitement to racial hatred.

Although the media appear to be less racially provocative at the millennium this may be because black 'quasi-rebellion', with its high news value, has been deconstructed off the agenda of the black communities. Paradoxically, a lack of journalistic interest in the black communities has not been matched by a lack of police interest in black individuals. Home Office crime figures for 1999, available on the WWW, show high and growing figures for blacks featuring in the Criminal Justice System (oddly much of the data relating to London's Metropolitan police is unavailable). Ethnically, proportions of arrest of black people per 1,000 of the population are twice as high as Asians, which in turn are approximately twice as high as for white groups.[11] Figures for the British Nationals' prison population show a decrease in the white male population from 87.8 per cent in 1993 to 85.7 per cent in 1996; for the same period the percentage of Afro-Caribbean men in British prisons rose from 5.9 per cent to 7.1 per cent.[12]

Figures linked to the operation of PACE 1984 for 1996/97 show numbers of searches per thousand of population. This is one of the few returns from the Metropolitan police who record four times as many searches of black suspects as compared to white.[13] Despite popular preconceptions about black violence, most white people are killed by white people (92 per cent). Black and Asian deaths are caused 69 per cent of the time by black or Asian 'principal suspects' but 31 per cent of black murder victims are killed by whites and 25 per cent of Asians are killed by whites.[14] In other words, whites are the more murderous ethnic group in Britain.

It is a priority of Tony Blair's Labour government to ensure that the principle of fair treatment remains central to the administration of British justice. But there seems to be a long way to go to achieve the Home Secretary's aim for the Home Office (see HMSO 1999) which was: 'In a multi-cultural society such as Britain today, it is essential that all sections of the community have confidence in the ability of the criminal justice system to protect the public and to deal effectively with offenders without unfair discrimination of any kind' (HMSO 1999).

It may be possible to reverse the concretisation of racism within the police that came about during the 1980s by reforming some of the most empowering legislation and introducing new internal practices and positive multi-cultural recruitment. The Blair Labour government at least seems willing to challenge racist policing, but changing cultural norms, either within or without the force, is unlikely to be achieved merely by legislation, though deconstructing institutional racism may be helped by recalling some of powers given to police under the 1980s legislative changes. But the Lawrence case is not just about a racist justice system. Racism simmers beneath what Hall called the consensual calm of everyday Britishness. The Commission for Racial Equality has received many more 'hate' letters and phone calls in the wake of the Lawrence case – including one stating: '"This nigger got what he deserved"' (*Guardian* 24.3.99). In the same article, Chris Myant, their Press Officer commented, 'despite thirty years of effort, there are still people who hold these ideas. You can't talk about British society without recognising there is this undercurrent within it and it has not gone away.'

3
Public Order: Criminal Class

At the outset of Thatcherism it was still valid to describe the cultural life of Britain as distinctly class differentiated:

> For the middle class culture is formalised and enjoyed privately in the form of theatre, ballet, opera, museums and art galleries. Working class culture on the other hand revolves around public and social relationships, often out of doors, at the public meeting, in the workingmen's club, at the Gala, in the fairground and most of all at the pub. (Coulter *et al.* 1984: 161)

Collective public culture can be threatening to the state. It generates cohesion around identity and communication that may bypass the mass media and commercialised leisure. Collective culture is often street culture. Public spaces occupied by carnivals, celebrations, markets, meetings, games and music can easily become sites of conflict of interest between participating groups and/or between street culture and the authorities, as happened in the racial disturbances in the inner cities form 1981 to 1985. This chapter focuses on two aspects of working-class life where such public, collective conflict was the pivot for major cultural decon-struction and reconstruction during the Thatcher government: coal mining and football. The maintenance of public order depends on the perceived legitimacy of control measures and therefore, also, on the way in which disorder is represented, so any analysis of disorderly publics must include work on representation. The chapter focuses on strikes and football hooliganism to try to show how any theory of violent collective behaviour is made more adequate through attention to mediated accounts of the communities, identities and contexts involved in conflict. It also argues that a research focus that concentrates too exclusively on the cause and prevention of conflict, alongside media preference for the 'violent highlights' diverts attention from the, sometimes, profound implications of political ideology and the exercise of power.

Causes of Disorder

Popular perspectives on public disorder derive mainly from two theoretical positions within psychology and sociology. It is worth briefly reviewing these because the remainder of this chapter suggests that, in contrast, work on culture is essential to the understanding of collective conflict.

Early psychological perspectives, deriving from the Victorian drive to civilise and control, viewed crowd violence as a return to barbarism. Individuals by the mere fact of being part of a crowd were thought to succumb to instinctual, animalistic behaviour (Tarde 1907). This view remains popular with the public and media a century later and is epitomised by the familiar description of crowd behaviour as mindless violence. In a crowd people are thought to lose their sense of individual responsibility, to cease to think for themselves and to adopt a herd mentality. There are many problems with such an approach but briefly not all crowds are violent, not everyone joins a crowd, people usually know others in the crowd and crowds are rarely spontaneous.

Another influential model focuses on personality types and suggests that some individuals are predisposed to aggressive behaviour and that this can be exaggerated by the crowd context. Such individuals, ringleaders, are then thought to prompt others into violent behaviour by stirring them up. They are often described as Jekyll and Hyde characters, for example, a man described as a 'quiet gentle young Dad ... was identified on video, masterminding violence' (*Mirror* 16.6.92). This explanation has always been popular with the press, who prefer to focus on individuals they can turn into personalities, whether heroes or villains, but was largely dismissed by Marsh (1978).

Marsh returned to violence as collectively generated but focused closely on the relationship of collective disorder to masculinity. For Marsh the crowd is neither an anarchic context nor a collection of lemmings, rather it is an event structured by 'shared meanings and social roles and a system of rules' (1978: 63). Crowds are not random or irrational but linked to and explicable by theories of group psychology. Group membership, role, status and relations between groups are central to individual identity. Marsh argued that most group activity remains within the 'limits of acceptable and sane behaviour' (1978: 70) and only involves the levels of rowdiness necessary for a member to prove himself a man. For Marsh a little violence is the mark of a man and a universal trait. Yet all men do not behave similarly nor is crowd violence the kind of regular, systematic event that marks out ritual behaviour.[1]

At the social end of psychological models of collective disorder other criteria come into theory that shift explanations towards sociological accounts. Particular groups may riot when they feel excluded from the mainstream or have a strong sense of being the victims of injustices. Such dissonance or alienation can erupt in aggression borne of frustration. Some broadly psychological models recognise the existence of divergent factors in disturbances. Smelser (1962) offered a multi-level account of the factors leading to violence that took account of macro components such as social structure, collective exclusion and 'political' critique alongside micro features such as particular context, situational event and moment of crisis.

Waddington, Jones and Critcher (1989) used a similar approach to analyse crowd violence in the UK, but with less focus on the deviant and irrational nature of it and more on the socio-political context. Sociological accounts see collective violence as conscious, perhaps rational, sometimes planned and sometimes legitimate. The three broad approaches are liberal, conservative and radical. The liberal model of explanation was characterised by the Scarman Report (1981) on the inner-city race riots (see Chapter 2) that focused on the deprivation and disadvantage of the black communities as an explanation. Street battles with the police were a frustrated expression of disenfranchisement and alienation. The solution is better conditions, inclusion and respect. Conservative models see little problem with the status quo, in fact they want it conserved. Collective challenge is seen as either mindless violence for no good reason and therefore requiring no action except legal control of the 'criminals' if adult, as in the race riots discussed in Chapter 2 (or to blame the parents or media if youths are disorderly, see Chapter 4), or conspiratorial attempts at political insurrection, usually led by outside agitators stimulating unwarranted anti-state activities, as in news about the anti-Vietnam protest at Grosvenor Square in 1968. Alternatively, the radical thesis explains crowd violence as a sometimes legitimate and informed political response when it arises from exploitation, discrimination or unjust coercion – an example where this thesis seemed to dominate accounts was the poll tax riot in 1988. The resolution is sustained, and appropriate, change in the socio-political order results.

Largely missing from both psychological and sociological theories is much work on the meanings associated with conflict, particularly in relation to the history of collective relations and the contemporary context of any specific clashes. This book is about the culture of conflict during Thatcherism, and this chapter examines two contexts of class conflict during that Conservative government in order to assess the extent to which the meanings associated with collective disorder can help explain its causes, resolutions and implications.

Class, Community and Conflict

The twin areas of work and leisure, illustrated here by mining and football, have a long history as sites of class conflict. They are seen in the late twentieth century as clearly demarcated areas with very different social roles. 'The patterns and rhythms of life are determined by work and its demands and any spare time, the residual, is labelled as a leisure period' (Jenkins and Sherman 1981: 1). Pre-industrially these distinctions were blurred and variable. People worked to sustain themselves and their families. Work peaked seasonally; society was rural and communal; intense periods of labour were punctuated with long holidays, frequent celebrations and flexible working arrangements. Workers had relative autonomy over their labour subject to, and dependent only on, the vicissitudes of nature. Communities were small and work was performed for self or group. Streets and commons were both marketplaces and play spaces where gossip and socialising interjected trade and labour. Alcohol was sold all day and business was regularly set aside for fairs and their 'temporary culture of licentiousness' (Malcolmson 1973: 76). This irreverence was also evident in the relationship between the social strata.

During festivities, effigies of local dignitaries were mocked or burnt, normal courtesies were ignored, as were poaching restrictions and the gentry tolerated petty crime and general rowdiness. This was early 'blind-eye' policing but not from choice because expressions of contempt for authority were as much part of leisure culture as was the sometimes violent settling of scores and in the renegotiation of individual and community identity. Malcolmson concluded that 'recreation was one major dimension of an established culture – it was woven into and derived its meanings from the total social fabric' (1973: 88). The gentry of an agricultural rural society depended greatly on the consent of the masses, as any means of directed coercive control were very limited.

The growth of industrial society informed dramatic transformations in the form, context and content of popular culture. Cities prospered and attracted the labour that was necessary for the newly emergent economies. These required reliable and trainable workers who would comprise a civilised and disciplined workforce. That need was paramount and led to legislation that was designed to deconstruct old cultural patterns amongst the new urban labourers. The new laws were backed up by the introduction of policing and a system of magistrates' courts; this was the process that E.P. Thompson (1970) called the making of the English working class.

Sites for spontaneous and public gatherings were quickly eroded from 1800 onwards. The Enclosures Act removed thousands of acres of land from common use. Crowd-attracting sports were curtailed because they disrupted work, led to drunkenness and sometimes damage to property. The Cruelty to Animals Act 1835 ostensibly stopped animal baiting but there was a hidden agenda as 'concern for cruelty and its consequences was strongly enforced by the solicitude for public order and discipline' (Malcolmson 1973: 27). The Highways Act 1835 introduced prosecutions for games-playing on thoroughfares. Football had to be forcibly terminated in some places because it disrupted business and blocked thoroughfares. Travelling balladeers and tinkers were returned to their own parishes under the Poor Law 1834 and fairs and markets were cut as holiday periods were reduced to enforce the labour needs of new industries.

Once the masses had been restricted physically by these impositions, it was altogether easier to persuade them of the value of work, especially because home in the urban slums offered little comfort. The next assault on popular culture was to implement the new home- and family-based middle-class pastimes as best practice for all. This involved a moral rather than legal crusade, though the law was sometimes drawn on as support, for example in the impositions of licensing laws to curtail drinking. Roberts (1981) saw this need to seek consensus to middle-class culture as explaining the provision of many of the municipal leisure and health facilities like parks, baths and public libraries. Pleasure was licensed and became an industry in its own right. Prohibition gave way to profitability in the music halls and gin palaces as popular culture was transformed to fit the needs of, and indeed become a site of, capital investment and growth.

In the early twentieth century, technology accelerated the process and cinema became the social habit of the age (Taylor 1970), offering leisure outside the home to women for the first time. BBC radio grew rapidly from meagre beginnings in the 1920s. After the Second World War, advertising sought larger home markets as the empire disappeared whilst concurrently the mass media became a central part of leisure as television was reintroduced first as the BBC public service and then commercially in the mid-1950s. Work and leisure were no longer blended but clearly segregated in time and often in space. Crucially, leisure was now something people were prepared to pay for, without which 'modern industrial capitalist society will be undermined or ruptured' (Jenkins and Sherman 1981: 43).

However dramatic, such shifts were by no means complete, as is evidenced by the continuing bare-knuckle fights, badger baiting, poaching, street brawls, 'sickies' and football 'hooliganism' that retain some part of working-class masculine affection. That may in part be due to the deep-rooted collective identity that is the legacy of trades unionism, and bonded workers together to improve the conditions of work and pay. The factory owners of the industrial revolution expected long hours in appalling health-wrecking environments with no job security or insurance schemes. Radicalism was fuelled, in the early nineteenth century, by the ideas of French republicanism and spread by the underground newspapers like the *Poor Man's Guardian* and *The Gorgon*:

> Many of the paid correspondents ... were also political organisers for the National Union of the Working Classes or the Chartist movement. They sought to describe and expose the dynamics of power and inequality rather than to report hard news as a series of disconnected events. (Curran and Seaton 1991: 18)

The radical press deepened class-consciousness by linking the struggles of disparate groups of workers across the country and promoting political organisation. Newspapers were the only source of information about the world beyond the local community. They were read aloud in public houses and private homes and played a major part in reorienting workers to the industrial context by challenging a social order that had previously been taken for granted as natural or pre-ordained. Early papers like Cobbett's *Political Register* assaulted the aristocracy but by the 1830s the focus was on 'the economic process which enabled the capitalist class to appropriate in profits the wealth created by labour' (Curran and Seaton 1991: 23). The radical papers were actively inciting insurrection despite punitive legislative attempts at control through taxation and libel suits. The aim was universal suffrage and the means was withdrawal of labour as in the 1842 General Strike.

Insurgent journalism was a problem for government and press regulation was seen as the key to controlling dissent. The taxes on knowledge designed to outlaw radical publications failed: if anything, the perceived injustice of controls on the press encouraged the outlaw printers and customers. The example of the USA informed a parliamentary challenge, ostensibly to encourage a cheap legal press to educate and inform rather than incite the working classes. But the cost of providing popular newspapers was high enough to ensure that such entrepreneurial opportunities would be taken up by the existing wealthy middle-class corporations not the political radicals. The repeal of the Advertising Duty, Stamp Duty and Paper Duty between 1853 and 1861 reduced the cover price of the mainstream papers and rapidly excluded the radicals from the marketplace. Effectively the populist press of the people became a popular press produced for the people. For Curran and Seaton this was an expression of the confidence of the Victorian middle classes that 'recognised in the expanding press a powerful agency for the advancement of their interests' (1991: 30). The culture that the masses had trailed with them to the cities and factories gave way to a culture provided for them.

> A large part of the impetus to cheap periodical publishing was the desire to control the development of working class opinion ... Respectable schemes of moral and domestic improvement became deeply entangled with the teaching and implication of particular social values in the interests of the existing class society. (Williams 1961: 73)

Home and family, the focus for middle-class morality and leisure, were packaged for the workers via the popular papers and new family magazines. The provision of schooling, public baths, libraries and parks improved education and health but the erosion of popular leisure activities that did not concur with middle-class work require-ments or moral values proved difficult. Church and employers funded brass bands, choral societies, Sunday schools and decent housing, this last most evident in the Quaker philosophy behind the construction of Bournville and Saltaire. Religious evangelism preached the perils of the bottle and prostitution; the latter to the extent that 'the general rule was that any woman in a public place of leisure unaccompanied – was a prostitute' (Cunningham 1980: 130). Activities that could not be stopped (or at least driven out of sight) by moral hegemony were controlled by licensing. Drink, especially, was subject to limitations under the Beer Act 1872 and taxes on alcohol to raise the price. This allowed containment of activities within the needs of industry, the growth of new leisure industries and the appeasement of the working classes by allowing rather than banning.

Football illustrates this process well. From a violent fair-day brawl on the streets involving whole communities, few rules and no organisation it became a fixed site, set time, spectator sport with rules, organisation and entrance fees. It was a form of commercialised mass entertainment to which the middle class brought the financing and organisation and the working class contributed the excitement, players and of course a paying public.

Leisure as a collective site of potential conflict, either through the political radicalism of the debates in the public houses and underground presses or the violence and immorality associated with street games and alcohol, was transformed by the outset of the twentieth century

> The outcome of a century of battles over the problems of leisure was that for the dominant culture leisure was safely residual, unconnected with and possibly a counterweight to new and socialist challenges to hegemony. (Williams 1961: 199)

Consensual values may not have been fully internalised but it did not matter because the means to express resistant politics or different culture had been largely eroded or controlled. Upsurges of disorder between the end of the nineteenth and the end of the twentieth century indicated that clear lack of internalisation but also the effectiveness of containment.

During Thatcherism, class conflict climaxed politically with the miners' strike from 1984–85, and football remained a site where clashes and efforts at control led to violence and death. From 1988 until 1991 I worked as a Research Officer in the mining communities of Yorkshire, Nottinghamshire and Derbyshire,[2] and became professionally, politically and personally involved with understanding the causes, processes and aftermath of class and community conflict.

The Miners' Strike 1984–85

Historically, miners have been considered the 'backbone' of Britain. 'At the industry's height on the eve of the First World War it employed more than a million men to work 3000 mines' (Thatcher 1995: 340). Margaret Thatcher felt that the conflict between miners and owners led to the 1926 General Strike but still in the 1930s the miners were the 'working-class heroes' of Orwell's *Wigan Pier* and were photographed by Graham Sutherland, who dubbed them as ennobled underground and considered their stature enhanced by their labour. The mines were the power source for Britain's industrial revolution and this in turn gave miners themselves considerable power. They could literally stop the wheels of industry turning. Friction between owners and miners was disruptive and commonplace until coal's essential place in the economy led to it being nationalised by the Labour government in 1946. For Thatcher, this signified the beginning of the end of the mines, in that reason did not apply and the pits and mining unions were given a privileged status and authority, because of their historic role, that undermined the need for efficiency. She blamed the National Union of Mineworkers (NUM) for the collapse of the Conservative Heath government in 1974 and Britain's label as the sick man of Europe in the late 1970s. In opposition, the Conservatives drew up the Ridley Report (1978) on how to deal with the NUM. In May 1978, *The Economist* listed its battle plan.[3]

> Building up national stocks of coal, switching to the burning of oil at power stations, cutting social security payments to strikers, recruiting 'reliable' non-union lorry drivers to cross picket lines and preparing large, mobile police squads to combat flying pickets. (Waddington *et al.* 1991: 7)

In 1979 the Conservatives were elected after the now legendary winter of discontent (Scraton 1985) when strikes had led to unburied dead, blackouts and rubbish-strewn streets. The new Prime Minister quoted from St Francis of Assisi: 'Where there is discord may we bring harmony', but admitted later that overcoming the perceived problems in Britain would not be possible 'without some measure of discord' (Thatcher 1995: 19).

After being forced to back down from a closure programme in 1981, by the National Union of Mineworkers (their leader, Arthur Scargill, had claimed there was a 'list of 80 proposed closures' – Coulter *et al.* 1984: 12), Margaret Thatcher determined to 'build up steadily and unprovocatively – the stocks of coal which would allow the country to endure a coal strike' (1995: 341). The 1983 general election put the Tories back in power with an increased majority and Peter Walker was sent to the department of energy reportedly to prepare for a miners' strike. Ian McGregor was installed as chair at the National Coal Board with a 'reputation for hard hitting, anti-union style of management' (Waddington *et al.* 1991: 7) and the closure programme was resumed – 20 pits and 20,000 redundancies by 1985. On 8 March 1984 the NUM made strike official.

The cultural position of miners had been largely overturned during the previous decade since they had been accused of holding the country to ransom during the 1973–74 strike. Their sheer weight of numbers lent substance to the myth that the NUM had the power to make or break governments (Thatcher 1995: 340). Ten years later the government was prepared to confront that power and the mass media had reconstructed the backbone of the nation as 'young savage toughs' (*Financial Times* 13.4.84) and 'threatening bully boys' (*Daily Express*). The media orchestrated a cultural demotion of the status of miners.

As the Ridley plan was enacted 'the government began to bring coal in using workers from other countries and scab labour' (Coulter *et al.* 1984: 15) at the ports, where the Union of Seamen supported the miners. From the outset around 75 per cent of the workforce at Britain's pits was on strike but 'several areas held ballots rejecting strike action and there were calls orchestrated by the government and the media for a national ballot' (Coulter *et al.* 1984: 14). Nottinghamshire had good geological conditions and high earnings and the men employed there felt safe from the threatened closure. A normally united union found itself split and that divide became the focus of media attention because the huge stockpiles of fuel reduced the potential of dramatic social effects.

Lack of unity became the fulcrum about which news could be made. It implied conflict – and conflict is newsworthy. Conflict was also central to the Conservatives' law and order mandate – conflict legitimated control. The issues were quickly defined as the right to picket versus the right to work and those definitions characterised the bulk of the media coverage for the remainder of the strike. That media discourse diverted attention from the actual strike issues – jobs, communities, economics, environmental concerns and political differences – and reduced the conflict of interest from between the power of state and capital and the workers to a squabble within the ranks of workers, who were quickly labelled, oppositionally, as scabs and pickets. Those labels became self-fulfilling prophecy because as every action was interpreted as internal division, so actual internal divisions appeared to harden. What the public 'saw' in the press and on television was not only the change of cultural status of miners but the emasculation and deconstruction of the previously most powerful working-class organisation in Britain. The National Union of Mineworkers was no longer seen as a credible oppositional force to political and economic dominance by either the media or the government. Instead, the main message was that a megalomaniac (Arthur Scargill) was leading a gang of criminal 'bully boys' in trying to force law-abiding working miners to join a strike they didn't support.

As the strike continued, the dominant political discourse paralleled the accounts of the 'riots' in the black communities, except the striking miners were the enemy within instead of an alien malaise. As with the black communities it was possible to see a process of mediating into the culture a revision of the meanings associated with the miners. Historically and collectively, representative of their class and democratic socialism they were divided into two groups: the good workers and the bad strikers. Working-class political action was reinterpreted as violence, terrorism and common crime (Fine and Millar 1985: 18), but it was also worth noting that by default, perhaps for the first time, working-class members who continued to work were associated with legitimacy, conservatism and moderation. Government contingency policy alongside a particular kind of publicity had largely undermined trades unionism, by removing its national power base of collective identity and united political and economic interests.[4]

The struggle to regain identity and unity became a community-based strategy. Broken down into local disputes around the eleven still working pits and survival tactics within the strike villages, the strike became much easier to police. Police were drafted in to keep the still working pits in production. Their methods were geared to preventing 'mass pickets getting to the coalfields using roadblocks,

and policing of pit villages was stepped up almost to saturation level'
(GLC 1984: 79). With no united power base or ideological cohesion,
strikers were refocused on defending their communities, culture and
identity. Striking miners were held, often literally, within their own
territory – by road blocks legitimated very early in the strike under
new laws introduced by the Thatcher government. 'On March 14th
1984, the National Coal Board was granted an injunction in the High
Court under the 1980 Employment Act restraining the Yorkshire
miners from picketing anywhere other than their place of work'
(Coulter *et al.* 1984: 19)

As in the inner cities, the victims of social change were readily
blamed for their own demise. Scargill's claim that 80 pits were due
for closure was an underestimate. 'By October 1989, some 94
collieries had been closed' (Waddington *et al.* 1991: 59), placing
hundreds of thousands on the dole and crushing communities.
Whether for political motives or genuine economic reasons, the representations of the miners' strike exacerbated the speed and volume
of intervention in the industry. Community by community,
dissenters were engaged and contained by:

> The emergence of a new kind of police force, arrogant in its
> usurpation of power, dismissive of democratic institutions,
> charged with political hostility to civil liberties and to the organs
> of the Labour movement. (Fine and Millar 1985: 14)

Now highly centralised via the National Reporting Centre, strike
policing, as in the inner city, resembled a riot force of highly mobile
Special Patrol Groups and support systems. As in the urban context,
traditionally perceived cultural and community rights became
deviant and even criminal activities. Striking, picketing, meeting,
coal-picking and street movements were suddenly targeted. Whilst
the state 'invoked civil law to curtail trade union powers' (Fine and
Millar 1985: 15) to sequestrate union funds and imprison officials,
the police used the criminalisation of previously everyday activity
to enforce actions against strikers and their families in the pit
villages. The eruption of violence that sometimes followed policing
of the communities, and was avidly reported by journalists, served
only to legitimate more aggressive and more intrusive efforts at
controlling the strikers.

The incident that gained the most notoriety became known as the
Battle of Orgreave. Orgreave was the site of a coking plant on the

outskirts of Sheffield that supplied fuel to the massive British Steel Scunthorpe works. Police blockaded the approach roads and frequently closed the M18 to normal traffic to maintain the supply route by using scab lorry drivers. Striking miners nonetheless tried to close the plant. Media coverage of the strike had already attracted considerable criticism from miners and from academics, who routinely claimed that the news was biased towards government perspectives. The most dramatic events at Orgreave occurred on 29 and 30 May 1984 and the way they were reported set the scene for much of the remaining coverage of the strike.

Coulter *et al.* (1984) saw events at Orgreave as a set piece, engineered by the government to teach the miners a lesson (a similar claim might well be made of the whole 1984–85 strike). Early picketing had been peaceful but events changed when miners' leader Arthur Scargill visited on 27 May. Police charged to break up an impromptu congregation and knocked Scargill to the ground in the ensuing scuffle. Escalation was inevitable and by 29 May large numbers of strikers had congregated, as had large numbers of police, many on horseback and many with dogs. The symbolism of picketing as a ritual of class identity and political commitment amongst workers appeared in this context to be a direct challenge to law and order. Pickets were not allowed to appeal to the scabs, instead they were confronted by police as if they were criminals.

The police equipped with masks and huge white riot shields literally whooped like warriors going in to battle – just as Scarman had described them in Brixton's Swamp 81. All the media accounts resounded with war metaphors the following day. The *Daily Mail* exclaimed, 'The thin blue line holds firm' amongst a press full of battle terminology. The strikers had become the enemy of the nation. Jones (1991) argued that: 'Violence is not only an essential news value but also a crucial term in political discourse, here it is contrasted with both law and order and democracy. To call the picket violent was therefore to condemn it' (Jones 1991: 8).

Scargill's presence also played into news values, allowing the press to personify the issues and to focus on the elite figures involved – the miners' leader and the country's leader. Scargill was systematically blamed for causing not only the violence but also the context of the picket in the first place. Orgreave became the *leitmotiv* for the whole industrial action and Scargill the cause. Jones (1991) pointed out that by 31 May the papers were cheering 'Arrest Him!' – on the grounds of obstruction of a footpath. The pickets were now a riotous mob and the *Sun* reported that Margaret Thatcher would not give in with 'Maggie raps "mob rule"'.

Reports consistently placed the pickets and Scargill in the agent's role, directing readers to interpret them as responsible for the ensuing action, which was frequently violence against the police. Images similarly depicted the lone figure of Scargill confronting the police or injured police officers (Jones 1991). Television similarly posed the police versus the pickets, although very little film showed the police cavalry charging the pickets, and little film from behind picket lines appeared at all. Few journalists were welcome amongst the pickets, not surprisingly given the bad press that miners were being given, so most news shots showed pickets confronting the police, particularly on the BBC, which tended to align closely with the establishment (government) perspective.

The news about Orgreave was so shaped by news values that it barely addressed the underlying grievances of the miners, the civil liberties issues associated with the heavy-handed law and order mandate or the implications or validity of the long-term pit closure plans. Instead, industrial action was repackaged as crime or insurrection:

> The media constructed the event as a morality play between the forces of good and evil and cast the strikers and their leaders as beyond the pale of legitimate politics and of civilised society itself. (Jones 1991: 48)

The rest is history, as these discourses of crime and violence provided the means of making sense of the remainder of the strike and legitimated the policing approach, which gradually alienated support for the miners.

Later in August, trouble flared at Markham colliery over rights and rules of interaction. Management and pickets had agreed on essential safety work being undertaken underground and only a token picket was mounted. This was quickly breached as management reneged on the arrangement and bussed in scab workers under a police convoy. Violence flared as reinforcement pickets arrived to find working miners boasting of their high earnings.[5] When the problem continued the following morning police returned in full riot gear prepared to take control of the whole village. The Public Order Act was used liberally with name-calling being interpreted as threatening behaviour. Markham was isolated by roadblocks and anybody on the street was stopped and searched until the protests were eroded.[6]

On Sunday 14 October 1984, day 210 of the strike, police officers swooped on the village of Grimethorpe and arrested women and children for 'stealing' coal – traditionally picking up the loose coal around the slag heaps and workings had been ignored. During the strike, when poverty added to the problems of the pit communities, 'picking' was transformed into theft. As in the inner cities, 'blind-eye' police acceptance of everyday rights became aggressive prosecution of the law. Rumours that a child had been injured by the police led to retributive attacks on the officers and an ensuing 'riot'.

Whereas the national media were almost uniformly critical of such violence and quick to blame miners themselves (Waddington *et al.* 1991) local journalists had to sell their products to these communities and occasionally presented a very different picture. The *Sheffield Star* printed a photo of the Grimethorpe incident on 14 October anchored by: 'Not even safe inside their own gate. Terry Green aged 17 with his father and mother at the gate where he was twice attacked by riot police.' A second story illustrated the way police were patrolling the streets and apparently randomly picking on inhabitants 'standing peacefully on the pavement'. The law invoked was a little used section of the 1875 Conspiracy and Protection of Property Act that allowed arrest on suspicion of 'watching and besetting' (Waddington *et al.* 1991: 120).

Such incidents were rarely foregrounded in the media, which preferred tales of overt violence but gradually began counting and reporting on the numbers of miners who were giving in and returning to the coalface. The drift back to work was often the opening information in press headlines and broadcast news until the magic figure of 50 per cent back was reached in late February 1985. On 3 March the strike was called off. The NUM had been defeated and the wholesale deconstruction of trades unionism, working-class politics and collective identity was underway. Ian McGregor, at the NCB, warned the returners that they would learn the price of insurrection and subordination. It was closure, redundancy, breaking up of work teams, union breaking, privatisation, higher productivity levels and intimidating management practices.

The disorder in the mining communities can be partially accounted for by the mainstream models of collective conflict, but the analysis is made much richer when events are contextualised in a history of class relations and conflict and against the cultural values and meanings that shore up identity. In contemporary contexts these are most pervasively and systematically disseminated by the mass media. During the miners strike the collusion of interests between the law, the government and news practices and institutions distorted the long existing cultural ideology of the miners, their class and their communities in the public eye. That distortion facilitated both the division of miners into good workers and bad pickets, and the subsequent use of the law to control and eventually defeat the strike. The extent to which that reconstruction of the meaning of coal impacted on the self-perceptions of miners, their families and communities is difficult to assess, but in terms of social power relations it is almost irrelevant, because the one subordinate group with sufficient power and political commitment to challenge dominance no longer exists in any influential way. Margaret Thatcher always claimed that the closure programme was based only on sound economic planning, but in the chapter in her memoirs titled 'Mr. Scargill's Insurrection' she could not resist pointing out:

> The coal strike was always about far more than uneconomic pits. It was a political strike. And so its outcome had a significance far beyond the economic sphere. From 1975 to 1985 the conventional wisdom was that Britain could only be governed with the consent of the trades unions ... that day had now come and gone. (Thatcher 1995: 377–8)

It was clear that such a 'victory' would have been more difficult if the press had been hostile to government policy. Many individual journalists like John Pilger were very unhappy about the news coverage but few found a means to tell a different story because those in control of the media uniformly stifled dissenting voices, and control was not based in Fleet Street. An industrial correspondent described:

> [h]ow his editor had been summoned to No. 10 Downing Street for a meeting with Mrs Thatcher. The Prime Minister told his editor that she was concerned about the tone of some of the newspaper's reporting. (Hollingsworth 1986: 285)

By 1990 pit villages were either becoming dumping grounds for problem council tenants or filling with 'commuters attracted by the low price of housing and easy access to the M1' (Waddington *et al.*

1991: 176). Collective conflict around work-based social relations was largely transformed by the integration of real power and ideological representation into the consensual beginnings of John Major's classless society (Seldon 1997). A similar process of containment and control can also be made out in that disruptive area of traditionally working-class leisure – football.

Terror on the Terraces

Pre-industrially, football was characterised 'by a lack of rules and conventions, mass participation, huge playing areas, very long games and an absence of external control agents such as referees' (Whannel 1979: 328). The game was an accepted arena of conflict involving 'blind-eye' judicial or magisterial policy to allow for the settling of interpersonal and/or intergroup scores. Participation was the key, not watching. Common land and the streets were the pitches and the team was drawn from the local community. The game was an anarchic release of tension and anger offering status to individuals and creating solidarity amongst community members, but it was not conducive to the requirements of the new urban industries. The emergent working class had to be enticed, cajoled or coerced into leisures and pleasures that fitted the rhythms of factory life.

Taming the game was part of the whole process of reconstructing popular culture during the nineteenth century – a process that was both about controlling culture but also about middle-class entre-preneurial drives to profit from the leisure arena. The Football Association was formed in 1863 and by the last twenty years of the century the game had been transformed into a popular, working-class, male spectator sport. Violence was not now amongst the participants but within a paying crowd who continued to indulge in 'fist fighting, swearing and occasional bottle throwing' (Whannel 1979: 329). The division between players and spectators was not well defined, with frequent pitch invasions holding up games.

Riots, unruly behaviour, violence, assault and vandalism appear to have been a well-established but not necessarily dominant part of crowd behaviour at football matches at least from the 1870s. (Dunning 1982: 219)

By the 1890s, however, the trend was towards respectability amongst the working class. Urban living had improved and the football stadium was part of the local community. It was a source of pride, identity, pleasure and escape from the dreary, routine drudgery of factory production that was both working-class life and predominantly male at the time. By association with their favourite players the crowd could vicariously be physical, be skilled, be winners and be famous.

Football and fans maintained some continuity[7] until the sharp decline in crowds linked to the increase in television sports coverage and ownership of televisions during the 1960s. During this period, gates fell from a peak of over 41 million in 1948–49 to around 28 million (Critcher 1979). *The Times* (11.11.61) noted: 'Once football was the opium of the masses. No longer. There is a greater awareness of standards and comfort now. So perhaps the real answer at last is a complete spring clean' (in Critcher 1979: 226).

That spring-clean might have considered returning the game to the format that had previously attracted huge, loyal local crowds, but instead there was an acceleration of incipient commercialisation, professionalism and internationalism. 'Football turned its attention to the provision of spectacle, skill and efficient performance – values understood to be important to the stereotypical i.e. middle-class supporter' (Taylor 1971: 363). The typical supporter was reconstructed according to the values of the providers of football rather than those whose sport it had once been. Concurrently, the early and middle 1960s witnessed the problem of soccer hooliganism (Critcher 1979).

During the 1960s and 1970s, as the game was 'civilised' with fencing, seating, separate enclosures, retentions and heavy policing, fans seemed to revert to the original football consciousness of capturing territory (the opposing team's fans' 'end'), street brawls and score settling without the game and outside of the stadium. Hooliganism was a sub-cultural phenomenon attracting interest not only from the police and the government but also from academics (Taylor 1982; Williams *et al.* 1984; Dunning *et al.* 1986). By the 1980s, 'terrace violence is out – you are going to get caught. It's on the streets at the moment' (*Guardian* 11.5.84, Chelsea Fan).

As with other collective violence the causes of hooliganism tended to be theorised as either sociological or psychological. The former stressed the commodification and embourgeoisment of the game as excluding the authentic interests and values of the working-class fan.

Players became stars in highly profitable performances, clubs became businesses and internationalisation broke the close links between supporters and local clubs. What had been free, participatory, violent clashes between local lads was turned into the profitable, passive, noisy appreciation of packaged, professional entertainment. Sociologists like Taylor (1971, 1982) theorised hooliganism in this context as an 'inarticulate but keenly experienced sense of control over the game that was theirs' (Taylor 1971: 163). Clarke (1979) echoed Taylor but included an account of the profile of the hooligan – working class but also male and young. Clarke focused on the traditional masculinity of working-class life, where being tough and looking out for your mates were part of male identity, to explain that profile. He argued that the siting of stadiums in local communities made them the 'physical and symbolic expression of local rivalries and identities' (Clarke 1979: 142), making matches an arena for conflict and machismo, mainly involving young males because of the fracturing of ties of family and neighbourhood, which had orchestrated traditional fandom. Marsh (1978) also focused on masculinity but in order to inform a psychological model of aggressive behaviour. Hooliganism was explained as a ritualised expression of masculinity in simple Darwinian terms of the survival of the fittest. What was not explained was why this manifested in relation to football, to class and to only some men.

Dunning identified 'age-grading, sexual segregation and territorial unity' (1982: 138) as relevant factors to hooliganism but argued that these variables must be understood historically as relating to the wider social context and part of British cultural heritage. Culture is where events, experiences and emotions are communicated and made meaningful and in contemporary life much of our culture is mass mediated. Dunning argued that the hooligan (like the mugger) was a media provided solution, in this case first applied to the embarrassing problem of the behaviour of English fans during the 1966 World Cup. The 'subterranean current of spectator misbehaviour that had never died out ' (Dunning 1982: 154) was antithetical to middle-class concepts of British sporting values and national identity. However, it was newsworthy and therefore reported, but as deviant and criminal, so dissociating the hooligan from the normal, respectable fan. The violent rhetoric of the press alongside the resurgence of working-class standards of masculine aggressive football support interacted to construct both good copy and a new set of cultural meanings, which could be drawn on to explain conflict.

The association of traditional football ebullience with criminality, danger and un-Britishness simultaneously legitimated the increasing levels of control of the game. In 1978, a Sports Council report *Crowd Disorder at Sporting Events* made the recommendations which were to characterise interventions in the game during the following years: the report recommended improving police strategies; promoting a sense of community through marketing, pressuring the courts to convict violent fans and co-ordinating information on hooligans through the Home Office. During the 1980s and early 1990s the working-class origins of football were finally transformed into middle-class family entertainment, increasingly watched on screens as well as at the ground. Fixtures and competitions grew in range and frequency; star players were bought and sold for millions in a global market place and the price of tickets escalated. The working-class male fans no longer simply identified with each other, their local club or the players but also with the ideals of middle-class leisure – comfort, style, safety and professional entertainment. Much of that process relates to the media both in terms of their accounts of football and their commercial reliance on it. In turn, those accounts legitimated the kind of social control the Thatcher government needed in place to finally re-invent football to suit the needs of both capital and conservative ideology.

Football featured as news during the Conservative government, as opposed to sport, in relation to two not disconnected news value criteria – violence (negative) or Britishness (elite nation). As football moved out of the community and became a national and then international event so team supporters turned into a sort of community on the hoof. Once football produced a paying public it was inevitable that those in the major cities with a larger local population would become more affluent, buy better players, provide more peripheral facilities for spectators and in turn attract more support. The rich clubs got richer and more successful both at the game and as businesses. New competitions were introduced at national and international level and fans followed teams, bound by loyalty and clever marketing – including the annual season ticket that much reduced the escalating cost of match attendance but meant that it was/is rare for a fan to attend a major match which doesn't involve their team.

In the early 1980s away fans travelled early, avoiding the heavily policed match specials, and chose designer gear over the 'colours' of their team to avoid standing out whilst they scouted out the 'enemy' territory. The antics of the Chelsea Mob included notorious behaviour at away fixtures: in November 1984 they were involved in an affray in Newcastle which left four men with knife and razor wounds. In 1985 Liverpool fans were widely held responsible for the fighting at Heysel in Belgium, which led to 39 deaths on the terraces. After Heysel, English teams were banned temporarily from playing on the continent.

At home, clubs stepped up security measures with extra fencing and policing. Police began to focus on hooliganism with operations such as Own Goal and Full Time infiltrating the gangs of supporters. The violence provided copious news stories but also fed the process. Chief Superintendent Mike Hedges remarked of Chelsea fans that this was a way of achieving some glamour and notoriety, which was precisely what the media offered through their publicity. Arguably, news about football violence encouraged a view of the terraces 'as a place to build and increase reputations for toughness' (*Guardian* 1.9.83). Accounts of violence were used to justify more interventions not only by the police but also by the football clubs and authorities. Sometimes such police interventions arguably actually contributed to disorder, most terribly at Hillsborough, Sheffield in 1989, when inappropriate efforts to police an overcrowded part of the stadium alongside high fences and locked gates were implicated in 96 deaths (ITV 5.12.96).

Football organisations were anxious to maximise returns on investment by attracting the higher spending middle-class fans and families, and selling broadcast rights without fear of interrupted play. Occasionally these needs to maintain the game at all costs led to conflict between the provision of spectacle and the more Olympian idea of what sport should be, particularly amongst sports journalists who regularly criticised clubs for not punishing player violence by bans (Rowe 1992). Yet, such criticisms were also about promoting a particular model of acceptable sporting behaviour in the tradition of British fair play and gentlemanly behaviour – the middle-class version of sporting behaviour.

Within the overt concern about violence from both directions, another invisible discourse was at work constructing an image for football conducive to the interests of middle-class society. The working-class, male rough of Matthew Arnold's (1869) *Culture and Anarchy* 'troubling the common course of business throughout the country' (in Storey ed. 1994: 8) was shown his proper place restoring our profound sense of settled order and security. That sense of order pivots around class interests but also around national ones – the sense of Britishness that was part of the reconstructive project of Thatcherism.

News about international matches and the World Cup during conservatism put British identity and reputation into the context of sport with its capacity to represent, both literally and symbolically, disharmony and conflictual identification (Rowe 1992). The construction of national identity seemed to take place in two distinct contexts: first British as different from other nations and second legitimate British[8] as opposed to yobs, rioters and thugs.

The first of these contexts has 'its referential base in a set of ethnic and cultural stereotypes' (Tudor 1992: 393). Tudor remarked that descriptions of other teams by sports commentators, in terms of their ethnic characteristics, works to reinforce those of Britishness, so the Latin temperament of the South Americans and Italians connotes the cool and control of the British approach. The high profile of African teams in the 1990 World Cup led to many examples of covert racism. Tudor (1992: 391–413) gives a range of examples of descriptions by journalists of the Cameroon, which relate directly to stereotypes of blackness and the country's emergence from a colonial past. Young boys in Cameroon 'played barefoot in the jungle' (Kevin Dunn, ITV 30.6.90) and the team 'do have a tendency to get excited' (Ron Atkinson, ITV 8.6.90). Reference to the English team was sometimes critical of the style of play but not of the Englishness, the old bulldog spirit was frequently mentioned in accounts where: 'Conceptions of "our" football, our history, its contemporary status and form blur into more general self-images of what constitutes our distinctive Englishness' (Tudor 1992: 404).

During Euro 96 that history and sense of Englishness was demonstrated by the consistent use of war metaphors to chart England's progress through the competition. The *Daily Mirror* (26.6.96) featured the 'Pride of England' with the players embellished with manes and fangs, alongside a song for supporters with the line, 'We'll send the Germans reeling'. The *Daily Mirror* (21.6.96) gave readers 'Gazza's Armada' to eulogise player Paul Gascoigne, who 'leads his crew into battle as England tune up to scupper the Spanish'. Football is defined as crisis – it is us against them. The media defined a confrontation by 'alerting the community', but by 'defining the crisis the media almost inevitably – by focusing national attention on it – amplify it' (Watson 1985: 35). Describing football in war-like language encouraged patriotic aggression that unsurprisingly was not always evidenced by a bit of harmless chanting and taunting.

Yet, off the field, bad behaviour was distanced in the news from heroic representations of national identity. Drunken 'hooligans' were labelled criminals or aligned with other examples of anti-social behaviour. After a chaotic match in Sweden in 1992 the headline, 'Rioting on £800 a week' (*Today* 16.6.92) was reminiscent of scrounger and beggar stories. The rioter/ringleader was exposed as having been previously jailed 'for causing grievous bodily harm in a vicious knife attack'. 'His family condemned him for the shame he had brought on them and his country.' 'He doesn't go to football that often.' In a few sentences this 'hooligan' is reduced to not being a football fan, not a proper family man and not patriotic. Frequently such activity was made sense of in the news by associating it with political extremism (neo-Nazis) or organised crime.[9]

These discourses split football supporters, as represented, into respectable and deviant, law-abiding and criminal, British and other, family men and yobs, heroes and villains, and led to police interventions, via the National Football Intelligence Unit and latterly the National Criminal Intelligence Service (NCIS), to seek out the leaders of what was widely perceived as organised activity. Gary Armstrong claimed this focus resulted from the way the media tend to pick on and personalise individuals, which created a supposed 'quasi-military hierarchical structure on hooligans groups' (1998: 18). In a decade of study, he found no evidence of such organisation but argued that the power of the myth has been sufficient to justify increased controls and policing, both within and without the football pitches.

Comment

It has become deeply unfashionable amongst academics to offer class analyses of socio-cultural phenomena but I can see no other way of accounting for the systematic symbolic and real deconstruction of working-class work and leisure practices and values. Nor, though, do I see how that process could be adequately explained without considering the role of the media in reconstructing the meanings associated with class identity. It was not simply that significant swathes of what characterised working-class life were associated with disorder, deviance and crime, enabling control and change through a range of policy and popular pressure during Thatcherism but rather that by inference other values were positively valued. Twenty years ago Hall identified much of this process when he wrote that media coverage of different behaviour 'stigmatises and degrades the actions of others – and implies that standards of conduct which guide middle society are universal' (1979: 29).

One result is tangible. In 1999, membership of trades unions had slipped from 13,289,000 in 1979 to 7,117,000. Membership of the mining and quarrying unions is down from 343,000 to just 8,145 (*Observer* 25.4.99). The remaining coalmines were sold in 1994 mostly to RJB mining. News about mining on the World Wide Web informs audiences that 'since taking on the business RJB has reduced coal production by 30% closing pits and cutting the workforce by 4000 to about 16000' (<the.herald.co.uk> 16.10.98). In March 1999 the first call for a pit strike since 1984–85 took place at Selby in Yorkshire.

Even those pits that were turned into tourist attractions struggle to survive financially. Caphouse Colliery at Ollerton, West Yorkshire became a museum in 1988 but was under-financed during the Conservative years. It has now been underwritten by the Department of Media, Culture and Sport as a nationally funded centre – ironically, nationalisation has saved just a memento of a once huge national industry.

In contrast, private business has made a huge industry out of football. The tragedies at Heysel and Hillsborough and the continuous focus on the violence and danger of uncontrolled hooliganism directed a push towards better stewardship, membership monitoring and all-seater grounds. The *Scotsman* online records that changes were underwritten by:

> [n]ew generations of entrepreneurs who have entered football to raise ticket prices and attempt to 're-position' the appeal of the game to a more middle-class market. The logic is that while some traditional fans may be alienated by the changes, they will be replaced by a new generation of supporters who enjoy the social cachet of attending games, while also possessing the disposable income to invest in shirts, glossy programmes and the limitless paraphernalia that marketing departments and club shops turn out. (<*Scotsman*.980.html> 4.5.99)

Football has been appropriately 'time-scheduled' and titillated with 'stars', to sell to the major television broadcasters, either match by match or as a wholesale deal. This appears to be the strategic plan of the industry and its association. Rupert Murdoch's 1998 bid to buy Manchester United for his own Sky Television was very much a symptom of the symbiotic relationship between the media and football industries. Central to these shifts is the remaking of football to fit the remit of the leisure industries – safe, clean, habitual family fun – so there remains a constant vigilance for the violence that might threaten pleasure and therefore profit.

'The national sport has made itself an adjunct to soap opera, sometimes a surrogate for war. It has embraced the vulgarities of celebrity' (J. Foster *Sheffield Telegraph* 9.5.99), but it has done so very profitably, and not without the fuel of publicity provided by journalism. That publicity stimulates desire for the game by cen-tralising it in our cultural records as integral to national and personal identity and legitimates the necessary controls to enable it to flourish profitably by highlighting the occasional disorderly conduct that accompanies a match.

It is worth noting though that the costly and interventionist NCIS set up in 1992 with 92 full-time Football Interventionist Officers and empowered by the 1997 Police Act arrested only 3,307 supporters (figures for successful prosecution are not published at the web site) in 1997/98, from 24,692,608 attendance (<ncis.co.uk> 6.8.98). The unit supports the tightening of legislation in the proposed Football Spectators Offences Bill perhaps because even with such a low number of offenders, closed circuit television and the high technology EPi-Centre for communicating supporter travel information throughout Europe, it has still not managed to catch those who leave a 'stain on England's reputation' (<ncis.co.uk> 6.8.98).

At the FA Cup in May 1999 tickets were priced from £20 to £110 and 'the 22 players on the pitch were probably worth as much as the 75000 in the crowd' (*Observer* 23.5.99). The TV audience was an estimated 500 million. *Channel 4 News* on the same evening as the match estimated that it would cost a Manchester United fan about £5,000 to travel to and attend every team event in a year. Sheffield Wednesday's fencing currently displays an advertisement to children inviting them to 'Bring an adult to the family enclosure for only £15', about the price of four cinema tickets.

Football is fashionable and for sale: to sponsors, in the stadium shop, the sports pages and by subscription on television. It is a momentous achievement for enterprise disguised as a celebration of identity and heritage. Mitchell (*Observer* 23.5.99) describes the FA Cup as the 'nostalgic centrepiece of perhaps the most unifying cultural force on our planet outside religion'.

When John Major claimed to be promoting a 'genuinely' classless society (Seldon 1997: 125–6) what he was actually describing was the decimation of the working class and its reconstruction in the image of middle-class aspirations, and commensurate acquiescence to the Thatcher plan for privatisation, deunionisation, individual responsibility and rampant entrepreneurialism – changes that were softened by the reassertion of the validity of Britishness and a call to heritage.

The Conservative years moved the class goalposts, directing the middle classes towards popular culture, reconstructing that to appeal to the middle class and reconstructing the meanings and realities of working-class lives to parallel and promote the pursuance of middle-class values and interests. Television's *The Fast Show* captures this well with excellent spoofs on the nouveau football fan as middle-class fashion victim. Increasingly we are consenting adults to a 'classless' society, in that there is only one class with which to identify – in Thatcher's terms, where there was discord there is harmony. To see a conspiracy would be to underestimate the complexity of the process and to see it as evolution would be to underestimate the symbolic–economic–political relationship and its endemic symbiotic power.

4
High Jinks: Youth, Crime and Community

Youth as opposed to children or adults is a category new to the second half of the twentieth century. From the early 1950s a succession of youth cultures is identifiable, starting with the Beats of the 1950s to the Greens of the 1990s. Each occupied a territory, marked out by symbols of identity – music, fashion, place, names, ideology and practices – that was different from, even opposed to, mature culture. This positioning outside of the norm heightened the visibility of youth and made it an object of curiosity, study and even fear. In 1973, Stanley Cohen identified the phenomenon of anxiety about troublesome youth:

> One of the most recurrent types of moral panic in Britain, since the war, has been associated with the emergence of various forms of youth culture (originally almost exclusively working class, but often recently middle class or student based) whose behaviour is deviant or delinquent. (Cohen 1973: 9)

In later years, some of the youth cultures of Thatcherism also took up positions that were outside of the mainstream, to the extent that their behaviour was not just disapproved of but viewed, in the public domain, as sometimes dangerous to the broader society.

The first of the inner-city riots, in St Paul's, Bristol in 1980, coincided with the first New Age Traveller Festival on Inglestone Common; the Battle of Orgreave during the miners' strike in 1985 was paralleled by the Battle of the Beanfields, when police sought to evict new age travellers from Stonehenge. From then until 1997 young people, moving around the country and defying 'normal' lifestyles, became the focus of the media and the law. Youths travelling and occupying 'common land' were clearly influential on the prevalence of rave parties in the late 1980s. The licensing laws were flouted by massive parties:

A decade ago Britain was in the grip of a Tory government obsessed with law and order. Then in the summer of 1989 a vibrant new culture of music, light and Class A drugs exploded. Throughout those balmy carefree months – in warehouses, clubs and open fields – rave promoters played a cat and mouse game with the authorities. (Garratt in the *Observer* 11.4.99)

The summer of 1989 was reminiscent of the summer love-ins of the hippie culture of the 1960s, originating with the Human Be-In in San Francisco in 1967.[1] Like the earlier events it was steeped in drugs and it pre-empted a wave of youth activity, but in the UK in the early 1990s much of this was riotous rather than revolutionary and violent rather than protesting for peace.

That youth riotousness occupied a different territory to the rural roads and commons; it took place on the streets of run-down council estates and the urban conurbations. in 'Homes Built for Riots' Burrows empathised:

More trouble broke out last week on several of those hideous housing estates that were designed to accommodate society's poorest in that familiar 'Early Ugly' style to which it was assumed they would, in time, become accustomed. Few people who have visited them will be surprised about what is happening, because most would regard having to live on one of them as the nearest thing to a life sentence. (*Sunday Telegraph* 26.7.92)

One of the other things that was happening was TWOCing, taking without owner's consent or joy-riding. Also happening was a very different group and type of youth protest, causing another kind of havoc on the roads by blocking road-building programmes in scenic Britain at Twyford and Honiton, in occupations to protect the environment.

This chapter begins by looking at earlier youth disorder in relation to theory in order to rethink that in relation to more contemporary events. It then focuses on areas of youth culture that were high on the news media agenda during the Thatcher/Major years, activities that bordered the criminal making them attractively newsworthy. These were: itinerant pleasure (raves and the new age), virtual pleasure (drugs), community crisis (joy-riding and street violence) and environmental protest.

Youth Culture, Crime and Class

The differences in these activities of the 1980s and 1990s appeared to reflect the differences between earlier youth disorder, with working-class groups tending towards parodic and destructive protests and middle-class groups tending towards hedonistic or political goals and practices.

Cohen says of the Mods and Rockers of the early 1960s, 'the young were highly visible: on scooters, motorbikes, packing the trains, hitching down the roads' (1973: 28). The two groups were distinct from each other in clothing and lifestyle; they moved around in large groups and set themselves apart from the ordinary, local residents. They were noisy on the streets, apparently aimless and had little cash to spend in the shops and/or on entertainment. Cohen reported that the 'typical Rocker was an unskilled, manual worker, the typical Mod a semi-skilled manual worker' (1973: 35).

The different groups were involved in scuffles on the sea front and beaches in 1964/65; these were reported as extreme violence in the press. 'The 1964 boys took over the beaches at Margate and Brighton yesterday and smeared the traditional post card scene with blood and violence' (*Daily Express* 19.5.64 in Cohen 1973: 32). Yet Cohen reported also that 'the number of deckchairs broken was not much greater than on an ordinary Bank holiday weekend' (Cohen 1973: 37). Police were called in to restore law and order, providing the bored and irritated youngsters with another target for abuse, and the press with more stories.

Cohen argued that the clash between youth culture and the police was exaggerated by being made newsworthy through acts of vandalism, mostly it seemed against deckchairs – which were/are the symbol of working-class family holidays at the seaside. Once amplified to the status of crime news, youths strutting and fretting in the sunshine took on a predictive quality for the press, who in subsequent years reported the fears of local traders and the threats of revenge from Mods and Rockers. Even when nothing happened the crime paradigm was used. The *Evening Argus* (30.5.64) sub-headed a piece with 'Violence' yet went on to state that 'in Brighton there was no violence despite crowds of teenagers on the beach today'.

Cohen argued 'the Mods and Rockers didn't become news because they were new, they were presented as new to justify the creation of news' (1973: 46). Youth was:

Defined as a threat to societal values and interests; its nature presented in a stylised and stereotypical fashion by the mass media ... Sometimes the panic passes over and is forgotten, except in folklore and collective memory; at other times it has more serious and long lasting repercussions and might produce such changes as those in legal and social policy or even in the way society conceives itself. (Cohen 1973: 9)

The way working-class youth was represented in the late 1960s made it the object of a moral panic. It also set a pattern of expectations in place for later news about youth culture. It would be mass, visible, loud, mobile, 'uniformed', disorderly and potentially disruptive, at least, dangerous at most (at least for young people themselves, deckchairs and policemen).

Whereas working-class youth has been called *sub* cultural, a term filled with the derision and denigration of the middle classes for the 'other', middle-class youth was called the rather differently loaded counter culture (Middleton and Muncie 1982). It was also afforded rather more impressive credentials by being dubbed politically or philosophically resistant to mainstream thinking, action and lifestyle. The affluence and materialism of post-war society was first challenged in the 1950s by the Beat generation, who, influenced by existentialism and nihilism, sought freedom of self and personal fulfilment in drugs, creativity and the rejection of industrial society.

The last of these foci informed the growth of the Campaign for Nuclear Disarmament and a powerful peace lobby based on moral rather than political ideals. This created a rather vague organisation and agenda. Disenchantment with its progress nourished the growth of the new left, a radical unification of Communists and intellectuals. This group was to emerge in the later 1960s as the political wing of the most influential youth movement of the twentieth century, the hippies.

Beginning from the same roots as the Beats, the hippy movement came from middle-class America. Drugs, Eastern religions, free love and music characterised the hedonism of a new Bohemia that was nonetheless also about disaffection with the current social order (Middleton and Muncie 1982). Change towards aggressive protest came in the late 1960s, with marches and occupations in the USA and Europe:

The three issues of American Imperialism in Vietnam, Black Civil Rights and educational control were to inform the spate of university sit-ins, marches and demonstrations in 1968, in which the strange agglomeration of black militants, students, drop-outs, draft dodgers, mystical hippies and women liberationists seemed to be momentarily united. (Middleton and Muncie 1982: 70)

In Paris and London the move was specifically counter to the existing order and highly politicised – originating in the universities and focused on higher education, yet also seeking alliances with workers under the broad banner of socialism and solidarity.

As previously that decade, such mass, visible and voluble youth activity drew the attention of both press and police, but this group of youths was described not as criminal but as revolutionary – *The Times* (5.9.68) warned 'Militant plot feared in London' (in Murdock 1973: 210) prior to the anti-Vietnam rally in London's Grosvenor Square in 1968. Murdock's study concluded that the volume of press coverage and the recurrent theme of 'them' and 'us' – the police versus the fanatical outsiders – served to reinforce the perspective of the 'legitimated holders of political power' (1973: 213) and that this was not accidental but 'the logical outcome of the present organisation of news gathering and processing and the assumptions upon which it rests' (1973: 223).

Subsequent theoretical approaches to youth have tended to divide into work on youth leisure, especially music, dance, sexuality, fashion and clubbing (Hall and Jefferson 1983; Grossberg 1986; Hebdige 1979; McRobbie 1982, 1991, 1997; McRobbie and Nava 1984; Garratt 1999) and on youth and crime (Pearson 1983; Campbell 1984, 1986; Griffin 1993). In relation to the media, work has focused on the young audience (Nava 1997; Gunter and McAleer 1997) but there has been relatively little work on the representation of disorderly youth[2] since Cohen (1973) and Middleton and Muncie (1982).

Clearly, major social discourses other than the media play significant parts in constructing and explaining youth in our complex society – particularly education, the law and medicine but also the less mainstream areas of activity and identity like music, dance and fashion. However, I would argue, and I hope other chapters show, that the media, and particularly the news, occupied a particularly salient place in relation to the emerging ideologies of conservatism from 1979 onwards regarding race, class, gender, sexuality and family. Youth as a whole is no elite institution with 'privileged access to setting the agenda for news' (O'Sullivan *et al.* 1994: 123); youth was and is no organised lobby, instead others shaped the topics within which the youth question was and is framed in the British press. This chapter investigates whether there is any evidence in the news that another major social variable, youth, was subject to a process of Conservative reconstruction.

New Age Travellers

The early 1980s were littered with public disorder, first in the inner cities, then in the mining communities and in the women's peace camp at Greenham common.[3] Some young people's collective behaviour at the time was reminiscent of the hippy project: rejection of the mainstream, freedom to travel, mysticism, drugs and music. Stonehenge had become a site for a pilgrimage to celebrate the summer solstice each year in late June.

In 1985 English Heritage and the National Trust took out injunctions 'preventing the staging of the unofficial festival, which has been held at Stonehenge for the past 21 years. The court action had been taken because of damage to bronze-age earthworks' (*The Times* 3.6.85) allegedly caused in the previous year's celebrations. The ban was imposed supported by barbed wire coils around the stones and by a policeforce newly experienced at controlling the roads from the miners' strike. After the strike, a report from the Association of Chief Police officers advocated increasing 'the numbers of officers trained in techniques to deal with public disorder' (*The Times* 3.6.85). The *Western Daily Press* (3.6.85) reported '520 arrests as police block hippy invasion BATTLE OF THE HENGE'. Some 630 police in 'full riot gear' outnumbered the travellers and the A303 'was blocked by tons of gravel' to keep the convoy of vehicles away from the monument.

There were several themes apparent in the news coverage, which was dominated by the kind of battle metaphors evident in the news about race disturbances and the miners' strike. The *Western Daily Press* (3.6.85) used the phrase 'Siege of Stonehenge' and referred to the 'high speed terror of the hippy army' who had an 'armoury of weapons'. The travellers are constructed as non-peaceful, despite their label 'Peace convoy'. The *Western Daily Press* commented: 'By no stretch of the imagination could these be called peace-loving hippies. These were not the lineal descendants of the sixties flower people. They are anarchic thugs.' Readers were told that '[A] thin blue line of just 39 policemen faced up to a rampaging mob of 350 hippies in the second battle of Stonehenge.'

Of the same incident, *The Times* (3.6.85) reported a 'victory for law and order' as 'hundreds of police with shields and visors ... engaged in hand to hand combat'. As in previous accounts of collective disorder the war metaphor allowed the journalists to draw a clear line of differentiation between us and them – it also allowed the mobilisation of another discourse around Englishness that constructed the travellers as somehow a threat to national identity and values. This discourse fitted neatly with the Thatcherite repro-duction of the heritage of British values that was drenched in Victorianisms and provided a kind of retrospective security, veracity and stability at a time of profoundly changing social relations and practices.

English values and symbols were pitched against the anarchy of the travellers. The hippies had 'battered vehicles'; they 'squatted' and they exhibited 'threatening behaviour' (*The Times* 3.6.85). The *Western Daily Press* of the same date noted 'gaily-painted lorries'; 'firemen had to be called to hose down burning vehicles'; 'it was another shocking example of how Britain now resorts to violence'. Such representations contrasted with the images of one of Britain's ancient landmarks, 'Mob that threaten Britain's most famous monument' (*Western Daily Press* 3.6.85), with the references to English Heritage and the National Trust and with the photos of 'PCs'. Villagers were 'trapped, cowering inside' by a 'ramshackle convoy' speeding 'down country lanes' (*Western Daily Press* 3.6.85). The resolution was 'a victory for law and order. The coils of barbed wire glittered in the sunshine, while at a road block nearby young policemen basked leisurely, in the afternoon sun' (*The Times* 3.6.85) in countryside that characterised England's green and pleasant land – symbolic of cricket, cream teas and English roses.

The third identifiable discourse was gender: one man has 'his hair in a ponytail' and a 'girl has a tattoo on her breast and a toddler at her knee' (*The Times* 3.6.85). One PC commented, 'This lot make the miners look like bloody angels' – strong criticism given that the miners were described as bully boys and young, savage toughs (see Chapter 3). 'Young, muscular men unafraid of the prospect of a fine or jail sentence went berserk' (*Western Daily Press* 3.6.85) and Hell's Angels revved up their bikes. There were a few references to police brutality in these accounts – 'women and babies had suffered the worst injuries' (*Western Daily Press* 3.6.85) – but in the parallel paragraph policemen were described coming down the road 'covered in blood'.

After the court cases following the disturbances a dozen children were thought to have been taken into care by social services suggesting inadequate parenting amongst the travellers. Women featured little in these accounts, but when they did their appearance, and the presence of small children, was always commented on, as if women were the 'camp-followers' of a raggle-taggle army. Descriptions of the men referred to their youth, long hair, joblessness and, almost as if a consequence of these, their violence.

These themes relate well to Chibnall's grid of British values[4] that 'provide criteria for evaluating existing and emerging forms of behaviour ... these background assumptions constitute the most unconscious part of any ideological system   Those actors who want their actions and beliefs signified as legitimate by the news media must contrive to associate those with the positive legitimating values' (1977: 21–2). These travellers had little access to the media to put their own spin on events and anyway their values were often too diametrically opposed to mainstream interests to be given anything but negative publicity.

Another discourse was only just discernible in 1985   in the 13 pages of news about Stonehenge in *The Times* and *Western Daily Press*, on 3 June 1985, there were just two references to drugs. The major themes in this journalism were characteristic of the conservative discourse evident in other crime, deviance and disorder news, reflecting the close alliance between news values and British values discussed in Chapter 1. But these were not static topics. As youth continued to be a problem, new labels and explanatory themes appeared in the news, perhaps influenced by or influential on subsequent popular and policy conceptualisations of youth culture.

Raves

Struggles with the traveller convoys informed a special section (39) in the 1986 Public Order Act. This clause reduced the notice to quit, required to evict squatters, to 48 hours. Nonetheless, efforts continued to conduct the illicit festivals, which were increasingly more about dance and all-night music than about any kind of pagan worship.

By 1989, in other parts of the world dramatic and violent political struggles were taking place. In February, Yugoslavia witnessed violent clashes between Serbians and ethnic Albanians; in China, students protesting for democracy in Beijing's Tiananmen Square were slaughtered by the People's Liberation Army; in August, P.W. Botha resigned in South Africa, pre-empting Nelson Mandela's release in February 1990; and on 9 November 1989 East and West Germans tore down the Berlin Wall. In contrast, in the UK, young Britons were partying until dawn at unlicensed venues that were kept secret to the last minute, and the police and government were incensed.

Margaret Thatcher had been in power for ten years when police tried to close down an illicit rave at Heston services on the M4. They blocked the entrance to the service car park but clubbers simply parked on the motorway blocking it completely as 10,000 of them flooded the warehouse for the event, 'the chaos caused delays to flights at nearby Heathrow' (*Observer* 11.4.99). Reminiscing ten years later, Barrat tried to explain events in this article. She wrote:

> The fight for the right to party may seem trivial compared to events unfolding in the rest of the world, but in 1989 it really felt like a cause ... People had begun to live for the weekend ... It was a mass movement without leaders, without manifesto, without any real aim except to have fun and stick up a finger at authority. (*Observer* 11.4.99)

The miners had been crushed, the inner-city black communities criminalised and the ideology of rampant individualism had put money in the pockets of many young workers. Suddenly these individuals began to act collectively and defiantly. With the growth of the rave scene, the drugs discourse, barely identifiable in the early accounts of new age travellers, became the rationale for trying to stop the 'unprecedented numbers of young people [who were] on the move at weekends' (*Observer* 11.4.99). Cracking down on drugs was the excuse made for the effort to control the dance scene at the 'pay parties' – the same excuse behind the ending of 'blind-eye' policing that led to the first of the confrontations between police and the black communities in 1980. But this time the disorderly crowd were young, working, white people and the rationale was not their criminality but their safety. The police assumption about drug

use, amongst the young, in such circumstances was and still seems
to be that:

> Drug use is not freely chosen but a result of corruption and
> innocence ... their own role is immediately defined by such an
> ethos; they must save the innocent (i.e. the drug user) and in a
> humanitarian fashion punish the wicked (i.e. the drug pusher).
> (Young 1971: 443)

Young was writing about marijuana, which was also the focus for
clampdowns on black culture in the early 1980s, but the preferred
drug of the ravers was Ecstasy. The ethos of intervention was broadly
similar to the earlier periods but the 'corruption of innocence'
motivation for police activity was hard to sustain. People wanted
drugs, 'they were willing, even voracious participants' (*Observer*
11.4.99) and they weren't 'estate dwelling lost youth. They were nice
kids. The kids next door' (*Observer* 11.4.99). The appetite for drugs
meant that soon organised crime began to target the raves, legitimating further the police effort to foreclose events. This effort was
supported by the media and employed tactics that most would
associate with the newly collapsed totalitarianism of the Eastern bloc
rather than England.

Fresh from policing the miners, the police blocked roads and
interrupted communication, especially the mobile phone networks
and pirate radios that were used for co-ordinating the production of
a rave. As police closed venues, so partygoers waited by their car-
phones and at pay-phones to be told where the alternative site was
to be. Concern was expressed in parliament:

> Yesterday Labour demanded a statement by Douglas Hurd, the
> Home Secretary, on the proliferation of Acid House parties and
> their alleged drug threat. The most extraordinary scenes came after
> 100 police stopped Berkshire's mammoth party. In a five hour
> country wide chase, several hundred packed cars sped in search of
> an alternative. (*Independent* 3.7.89)

Those entrepreneurs organising the parties – dubbed 'Sloany'[5] in
the *Independent* (3.7.89) – argued for more lenient licensing and
dancing laws but were initially only rewarded with a tightening of
legislation in 1990. However, after a decent period of clampdown, the
government relented in the face of pressure from the leisure industry

and late-night licences and all-night raves joined the range of entertainment legally available. Respectable youth went back indoors,
paying lucrative entrance fees for the privilege. Others were less
compliant and the streets of cities and the countryside remained sites
of struggle between youth and authority throughout Thatcherism.

Taking the Streets

In 1991 tensions on a Cardiff Estate focused on an ongoing dispute
between shopkeepers, which 'hovered on the raw edge of race'
(Campbell 1993: 5). An attempt by an Asian grocer to foil shoplifting
led to racist taunting from a crowd of mostly young men that turned
into riot as police arrived to clear the area as the pubs closed. Over
the weekend of 1 September police in riot gear were deployed on the
estate, supported by a helicopter and dog handlers, to deal with the
youths who 'were having the time of their lives shouting anti-police
and anti-shopkeeper slogans, like "Paki out"' (Campbell 1993: 21).
Also enjoying the spectacle were large numbers of residents and
others, especially the media, who had come along for the show and
the story – this crowd was milling about on the streets waiting for
some hot action, on a hot night. In the chaos, police cleared the area
by cordoning off routes and sending people home – a process
highlighted by a helicopter's spotlight. Floodlit youths ran the
gauntlet of police lines hurling bricks and insults and many ended
up under arrest under the Public Order Act.

The local press initially reported the events as a race riot but
nationally the emphasis was on the original dispute between shops
about trading regulations: 'Bread dispute brings new bout of summer
madness' (*The Times* 3.9.91) or drunken, generally discontent youths.
There was also in *The Times* (3.9.91) a leader article that denied any
political motive for riot at all: 'a riot is not a political event. It is a
phenomenon of crowd psychology' (see the discussion in Chapter 3
on Marsh, 1978 explaining riot) very often influenced by television.
Alcohol, testosterone and the heatwave often featured in explanations for the violence on the council estates in 1991 and 1992.

The same weekend that police went into Cardiff in riot gear they
also decided to act on the Blackbird Leys Estate in Oxford. The estate
had experienced more than a year of car crime problems amongst
young men, who were often unemployed and dependent on their
mothers (Campbell 1993). With no job and no money there was

little to give them any kind of mark of manhood – there were few enough men around the estate anyway. So what they could not realise, they symbolised.

The fast powerful car was the sure sign of a young upwardly mobile, thirty-something man during the booming entrepreneurialism of the 1980s. High-powered car dealer Robert Frige described his wealthy customers in London as traders and dealers, 'they're very fast and aggressive people ... they want the fastest, flashiest most aggressive looking car they can get ... at the end of the day it's just like penis size' (*Guardian* 14.11.92). Taking without owner's consent was the one way the boys of Britain's poorest communities could pretend, however briefly, to be mature, middle-class, heterosexual men – in other words, joy-riding briefly gave them power. Late at night, they stole fast cars and drove them hard and dangerously for an audience of admiring teenagers.

> All these boys becoming men, stealing and steering an object impregnated with fantasies, doing nothing more useful than getting high on a machine and nothing more useless than demanding to be seen doing it. There is something ultimately transgressive in their culture because, of course, they are connoisseurs of cars – but they can't keep them. (Campbell in *Marxism Today* December 1991)

At Blackbird Leys the 'displays united thieves, drivers and audiences in an alliance against the authorities' (Campbell 1993: 33), yet the police decided to move onto the estate only after events at Cardiff had developed to riot proportions. The police officer in charge in Oxford had served in the St Paul's area of Bristol during the 1980 disorders – he was what Campbell called a public order man. As in Cardiff, the media also became part of the audience and the boys performed for them. There were claims that journalists even paid the lads to do the business, so they could get photographs and stories.

After a week of skirmishes and dozens of arrests, peace was restored; the roads were rapidly adapted to slow traffic with 'sleeping policemen', but the people on the estate were confused and angry – nothing had been done about the joy-riders before and when it was dealt with it was by police invasion and intrusion. Moreover, joy-riding was not over – it was just beginning. For Campbell (1993) explanations lay in emasculated white, working-class youth refusing to accept the rotten deal handed out to them by Thatcherism and taking what they hadn't got the means to buy in a struggle for consumer enfranchisement.

Jefferson (1992) agreed that class was a partial explanation but only when linked to masculinity, because crime is quintessentially masculine to the extent that boys who never challenge authority are regarded as wimpish or girlish. Grown men often boast of their youthful deviancy and it was such deviancy that Jefferson focused on rather than any class political action. For Jefferson, class merely meant that for these lads their deviant rite of passage was worked out by assaults on middle-class possessions, not for political reasons but for machismo, and the challenge by police was the highlight of the process, especially if the media covered the 'battle'.

Neither the class nor the masculinity issue was addressed by either journalists or politicians as possibly relevant to explanations for joy-riding. There was no integrated discussion about the implications of removing any legitimate access to both class and gender identity from a whole generation of young men. Instead, what began to emerge was the wholesale condemnation of the communities where these young men lived. Poverty, unemployment, lack of facilities, policing were only addressed as a result of already 'dangerous places' (Campbell 1993). More commonly, youngsters, especially young men, were perceived, across a range of authoritative discourses, as out of control. Blame for this was often directed at the parents – or rather, given the constant references to lone parents, the mothers.

For example, when trouble flared in Newcastle on the Meadowell Estate in mid-September 1991 much of the reporting focused on the responsibility of families: 'children as young as eight were reported to be taking part in the disturbance' (*The Times* 10.9.91).

The Home Secretary is to support action by courts and the police to keep rioting youngsters at home at night. Mr Baker last night encouraged police forces to ask the courts for curfew orders as a condition of bail for any youngster arrested in the sort of riots seen in Newcastle, Cardiff and Oxford. His message to police was to clear Britain's streets of troublesome youngsters by ensuring they stay home at night … it is the lack of parental responsibility and control, a significant feature of the recent rioting, that has appalled ministers. (*Sunday Telegraph* 15.9.91)

Communities curfewed to enforce parental responsibility became common in the early 1990s as the pressure on families to conform to the Conservative model and the publicity about the problem associated with 'other' families increased (see Chapter 7). It climaxed in Liverpool within explanations for the murder of a toddler by two pre-pubescent boys.

'The devil himself couldn't have made a better job of raising two fiends' (*Sun* 25.11.93)

In 1993, the Bulger case became the pivot for discussions of youth, family and community. Eight-year-olds may have been rioting in Newcastle but in Liverpool two ten-year-olds, Thompson and Venables, kidnapped and killed a toddler, James Bulger, whilst playing truant from school on 12 February. After their trial, the press launched into a desperate attempt to explain what was probably inexplicable – but to say something is inexplicable doesn't generate weeks and weeks of high-selling salacious crime journalism. Instead, journalists drew on other recent news stories – the riotous estates in the inner cities, single parents jumping housing queues and John Major's back to basics drive.

The *Sun* (25.11.93) reported Thompson and Venables 'running wild ... the boys roamed the streets looking for trouble and causing terror', they 'urged school pals to join our gang'. They were truants who 'stole sweets and toys from shops, threw stones at windows, swore at shopkeepers'. The whole of Liverpool was found wanting as it emerged that James was dragged through the streets in tears before his death with no intervention.[6] 'They had walked these two and half miles and been seen by dozens of people' (*Independent* 25.11.93). The television news showed image after image of run-down housing, railway sidings and mean backstreets. One boy's home was 'in a badly built, badly maintained, badly kept council red brick terrace house ... Anything could happen with those kids, they ran riot, were playing on bikes at 1 o'clock in the morning' (*Independent* 25.11.93).

The *Independent* revealed: 'Killers from broken but contrasting homes'; Thomson had '6 brothers ... the father of all bar the baby, left in 1988' (25.11.93). The *Sun* (25.11.93) headlined a story: 'MONSTER'S MUM: I'M NOT TO BLAME', followed by the comment, 'Thompson's mother has blamed everyone but herself'. Venables' parents also separated in 1988, his mother was a disciplinarian and the boy 'was disruptive at junior school' but his relatively normal life compared to John Thompson's placed him as the accomplice to Thompson as the 'weirdo'.

The collapse of the family as causal of violence featured twice: first in articles such as 'Break Up of Family Leads Kids to Crime' (*Sun* 25.11.93), juxtaposed to the Bulger reports; second in the furore that raged after the judge in the case made a post-verdict comment on video-nasties. The press sifted through all they could think of and came up with *Child's Play 3* as having scenes similar to those of the murder. The *Sun* (26.11.93) insisted 'Burn this evil video' in an article stressing the large numbers of videos in Thompson's house and warning 'millions to think seriously about the kind of material they let into their homes'. A throwaway remark became a means of blaming deviant, neglectful families and video-nasties for youthful violence and enabled a calling for censorship – even though 'despite police efforts there was not a scrap of evidence that the boys had watched the film' (Barker and Petley 1997: 13). The *Sun* preached a 'Grim warning of nightmares to come' because 'Liberal permissiveness is eating the fabric of our society' (25.11.93).

Drugs

Although the huge council estates of the post-working classes were and are sites for dealing and using drugs like marijuana and heroin, it was Ecstasy, the designer drug of the club-scene, that featured high on the news agenda as it became clear that moving the pay parties of the late 1980s to the all-night clubs of the 1990s had done little to inhibit the appetite for Ecstasy. Any theory that innocent, raving youth were being preyed on by drugs barons at illicit venues was scotched by the ongoing popularity of the drug even in the licensed clubs. Its illegality was clearly no deterrent simply because it is swallowed not smoked or injected, making detection by simple searching a major problem.

In 1995 the deterrent discourse changed after the death of Leah Betts: 'Pretty Leah collapsed at her eighteenth birthday party in her own home four hours after swallowing a £10 Ecstasy tablet' (*Daily Mirror* 13.11.95). As crime journalist Duncan Campbell pointed out, 'an attractive young white woman remains the likeliest person to attract media coverage' (*Guardian* 4.8.92) and this was certainly the case with the Leah Betts story, which 'conformed so perfectly to the mechanics of the tabloid machine' (Bellos in the *Face* April 1997).

In news values terms it was negative, sudden, dramatic (especially as her father gave the photograph of her on a life-support machine to the papers), it fitted with prior knowledge about the dangers of drugs and it was a personal story (Galtung and Ruge 1965, see Chapter 1). It was a crime story with many of the elements Chibnall identified in 1977: illegality, destruction, irresponsibility, irrationality and corruption.

The effort to convince young people that drugs are bad because they are illegal was becoming increasingly difficult to maintain in the early 1990s, as the experience of youth was that Es were cheap, pleasurable, easy to get and, given the millions using the drug, relatively free of side effects, especially addiction. Alongside this experience was a growing campaign to decriminalise drugs – partly relating to the increasing evidence of the benefits of cannabis to multiple sclerosis sufferers, partly to destigmatise users and control quality as does Dutch policy, partly to reduce the crime attendant on illegal drug use such as prostitution and theft and partly because of the clear hypocrisy of the legality of alcohol and tobacco.

Young argued that illicit drug use is news because it is crime, but it is awkward news because it is about pleasure – 'alternative realities, violations of the consensus image of society' (1971: 330). However, when a drugs story results in pain rather than pleasure it becomes much easier for journalists to deal with. The negativity of a painful outcome fits newsworthy criteria and also allows journalists to condemn and moralise around the theme of undeserved pleasure leading to pain. However, the constant stress on the illegality of drugs had become a tired story in the 1990s – given the tiny numbers of prosecutions and the slight pain of the punishments (there were four drugs arrests at the party by the A34 with 2,500 ravers, *Independent* 3.7.89), making the construction of drugs users as deviant pretty ineffectual. The alternatives according to Young were to present drugs users as either mentally ill (so not normal) or corrupted innocents (so blaming someone or something else). This last was the route taken by the press in the Leah Betts case.

The story contained elements of cultural value particularly resonant to a contemporary audience: Leah's father was an ex-policeman; it was her 'coming of age party' at 18; she was an innocent – it was her first drug experience, 'she may have been tempted to try one of these tablets without really knowing what it is ... she comes from a good home and a nice respectable family' (*The Times* 13.11.95). It happened in her own home in the South East;

she carried a donor card and her heart was given to another young woman, leaving Leah 'living on in some way' (*The Times* 15.11.95). It was these latter values which dominated the press accounts.

Leah was 'poisoned': she was a victim because the drug was 'spiked'; her father was 'heartbroken' and her mother 'anguished'; a 'dealer out there is selling this poison to unsuspecting young people' (*Daily Mirror* 13.11.95). *The Times* quoted Mr Betts copiously: 'Anyone who supports drug use and thinks drugs should be legalised only has to look at my family and my daughter in particular' (13.11.85). This kind of coverage amplified the story to a higher level of cultural resonance. This was an assault on virtue, on the British police, on the home and on the family by an evil drug dealer selling poison. These were normal people treated criminally.

The impact of such a discourse is hard to assess. Teenagers probably saw straight through it from their position as oppositional readers (Hall 1973); some features' journalists were also sceptical but found it very difficult to blame the dead girl (Burchill in the *Sunday Times* 19.11.95); the youth press stressed the need for teenagers to be informed not frightened (the *Face* February 1996), particularly as it soon emerged that Leah died not from Ecstasy but from water intoxication (the drug can lead to dehydration so ravers need to drink fluids, but in moderation).

As a media analyst, I was less interested in the angle, accuracy or effects of the reports than in what the stories revealed about the British news media. My feeling was and is that there is less of an effects debate to be had about this kind of news than an ethics debate – if journalism risked the anger of the moral majority and offered decent drugs information instead of salacious, emotive condemnation then maybe parents might be in a better position to talk to their kids. The need is to know, not to be told to just say no.

These stories reinforced middle-class, traditional family values – there was no criticism anywhere of the family, the community or Leah herself. Neither was there any criticism in the national papers of the policing of drugs crime, nor much discussion of the discontinuity between drink and tobacco legislation and other drugs, nor any information on how to be safe using drugs. These news reports were ideologically mainstream both in terms of law and order and middle-class culture, partly due to news values, partly perhaps due to the remaining class profile of national press journalists – 'new entrants to journalism are better educated, increasingly likely to have middle-class backgrounds ... than a decade ago' (Franklin 1997: 64)

– and indicative of a continuing reciprocity of interests between the
law and the media (Erickson *et al.* 1991).

Protest

The most recent site of troublesome youth also revealed those
middle-class interests, but in a far more subtle interplay of discourses.
Gradually in the 1990s, the new age travellers' focus on common
land transformed into or was partly replaced by a more politicised
youth action, in defence not just of access to the land but of the land
itself against commercial or state development. In 1993, Green
protestors occupied a site at Twyford Down, to try to prevent the
building of a new extension of the M3. This occupation was defeated
by police and private security guards and marked the beginnings of
a new kind of eviction process, a new kind of mainly youth activity
that for the first time since 1968 claimed to be overtly political, a
new kind of occupation of trees and later tunnels and an apparently
new kind of 'news'.

It was the new kind of news that drew my attention to the green
protestors, mostly because it was, at first glance, benign at least
towards this example of disruptive youth and in some cases seemed
to be positively supportive of this new cultural form. The first road
protestors occupied trees to try to prevent land being cleared with
chain-saws – the authorities responded by bringing in expert
climbers to clear the area in what sometimes appeared to be a wildly
dangerous air ballet as the trees were sawn away from beneath them.

At Newbury in 1996 Greens tried to stop the clearance of ancient
woodland in a scheme to build a bypass. Again the trees were
occupied to try to save them by protestors 'cynical of mainstream
politics' and blaming 'the state for a massively destructive roads
programme' (*Guardian* 7.2.96). Newbury was eventually cleared by
'700 guards moving like an organism through the woods, destroying
everything in its path' (*Guardian* 7.2.96) but the protestors had learnt
a new occupational technique – tunnelling.

In 1997 they tunnelled first at Fairmile in Devon and then at the
site of the proposed new runway at Manchester airport. Again, the
journalism appeared broadly sympathetic. Out of curiosity, I
collected the press and TV coverage of the Manchester protest.[7]

The positive press given to these young, dishevelled, single-issue
protestors who were both trespassing, causing delays to development

work and costing huge amounts of money to police and evict, was puzzling, given that the profile of British journalism hadn't changed significantly since the 'Battle of the Beanfield' at Stonehenge. I couldn't believe journalists were aligned with the views of the tunnellers and tree dwellers. There was no evidence of them abandoning their company cars for bicycles and recycling their booze bottles.[8] Yet the press effectively turned the tunnellers into eco-heroes.

Swampy, one of the prominent activists, was dubbed an icon of masculinity, the successor to the new lad. 'Women have decided that what they really, really want is a good old fashioned hero with a soft centre' (*Independent on Sunday* 13.4.97). Once the heroic motif was in place, other romantic metaphors were readily mobilised. The *Observer* offered the headline: 'Tunnel of Love: for Denise and Grandpappy the earth moved under Manchester airport' (15.6.97). Denise reads 'Watership Down' underground and is pregnant – a subterranean conception resonant with earth mother connotations. If a boy, the child will be named Clay or Doug. Journalist Nicci Gerrard in the *Observer* was very concerned about health risks and sanitary arrangements. The liberal broadsheets uniformly followed this line of reporting: sympathetic, personalised, prurient, focusing on the risk from nature and dirtiness rather than from the bailiffs and police.

The usually incisive *World in Action*, ITV's groundbreaking documentary series, approached the tunnellers similarly. Interviews emphasised the risks to the tunnellers, the support given to them by local women, the dirt and the same love affair identified by the *Observer*. The programme included a sequence of about ten minutes showing the couple taking a bath, with a long, lingering shot of dirty soapy water going down the plughole (May 1997). This was very much in line with Franklin's (1997) argument that news journalism is 'dumbing down'. Our flagship press and television personalised collective activity, cleaned dirty bodies and hardly addressed the issues of environmental politics or the economics of development at all.

Oddly, the tabloid press told different stories or rather didn't tell the story at all with one exception. The *Sun*, *Daily Mirror* and *Daily Mail* ignored the young Greens in favour of football, soap opera, pop stars, the Royals and the election. Journalists write for an audience and editors need to sell papers – clearly those working on these tabloids didn't see environmental politics as an issue for which their readers would rush out and buy papers. McNair stressed that 'the journalist is a cog in a wheel over whose speed and direction he or she may have little or no control' (1998: 62). Unless a story fits within the routine and requirements of a particular paper, it is unlikely to be reported. Some of those requirements are news values and cultural relevance, others are more ordinary issues of time, cost, access and the model of the audience. Environmental issues appeared to be perceived by journalists as middle-class – but there have been exceptions. The *Daily Mirror* effectively broke the Brent Spar story[9] and covered it copiously, but the other tabloids barely addressed it at all. The broadsheets covered the story and:

> TV journalists saw it as fascinating and bizarre that people were willing to stand in front of whaling harpoons or under a barrel of nuclear waste being dumped at sea. These activities were seen as heroic and they were an absolute gift for the media. (Porritt and Winner 1988: 94 cited in Anderson 1997: 35)

Yet, it was obviously seen as outside of the range of interest of most tabloid readers as the other popular papers hardly featured it.

The tabloid exception for the Manchester story was not the *Mirror* but the *Daily Express*, which more or less confirmed my suspicions about the relevance of class by calling the Greens '[m]iddle-class warriors' (28.5.97). However, the *Express* took a very different line to the quality papers in that it focused not on the romance, nor on the environmental politics, nor on the natural danger from the earth, but on the policing and organisation of the protest. The issues for the *Express* were the use of private security firms to enforce evictions – 'There is something alien and un-British about these squads of mercenaries ... Why can't the job have been given to the police ...?' (22.5.97), and the theorised extreme left influence behind the protests – 'The hard left is wooing green protestors to take on other issues' (28.5.97). The paper sympathised with the protest but disliked the lifestyle of the empty-headed hippies. The only explanation for this approach I could think of was the need to satisfy a readership of rather conservative, nationalistic, green-belt dwelling, 'not in my backyarders' (NIMBYs), some of whom might well have been supplying hot baths to the young protestors. The coverage embraced law and order, condemned the left, showed concern that middle-class youth was being led astray and sympathised with environmentalism at a stroke.

News about Green politics was transformed by journalists to news about sex (the broadsheet liberal papers) 'n'violence (*Daily Express*). The threat to the establishment from collective, politicised, angry young people challenging state, authority, capital, lifestyle and hygiene was diffused into a story about vulnerable, nice middle-class individuals: idealistic, perhaps led astray by the wrong crowd, falling in love, looking for excitement, not minding being grubby and being dealt with by 'questionable strong arm tactics' from 'hired gun skinheads' (*Daily Express* 22.5.97).

This was complex news – there is no clear propaganda (Herman and Chomsky 1988), no shared agenda amongst all the British press (McCoombs and Shaw 1972) and no pluralism (Tunstall 1996), because there is no political account of the environment. I found evidence here of a calling to consensus not simply to the state or to capital but to British middle-class cultural values. It seemed to me that the middle classes closed ranks around cultural norms and values – lost children were brought safely home, dirty bodies were scrubbed clean, legitimate law and order were restored and individual heroes were paraded in public. In this fairy story, middle-class interests of all types justifiably live on happily ever after.

Comment

Identifying in any media text choices between available discourses that benefit, legitimate or seek consensus for the ideas and identities of the particular social group(s) producing the text make it reasonable to claim ideological bias. When such analysis links these discursive choices to the cultural values (or political and economic values) of already powerful social groups then the exercise of power over meaning is made evident. That seemed to me to have happened consistently in the accounts of disorderly youth during the period of the last Conservative government. Fairclough argued that language is a 'social barometer' in that uses and meanings shift relative to human relations:

> Representations, relations and identities are always simultaneously at issue in a text ... The value of such a view of texts is that it makes it easier to connect the analysis of language with fundamental concerns of social analysis: questions of knowledge, belief and ideology (representations – the ideational function), questions of

social relationships and power, and questions of identity (relations and identity – the interpersonal function). (1995: 17)

This is not a chapter about youth culture but about news that represents youth culture as deviant or criminal. In other words, I am analysing and writing about the news media not British youth. There may be implications of course for the practice of youth in its representation but effects research is neither my interest nor my focus here. In fact I would go so far as to argue that too great an emphasis on ethnography and effects can produce in the first case an apparently delightfully differentiated and multiplicit youth culture, particularly in relation to leisure or, in the second, a model of youth as more or less constructed relative to their visual media experiences (few undertake effects research on books or radio or even music).

My hypothesis is that regardless of difference or effects those with power will seek to maintain it – difference and effects are only relevant to power if they threaten power, if they can be exploited by power or if they can be used to justify power. Power is hierarchical and operates in different ways at different levels, contexts and epochs but it would be naïve, ignorant or misleading to assume those operations as equal in socially and economically stratified societies (and even the most committed post-modernist could hardly claim their equity is the British reality, however admirable the theory).

In terms of the context of communication, the media are the most prolific, systematic and pervasive source of information, and information is power in our post-industrial Western world – that for me is sufficient reason to scrutinise them.

One of the easiest ways to make sense of who has authority over the media is to consider not whose views are given publicity but who could stop that process. In terms of the news media, the power to stop the presses and blacken our screens lies ultimately with the state, secondly with capital (though this power relation is changing rapidly as transnational media groups increasingly operate beyond national boundaries) and thirdly with journalists and media workers themselves. The only current source of global information, relatively free of the threat of closure, is the World Wide Web and millions are currently being spent by commerce and the government to find means of controlling it. The fact that empowered groups seek all sorts of means and authority to control mass information sources is a good enough reason for me to analyse the representations available through those sources.

When Cohen (1973) and Middleton and Muncie (1982) analysed news about youth they noted class differentiations. Young (1971) found a tendency to label youth drug use as innocence corrupted or evil manifested. All three approaches saw the media as actively defusing the activities of rebellious youth by defining and castigating criminal tendencies and clarifying the value and desirability of mainstream culture. It seemed to me that however else youth was expressing itself during the 1980s and 1990s, once those activities crossed, or potentially crossed, the boundaries of illegality the news media continued to deal with them in a broadly similar way. Although the earliest disturbances around the new age travellers provided an opportunity to reiterate English values and show off the newly empowered police force's capacity for restoring law and order, most of the news about youth high jinks remained class differentiated in the press of the Thatcher/Major years – though the model of class is very different and gender is still barely addressed compared to the pre-Thatcherite examples.

Whereas the Mods and Rockers of the 1960s could be described as working class – because they were working in manual or semi-skilled jobs and came from families with similar work histories – by the time of the riots on council estates of the 1990s few young men living on the estates were working. At Meadowell 'between the sixties and the nineties the region lost most of its staple jobs for men in the shipyards' (Campbell 1993: 49). In many instances the fathers were also unemployed, if they were still around the family home. There was no construction of these youths as corrupted innocents, not even much mention of the levels of heroin, crack cocaine and solvent abuse on these estates nor of the endemic poverty and lack of any potential for gaining from anywhere a sense of self-esteem and positive identity. Joy-riding was just seen as crime, not in any way relative to the need for some kind of masculinity – however parodic, symbolic or brief. The condition of these estates was portrayed as an effect of the lawlessness of their youth rather than cause. Like the miners in the mid-1980s these lads appeared to be the authors of their own misfortune.

Classless and emasculated poor white youth of the urban estates are doubly socially excluded – the best the press managed by way of explanation was the usual cant about failing families and single parents (mothers). Bea Campbell asked 'why masculinity takes such spectacularly destructive forms when it loses its power' (*Marxism Today* December 1991) – the answer is because it is the one thing it can do that remains a marker of manhood on these estates where work no longer exists and women occupy the domestic sphere. Criminalising a group with no other means of establishing their maleness actually makes the press and police complicit in producing crime – hence the performances for the cameras and the floodlights during the disturbances.

The class base for these representations becomes clear when the news about other groups of deviant youth of the period is considered. The raves involved working and otherwise respectable young people – they were also potentially highly profitable. The resolution to the deviance was to license clubs to provide the same experience but in a controlled and taxable way, but the rationale provided through the press was that criminal activity was making the raves dangerous places for our young people, especially around the sale of illegal drugs. The fact that these drugs, especially Ecstasy, have simply increased in popularity throughout the 1990s suggests that the working, aspiring young are not the innocents the press prefers. Even the treatment of the Leah Betts case failed to stem the tide of recreational drug use, despite the range of familiar discourses around family, innocence and the criminal supply of drugs.

When middle-class youth became politically active against the interests of state and capital in the environmental protests of the 1990s, the press (or at least those who reported it) gave them some sympathetic support, but it was sympathy fuelled by romanticisation, personalisation, a British dislike of privatised security forces and quite possibly an identification, as many current journalists would have been part of the rebelliousness of the 1960s. Environmental youth protest was reported with benign prurience and without much debate on either politics or the environment, at the close of the Conservative period in office.

At the cusp of the millennium, youth remains a problem for the Blairite government mostly because of drugs, partly because of sex, both of which coloured the news about the eco-warriors. Now that the children of the middle classes are clearly choosing narcotic pleasure, the Home Office has directed significant research funds towards drugs education and research. However, 'Anti-drugs Drive Fails to Stem Abuse' (*Guardian* 22.3.99). Increasingly high profile middle-class kids are featuring in the media as drug users, including the son of Jack Straw – the Home Secretary of Tony Blair's 1997 government and the son of Camilla Parker-Bowles (the heir to the throne's partner). Finally, middle-class journalists are objecting to the criminalisation of young drug users, so long of course as they are working, white and well-spoken. *Guardian* journalist Libby Purves admits as much when she claims that 'the unprecedented popularity of Ecstasy brought drug use off the streets and into the homes and gardens of the middle-classes' (20.5.99). But Ecstasy is illegal and reliance on dealers for supplies created a space for the marketing of more dangerous highs. Purves argues that the legislation is now incompatible with the current morality of drug-taking and should be changed – now that it isn't just the 'socially excluded' who are facing street violence and heavy-handed criminal justice – and argues for challenges to the 'immovable assumptions of right and wrong' that are the Thatcher legacy on drugs legislation. Although one or two articles in the liberal broadsheets do not amount to an onslaught on policy, it seems increasingly likely that there will be one and that decriminalisation of the possession of some classes of illegal drugs will come first, followed at a decent interval by some form of licensing. Now that drugs are coolly central to middle-class youth culture they must lose their stigma. Legitimised, they could also prove a very useful source of tax revenue and new enterprises, whilst cutting the health and welfare costs of the current major (legal) drug killers: nicotine and alcohol.

In the news about youth, the middle-class family is found faultless and offered as a model to the post-class communities, excluded from class identity by the deconstruction of working-class work and community and from the middle classes by geography and poverty. Gender was central to these disturbances yet was rarely addressed by the media. There was an assumption that the trouble was boys, with girls only mentioned in relation to their looks or their motherhood. Yet, there was no interrogation of this, leaving norms of masculinity – aggression, dangerousness and irresponsibility, in place. The implications of such representations are difficult to assess because:

> Untangling the relationship between culture, structure and agency ... reverberates with contradictory and complex arguments drawn from post-structuralism and feminism and other radical perspectives shaped by the rise of the New Right and the crisis which faced the left during the 1980s. (Griffin 1993: 211)

But when the news media representations of deviant youth are taken alongside those other major discourses considered by Griffin (1993) they accumulate to a profound amount of cultural knowledge informing young and old alike about what is acceptable youth behaviour; that knowledge remains class and gender differentiated in ways that relate to a very conservative model of mature identity.

The political parties lost their young members and voters during Thatcherism, perhaps because the government's longevity belied the possibility that change could be achieved so activism seemed pointless. 'At the time of the last census (1991) nearly 20% of 18–25s were not registered to vote compared to 2% of those aged 55 or over' (*Guardian* 29.1.98). Tory policy and ideology also effectively deconstructed some of the venues of traditional politicisation, especially the trades unions, and promoted an entrepreneurial and individualistic culture. Thatcherism sidelined collective political involvement for young people, rendering it trivial, hedonistic or criminal.

5
Beggars Not Choosers

1918 Lloyd George promises homes 'fit for heroes who have won the war'.

1933 Ministry of Health promises to clear 'all areas that require it, no later than 1938'.

1946 Aneurin Bevan: 'I give you this promise; that by the next election there will be no housing shortage'.

1950 Lord Woolton boasts: 'We have done more things than re-house a nation'.

1961 Housing White paper promises: 'with the exception of a few areas unfit housing should have practically disappeared within the next ten years'.

In 1967 the Ministry of Housing stated that in Britain more than 3 million people were living in unfit homes.

(Shelter Campaign poster 1967 *Britain: The Promised Land* in Wilson 1969)

In November 1966, Ken Loach's shocking and poignant BBC Wednesday Play *Cathy Come Home* sought to deconstruct one of the most powerful and prevalent myths that the homeless were largely personally responsible for their situation through 'bad luck, irresponsibility and incompetence, sudden financial crisis, relationship breakdown or just wilfulness' (Booth 1989: 47). Prior to that screening, homelessness had tended to be equated with 'rooflessness' and the plight of some three million people living in appalling conditions was largely invisible to the public and ignored by politicians. Any press coverage focused on beggars and vagrants as in Moorhouse's description: 'A hunchback shuffles up to a bench opposite platform 10. He discovers a long fag end in his pocket, lights it and looks at nothing in particular' ('Whose Waterloo', *Guardian* 22.10.65).

In contrast, the focus for *Cathy* was the lack of affordable housing for families. The public reaction impelled huge support for the charity Shelter, created just a month later, which, 30 years after *Cathy*, retains that motif, 'affordable housing', as central to their campaign for the provision of decent homes for all. Yet government was and is resistant. The programme prompted a great deal of blame-attributing but much less action: 'Homelessness is something of a political football – the result, say the parties, of their opponents' incompetence or inhuman housing policies' (Ferguson 1968). One result of that inactivity and bickering is the ongoing involvement of the voluntary sector in the provision of accommodation – from the night shelters of the Salvation Army to the self-contained flats built and offered by the St Anne's Shelter in Leeds. Despite *Cathy*, housing problems increased during the 1970s, with many local authorities resorting to placing families in bed and breakfast accommodation. Any such housing initiatives were not always welcome by local residents, whose sympathetic views of the televised homeless became denigratory if the homeless appeared next door. Cook quotes one such resident in his study of vagrancy: 'If you think there are plans to store refuse in an expensive box in your street you scream, and the powers that be are frightened by the din' (1979: 9).

The total cost of homelessness to local authorities was £260 million during 1994 (Shelter 1996). Other costs are more difficult to measure as 'the homeless pay a heavy price for Britain's failed housing system – the daily horrors of insecurity, squalor, disruption to jobs and education, damage to family life and ill health' (Shelter 1996). Homeless people, perhaps more than any other social group, are routinely blamed for their own predicament. During the Conservative governments from 1979 to 1997 that predicament was exacerbated by a range of legislative change alongside the deconstruction of welfarism and the promotion of home-ownership. By the early 1990s, begging was a common sight in London and other major cities. When Prime Minister John Major denounced beggars as 'offensive eyesores' in May 1994 few newspapers disagreed: 'Prime Minister John Major today called on people to "shop" beggars and drive them out of the city' (*Evening Post* 27.5.94). The occasional liberal exception was damning of the Conservative government:

> Mr Major insists that all begging is wrong. It is not as he puts it 'necessary'. One can only reflect, with J.S. Mill, on the 'inability of the analytic mind to recognise its own handiwork'. (*Independent* 29.5.94)

Failure to improve Britain's housing record was insufficient for the Conservatives – they not only increased homelessness but promoted the kind of popular discourse that ensured there would be little public pressure on the state to improve matters, and much pressure on individuals to accept responsibility for their own fate.

Two particular models of the homeless prevailed during this period. First, the single homeless, usually referred to as beggars and often described as scroungers – 'Beggar Had £200 in His Pocket' (*The Times* 4.1.94) – or mentally ill, as in 'Street Army of Broken Minds' (*Daily Star* 29.4.94) or addicts of some kind:

> Back at the Centrepoint shelter, 21 year old Richard told of begging £20 down at Victoria Station that day. 'I've bought myself 12 cans of beer and two tabs of speed. I'm wasted', he groaned. (*Daily Express* 9.5.94)

The second model was the single parent or more specifically the perceived problem of young women becoming pregnant in order to be offered council accommodation, ahead of others on the waiting lists. This focus developed following the Tory Party conference in October 1993 where the concept of 'back to basics' morality was mooted. By January we saw headlines such as: 'We'll Stop the Queue Jump Mums' (*Daily Mail* 19.1.94). The government discussion paper 'Access to Local Authority and Housing Association Tenancies: a consultation paper' (January 1994), proposed to introduce much tighter controls on the definitions of homelessness necessary for consideration for social housing. It also specifically suggested that local authorities should be obligated to provide only temporary accommodation, that the only route to permanent rehousing should be the waiting list and that the private sector should be more systematically used.

An Englishman's Home

After the emotive reaction to *Cathy* the Labour government effectively exacerbated a growing housing crisis because 'housing issues were left to the management of local authorities who failed to recognise (or chose to ignore) the fact that the problem of homelessness could be solved simply by using unused publicly owned resources at a considerable saving of public money' (Bailey 1977: 17). Whereas Labour's failure was one of indecision and inaction, in Britain in the 1990s Shelter argued that the political context of the housing crisis was firmly grounded in Thatcherite economic policy.

The selling of council houses and promotion of home-ownership as the ideal housing model had reduced the available stock of public housing to rent and excluded the poor, the young, the single and the highly mobile from access to a home. By the 1990s the housing situation and social distress had reached crisis point, to the extent that Booth argued 'poverty and bad housing are as inextricably linked as they were a century ago' (1989: 71).

By turning houses into commodities, the ability to make a home became linked to economic power. The Conservative government argued that more people than ever had become home-owners, but it was also true that during the economic slump in the early 1990s more people than ever were in significant arrears with mortgage payments (more than six months behind), more people than ever had had their homes repossessed by banks and building societies – 'Societies Seize 60,000 Homes' (*Observer* 21.3.94), and more people than ever were living in houses worth less than they paid – 'at its peak about 1.8 million households were affected with an average negative equity of £6600 ... two thirds of those affected are first time buyers' (*Daily Telegraph* 9.5.94). The situation was made worse by the Conservatives' commitment to the sale (sometimes in highly contentious strategies to retain votes[1]) of council housing. This strategy both increased the opportunity for those on lower incomes to buy and diminished the amount of cheap housing available for rent for those pushed out of their bought homes by repossession orders. As a result, people were forced outside of the housing mainstream by bad debt, into homelessness and sometimes into desperate acts.

Before the election of Margaret Thatcher's government, the Homeless Persons Act (1977) had been supported by all political parties. It put the duty on local authorities to house homeless people and provided strict guidelines for assessment and qualification to prevent abuse. However, the Tory government, whilst repeatedly recognising that homelessness was a problem, consistently failed to address the underlying lack of decent, affordable, secure homes; rather, it introduced controls over local authority provision which systematically exacerbated that lack. Instead of addressing the structural issue of housing, the 1994 consultation document attempted to rewrite and so misrepresent the problem of homelessness by excluding large numbers of people from eligibility. Concurrently, schemes like 'Care in the Community', the cutting of benefit to under-18-year-olds and the creation of high unemployment as an inflation-beating tactic, alongside the promotion of home-ownership, impelled more and more vulnerable individuals and families onto the streets. Such policies directly caused the increasing numbers of people with nowhere to live and the daily evidence of this homelessness on the streets of all major cities. Yet, the issue was seen as one of queue jumping for homes and criminality, not poverty, policy or lack of houses.

Homelessness and the Media

During this period, I was working in Leeds in a Cultural Studies teaching team that had devised a new course module called 'The City Project'. Some students focused their case-studies on the rapidly growing and hedonistic club scene in Leeds, but many became involved in social issues, some continuing that involvement in the longer term. One area of study that led to some of the most impressive coursework was housing and homelessness in Leeds and the surrounding areas. Drawn in by the students' commitment, and by growing links between the department and a wide range of charities and agencies working in the area of homelessness and housing, a colleague and myself applied for some research support to investigate 'Representations of homelessness'.[2]

That project was funded in 1994/95 by Trinity and All Saints College, University of Leeds, and was concerned with the possible repercussions for homeless people of representations of their situation in the media, policy documents and housing information material. It sought evidence of discontinuities between the 'real' cases presenting at a Housing Advice Centre in Yorkshire and 'representations' of the homeless. Part of the project involved discourse analysis of a range of texts, including the press, in order to develop a profile of the language style, structure and semantics in relation to issues around homelessness. A major concern was that there might be gaps between people's real experience of homelessness, media coverage of housing and homelessness issues and the treatment of people presenting for aid and advice on housing.

The anxiety was that, whatever the source, very particular media models of the homeless were being internalised and reproduced in other discourse types such as public opinion, advice offices and government documents. The objective was to identify the most prevalent models in the press, to assess whether they occurred regularly enough to be systematic and to measure their accessibility to readers and the likelihood of influence.

The press offers to many of us the means of accessing events such as violence, starvation and homelessness, which most of us may never personally experience or even witness. The extent of that access to events beyond our experience is simply demonstrated by the fact that each week some 22 million newspapers are sold in this country (15 million national dailies), many of which are likely to be read by more than one person (Tunstall 1983).

During the period of the research, the broadcast media covered issues of homelessness quite extensively in in-depth documentary programmes. On the other hand, the press reported the problem of 'the homeless' as identified by various politicians. Many of the images used to support homelessness stories were poignant and resonant with a tendency to present people in housing difficulty as victims, but there was much also that was inflammatory, denigratory and criminalising. The research mapped the kind of language used in the media and tried to relate it to the broader interests of state and capital, the real experiences of the homeless and the accounting discourses used by those working in housing support and advice.

Housing Advice

The research team spent time in a Housing Advice Centre (HAC) in Yorkshire, examining two aspects of client case records for the end of 1993: the nature of the client's experience and the language of the advice worker's account. The cases were assessed under Section 64 of the Housing Act 1985 that provided four hurdles through which applicants must pass in order to qualify as homeless. A statutorily homeless person had to:

1. Be homeless or threatened with homelessness;
2. Have a priority need for accommodation;
3. Not be intentionally homeless;
4. Demonstrate a local connection.

If these conditions were satisfied the local authority was obliged to make 'one reasonable offer only' of housing. The research was intended to identify the dominant discourses informing these processes and try to relate them to the discourses in the press and policy documents of the period.

Some 2,372 people presented themselves to the Yorkshire Housing Advice Centre, featured in the Leeds research, in the month before Christmas 1993. The overwhelming number of enquiries was simply requests for advice and information and only 178 clients formally asked to be considered homeless. Cases were read and identified, as far as possible, by client type. The confidential and complex nature of some applications, alongside the need to respect our responsibilities to the housing advice workers and the exclusion of 'live/current' cases for reasons of confidentiality made it impossible to be very systematic. We elected to take ten cases randomly from each of the representing client types and to examine each one looking for the same issues. Our interest was in the qualitative nature of the reports and experiences of the individuals involved, so we noted biographical information, references to the legislation, ambiguity and contradiction, moral judgements, labels, referrals to other agencies and any implications relating to the proposed legislative changes. In this chapter, I focus on the two groups which dominated the press homelessness discourse at the time, single people and single parents, to try to elicit evidence of those discourses in the housing reports and to test out the validity of the press accounts in relation to the real experiences of the homeless.[3]

Media, Myths and the 'Real' Issues of Homelessness

At the outset of the Leeds study there was a brief period of Christmas charity towards the homeless evident in the press in December 1993. Immediately before the festivities there were several articles focusing on the plight of children and young people, though even these managed some innuendo about poor mothering being to blame for a young runaway's story. The *Sunday Times* launched its 'Crisis at Christmas' appeal by telling the story of Debbie, whose real mother gave her away 'when she was barely a day old', who was looked after by a woman she thought was her mother 'in a haphazard fashion until she was eight', and who was eventually thrown out by her adoptive mother via a note on her doorstep saying 'go away, you are not my daughter' (12.12.93).

After the seasonal peak,[4] homelessness remained newsworthy into the early summer of 1994, due to the planned introduction of changes in the legislation relating to housing provision. But in all the discussions in the media, little connection seemed (seems) to be made between the commodification of housing and the rise in homelessness. The focus was certainly on some of the victims of the housing crisis but not on the thousands of families made homeless by repossession orders (this information was offered but usually as part of the financial and business agenda). Instead, single people and single parents became the motif for homelessness during 1994.

In the press, single people were described as either young petty thieves, layabouts, prostitutes and/or drug users – justifying the headline 'Major's War on the Beggars' (*Evening Post* 27.5.94), or older alcoholics, mentally ill people and tramps – 'the forgotten flotsam of our streets' (*Today* 20.4.94). In either case the press claimed that such people frequently chose to live rough: 'Plug is 33 but looks 50 ... Members of the homeless unit have tried to coax him into a hostel but he is not interested' (*The Times* 31.3.94). Youngsters were portrayed as 'leaving home for the bright lights of the city' (*Daily Star* 22.3.94).

In the 1990s, the single homeless were depicted as 'roofless' and either mad, bad or dangerous. Thirty years after Moorhouse's 1964 article, the *Daily Star* described the scene at Waterloo station: the homeless were not 'pan-handlers on the make but mad – part of an army of poor, demented people with broken minds' (26.4.94). A woman was described as 'filthy and bedraggled, with a rope tied where the belt used to be of her army surplus greatcoat, she marches up and down the pavement blowing a whistle and shouting at passengers'. Changes in health care policy, under Health Minister Virginia Bottomley, had led to closures of institutions for the mentally ill 'leaving needy patients to fend for themselves' on the streets and turning remaining inner-city mental hospitals into 'crowded, crumbling madhouses' (*The Times* 20.4.94). Care in the Community schemes merely shifted the 'problem' of the mentally ill from the health service to housing services and whilst the press was highly critical of this process it also reported cases of extreme behaviour in ways which implied that all homeless people (and all mentally ill people) were disruptive and even dangerous. These people were an army, a menace, dangerously ill, psychiatric offenders, potentially violent and 'discharged abruptly, inappropriately and without adequate support into the community' (*Evening Standard* 20.4.94)

Begging was dubbed not mad but wilfully bad. During 1994, terms last used in the press during the 'scroungerphobia' of the mid-1970s (Golding and Middleton 1982) resurfaced. Golding and Middleton quote from the *Daily Telegraph* in July 1976 '£10,000 a Year Lifestyle for Dole Fiddler', whilst in 1994 the *Daily Mail* offers 'Costa del Dole Invasion' and 'Scroungers Bring Threat to Tourism and the Good Life' (6.5.94) in a story about the large numbers of people in temporary housing accommodation in seaside resorts. These are described as young 'drug addicts, thieves and drunks' who will only work for cash in hand. Articles on beggars boasting that they make 'between £40 and £80 begging on Thursday, Friday and Saturdays' and claim '£44 per week in benefits' (*Daily Express* 9.5.94) were commonplace. Soon after the end of the Christmas charity, home-lessness and scrounging became intertwined in the press discourse, making it possible to report homelessness as 'crime news'. The streets became dangerous places full of threat. The concept of the violent society was invoked again with stories such as:

Life on a knife edge for doorway drop-outs: For the homeless on the Strand, where a policeman was stabbed on Monday, each day is tough, brutal and getting nastier ... An 18 year old of no fixed address has been charged with murder. (*The Times* 31.3.94)

The 1986 Social Security Act removed benefits from under-18-year-olds making the young homeless particularly desperate. Criminal activity, particularly prostitution and drug dealing, became sometimes the only way of getting by. The *Mirror* tells readers about Georgie aged 15 who knows 'girls who get eighty pounds a night on the game, and I have seen people go down through drugs' (5.12.94).

Squatting was a popular option for youngsters in one of the record number of empty houses – probably over a million – which litter the landscape (*Guardian* 15.4.94), yet it was also the route to a prison cell and a criminal record. The paper also quoted Home Secretary Michael Howard as saying: 'Squatting can never be justified, squatters should face tough criminal sanctions and it is quite unac-ceptable that squatters should be allowed to jump the council house waiting list.'

Beggars were related to a 'cancer eating away at our society and that is fear of crime ... our streets and cities have become nasty places ... They now represent a gauntlet of fear to be run daily' (*Independent* 22.6.94). The press found proof of the validity of these fears when in

August 1994 '[a] girl's innocent familiarity with the street vendor she passed each day led to a horrifying rape and knife attack' (*Daily Mail* 2.8.94). The headline was 'The Big Issue Rapist' (*Daily Mail* 2.8.94) and readers were told that vendors 'sign a code of conduct' but 'police records are not checked'.

These news stories about the single homeless were often extreme, out of proportion to the problem of single homelessness in relation to homelessness as a whole, concerned with a narrow definition of homelessness as rooflessness and centred on London. The contrast between the media myths and the real issues was a stark one.

Single and Homeless in Leeds

Some of the applications for help under the homelessness clause were made by single people during the period of the Leeds research. Ten cases of single homeless were randomly selected and examined.[5] Only three were eventually deemed to be in priority need of housing, allowing them to 'jump' the waiting list queue. Three had been considered homeless but not in priority need and these were sent standard Section 64 letters, describing the priority need categories and suggesting the applicant register on the council waiting list. Four others were deemed not homeless: one applicant had returned to the tenancy, one to the marital home, one had accepted a council tenancy and the fourth had not been in touch with the HAC again.

The remaining three had all been accepted as homeless and in 'priority need' due to their 'vulnerability', in one case because the client was very young, and in two cases because the clients were considered to be at risk of violence; one of these was also in poor mental health. Of the accepted cases, the two applicants fleeing violence had arrived from other local authorities. In one case a relative lived in the HAC area but in both cases it was considered unsafe for clients to return to their 'home' authorities. For example, the note 'wishes to be re-housed in H as does not believe boyfriend would trace her' was written on one file.

The terminology used within the case notes included direct reference to the Housing Act in one case, the phrase 'not in priority need'[6] was used three times, and in another case 'accepted as priority' was used three times. In two cases, there were references to intentionality as in 'homelessness direct result of his actions?' Where there was loss of contact the HAC considered that it had 'discharged its duty'. Legislation, council policy and the organisation culture of the HAC limited the scope of assistance available. Yet, there was evidence within the case-studies that officers had actively pursued their enquiries; there were several references to the difficulty of contacting agency workers who had direct knowledge of clients as 'social services involvement difficult to track', 'police officers with knowledge of incidents difficult to contact' and 'HAC made enquiries of doctor. Letter to GP returned unanswered.' HACs aimed to complete their procedures within 30 days from initial contact so these kinds of non-co-operation on the part of other agencies caused real problems for their clients. Evidence of medical conditions was given priority with this group of clients, since only 'vulnerable' single homeless can be offered permanent accommodation. Supporting evidence for vulnerability was obtained from doctors, social services, police, probation officers and any other 'professional' agency that may have come into contact with the client. Occasionally clients would take extreme measures to find a home as in 'committed crime to be housed in bail hostel for six weeks'.

Most single people approaching the HAC were going through a crisis in their lives – in most of the ten cases of single homeless applications their need was the result of the breakdown of a relationship with either a partner or parents. Yet, even when staff were faced with a client fleeing violence, they were still required to make enquiries to confirm the situation. In some cases, this duty was delegated to the Women's Refuge since anyone referred to the HAC from the refuge was considered 'proven' vulnerable.

Moral judgements about appropriate behaviour did impinge upon the action of support staff. The proprietors of the hotels and the hostel wardens preferred clients to 'fit in' with the regime and not to upset other residents. This meant that some vulnerable people did not receive as much support as they might need. The case of a young girl whose family would not house her any longer illustrated some of the difficulties. The proprietor of one hostel evicted her for allowing her friends to share her room. She then moved to a hostel where the warden became very concerned about 'getting obscene phone calls at hostel'. The HAC sent this client a standard warning letter about drug abuse, following the arrest of her young female friend for 'possession of illegal substances'. The moral assumptions about family life made by government, and disseminated through legislation and guidelines, were/are that children would be raised by two-parent families until they are of an age to earn their own living and be financially independent. There was little evidence of concession to the decreasing stability in family relationships, the increase in numbers of children who spend at least a part of their childhood in care and of those who leave home following various forms of abuse or a final rupturing of family ties that may have resulted from the problems of adolescence.

In contrast to the presentations of single homelessness preferred by the newspapers, none of these ten cases was 'roofless' since most had temporary space in 'friends or families' houses. None could be described as beggars and although only two appeared to be working, the others appeared able to survive on their benefits; there was no evidence of 'dole-cheating or crime'. This sample provided only a small amount of qualitative data. It did, however, illustrate that not all the cases presenting as homeless required a local authority solution. Four applicants solved their own problem and a further three were considered able to do so since they were 'not vulnerable'.

Single people had to prove their vulnerability to obtain housing under the legislation and were dealt with carefully but rigorously by the HAC workers. The ages of our sample ranged from 16 to 46, with four women and six men. None was technically on the streets, though the changes to the Housing Act (Consultation Document clause 28.1.v) would make it less likely that friends might offer temporary shelter if it disqualified people from being homeless. Only three were offered priority housing and none fitted the stereotypes that the government and media were presenting. These were not young able-bodied men who preferred to scrounge rather than to work or young women who became pregnant deliberately to obtain housing priority or violent criminals, but a vulnerable under-age girl, a woman fleeing domestic violence and a man with poor mental health who needed 'to be near his sister for support'.

Lone Parents in Leeds

Single parents bore a considerable burden of blame in the panic about housing (and were singled out in the consultation document to be excluded from priority consideration for housing). 'Blitz on Single Mothers' (*Daily Mirror* 19.1.94) and 'Back in the Queue: Action on single mothers reinstated' (*Daily Mail* 19.1.94) were the jubilant opinions of the conservative press when reports that the government might waver in its plans to offer only temporary accommodation to single mothers were denied by Housing Minister Sir George Young. Single parents became the signifiers of the collapse of personal morality, which had informed the Conservatives 'back to basics' campaign designed to regain the political initiative after the party conference in the autumn of 1993. The *Daily Mail* claimed in the same article that 10 per cent of the 140,000 'declared homeless' claims to councils each year were 'young mothers' or 'teenage runaways'. It neglected to do the sums and tell readers that 90 per cent were therefore families or older single people. In terms of numbers, the *Guardian* (23.11.93) noted that '750,000 families are at least two months in arrears with their mortgage and in 1991 alone 77,000 had their homes repossessed'. For them, home was no castle but a debt trap.

The media focus on single mothers' applications for council housing (usually made during the first pregnancy) created a moral myth that diverted attention not only from the issue of commodification of housing but also from the fact that many one-parent households were/are not one-parent families but abandoned, bereft or 'in flight' parents. They were usually women, usually over 30 and often working. In 1991 only 18 per cent of all households were one-parent and some 70 per cent of those were divorced, separated or widowed women (so by no means queue jumping mums) according to the National Council for One Parent Families (*New Statesman and Society* 8.10.93).

Clearly there was an ideological agenda, whether conscious or not, operating in the selections and representations of housing issues, which had more to do with reasserting traditional, familial and moral paradigms than solving the homelessness problem. Real one-parent families did not comply with the press model of 'girls being rewarded for being pregnant' (*Sun* 19.1.94). In the month before Christmas 1993, only one of the ten cases randomly extracted for examination involved a single parent with a child; the remaining nine were all ex-married (including one male). Nine of these cases were deemed homeless under Section 64 of the Act.

The one deemed not homeless was a woman of 21 with two children. The woman was first deemed homeless on the grounds of mental/physical violence but this was withdrawn after it was found the woman had accepted a tenancy in her married name. So it was deemed that no threat of homelessness applied in this case.

Of the homeless group, the only never-married, female, single parent was offered and refused two properties and was therefore moved onto the waiting list. A letter informed her that the 'council had performed its legal obligations'. The male single parent (already a council tenant) was first deemed not homeless 'as enquiries had been unable to identify any incidence of or threat of violence'. Later investigations under the Housing Act 1985 Part iii agreed he 'could no longer reasonably continue to occupy because of violence' but no house large enough was available and the client refused temporary rehousing so the HAC wrote to him stating that he 'no longer wished to be considered for rehousing'.

Each of the remaining seven cases received a Section 64 letter with priority need established due to dependent children (Section 59) and local connection (Section 61). All were women applying after relationship breakdown (Section 58–60): one left an alcoholic husband and was in a damp one-bedroomed flat with two children; three were fleeing violence and three were facing eviction – one for rent arrears in the private sector (fled a violent relationship) and two for mortgage arrears (after husbands had left for new partners/families). These last three were each sent a letter stating 'we are in receipt of a possession order and confirm homelessness through no fault of your own'.

All applicants were interviewed in the first instance and then the HAC conducted a follow-up investigation that might have included approaching family, schools, GP, police, social services, building societies, loan companies, Child Support Agency (CSA), other local authorities, battered women's hostels and the courts for relevant information. HACs also counselled applicants to consult Citizens' Advice Bureaux (CAB), the police and other organisations as appropriate.

The claim of fleeing violence appeared generally to be accepted without need for corroboration although files contained much subsidiary material that indirectly supported or cast doubt on women's claims. Such comments were often housing officer opinion rather than the result of procedural investigations as in, 'partner supposed to be nasty' and woman 'suffers flights of fancy'.

In contrast, repossession produced a vast array of detail and evidence of detailed and thorough procedures. A woman earning a 'good salary' had to provide a full monthly breakdown of expenditure – salary slips, bank statements and employer's statements – before it was accepted that she had been left with outgoings that were higher than her income. Debt had to be demonstrated, as in: 'ex-husband not contributing – left massive debts'; 'mortgage £600 pcm'; 'second loan £140'; 'serious difficulties with two loans'; 'bought a car and financed his own business, which failed, and left'; 'landlord claims debt of £7528'.

Any investigative procedures had to be completed within the time scale of the act and even the most complex of the repossession cases was resolved in twelve weeks with a property offered and accepted. The time pressure meant HACs only allowed a seven-day response time for any communication with a client. Several cases were closed by letters stating: 'you have not been in touch with this department since [date] so I must assume therefore you have resolved your housing problem', only to be reopened by a second application for advice within a short time. Loss of contact with the client was one procedural problem; difficulty in contacting other relevant agencies, whose opinion or action was often vital, was another.

Referrals were made to financial organisations, CAB, schools, police, hostels, other housing agencies and social services for this group of applicants. In some instances workers came up against confidentiality within other agencies. The CSA seemed particularly unforthcoming as in: 'have been unable to determine exact story from CSA (confidentiality barrier)'; 'CSA have not/cannot enforce at this stage – whereabouts unknown not even paying their bills'. The police and/or social services were often cited and their information included even when it seemed not strictly relevant. For example, a woman fighting a notice to quit and harassment from her landlord was described as having been knifed by her ex-husband who is now in jail for attempted murder. In this case, the 'two younger children are being assessed by social service for a supervision order'.

The male single parent's situation was first described by police as: 'no different from other families in the area – name calling, petty vandalism, no evidence of violence' and he was deemed not homeless. He appealed and the HAC went to the school to discover: 'children vulnerable – girls are nervous and scared – daughter suffering'. A client with a very long, confidential file was known to police as someone who: 'lies a lot and has made fraudulent credit agreements'. Police were quoted as being: 'increasingly sceptical, problems are of her own making'. The HAC also checked whether any social worker was involved with families. Several files contained comments that *no* evidence has been given by police, medical or social services – suggesting that such contact is normal.

There seemed to be some animosity with other housing areas. Bradford was accused of offering 'red herrings to avoid rehousing' a woman fleeing violence. Section 61 (local connection) was firmly adhered too because of a suspicion by the HAC that she was 'jumping the transfer list and trying it on with the claim of violence'.

There were both ambiguities and contradictions in the case notes, sometimes deriving from structural factors and sometimes indicative of particular readings or views of an applicant's situation. For owner-occupiers one of the major contradictions related directly to the law: in order to be rehoused clients have to be 'unintentionally homeless'. So people need to be in arrears, to be in debt and to have evidence of this and of their real hardship, for example, unemployment or abandonment, and be threatened by court procedures for repossession before they can be rehoused. It followed that willingly selling a property to avoid huge debts may prevent a family being rehoused by the councils as they would be deemed 'intentionally homeless'.

The single mother offered a house presented herself as contradictory because she claimed homelessness – 'her sister's house is for sale – she was thrown out by parents' – but rejected two properties offered. When refused further offers and placed on the waiting list, she threatened the HAC 'with exposure to the media'.

Most of the moral judgements implicit in these case reports were reserved for errant fathers (there was no such discourse in the press), to a lesser extent duplicitous mothers (particularly around money) and private landlords. The two repossessions of owner-occupied houses affected women of 30 and 40, who were working with children. Each father had abandoned his family with huge arrears on mortgages and other loans – both men had new partners and babies. One was in serious financial difficulty; the other was being pursued by the CSA and was a 'chronic alcoholic, prone to go on binges'. The HAC advised women fleeing violence to 'seek injunctions' preventing violent men access and concern was often expressed for the welfare of children in violent relationships – though not in cases of debt/repossession. Poverty was rarely seen as an issue.

Generally, there seemed to be some disapproval of those owning homes who got into debt – in spite of the commonly experienced issues of negative equity and the profound level of redundancy. There was often suspicion of home-owners who applied for advice as in: 'If we accept the couple now they could end up with two homes'; 'if homelessness is inevitable why does the CAB solicitor think he can delay the eviction. Why shouldn't we hang on for a few days?' Women owners in debt were investigated very thoroughly and comments included: 'she is earning good money';

'why is there such a long period of arrears?'; 'why is there so little information on the ex?'

The two cases involving private landlords involved strong moral judgements – in the HAC concern over 'illegal' tenancy agreements being forced on tenants was very evident. Housing officers genuinely seemed to consider the plight of children as of most importance. Real effort was made to check with schools, social workers, wardens and doctors about the impact of housing on children. There was little evidence of moralising over the collapse of relationships, only efforts to comply with regulations and not be duped.

Contrary to the media and government representations this small random sample of families presenting as homeless to a Yorkshire HAC was very diverse. Most significantly, only one case was a single mother and she was eventually not housed by her own choice. Three were owner-occupiers in difficulty and two were in sub-standard private accommodation (perhaps embarrassing for the government to publicise). One lived with family, a second in a hostel, one in a battered women's refuge and two were in council property but seeking transfers and claiming unsuitable housing.

Under the changed legislation, none of these cases would have been offered secure accommodation in the first instance. They would have been put in temporary accommodation and added to the waiting list which would be their 'sole route' to full council tenancy. Yet each was carefully investigated and considered; these were not cases of people simply being 'given' homes undeservedly. As with the single homeless cases, none of these cases was roofless, that is left living on the street. The single-parent families considered here seemed mostly to have suffered from masculine dysfunction – violence, infidelity, alcoholism, abandonment, financial recklessness or irresponsibility – or from poverty due to low wages, child-care costs or unemployment. The absent father in most of these households was also absent from the press accounts of 'single' parents.

Press Ideology

The press seemed to be dictating an agenda for concern that was quite different from the real experiences of the homeless in Housing Advice Centre cases. Their focus was London/South East centred, yet in 1992, 33,950 applications for housing were made in Yorkshire (*Shelter* 'Homeless Legislation: made hopeless' 25.1.94) and '8600 people were sleeping rough last year, including some 5000 outside London' (*Guardian* 23.11.93). The press also preferred to interpret homelessness as rooflessness, justifying their close attention to those 3,600 on London's streets, as opposed to other groups such as the 64,500 'short life housing tenants' (*Guardian* 23.11.93).

Although much media analysis (Murdock and Golding 1977; Hall *et al.* 1978; Garnham 1990) has argued that the explicit mutuality of interests between the media, the state and capital is sufficient to claim that the press actively represents the interests of oppressive power, others have claimed that our press is broadly pluralistic (Tunstall 1983) whilst the cultural populist view argues that audiences may find ways of being individual and creative regardless of the operation, or not, of powerful ideologics (Curran and Seaton 1991: 126). News about homelessness in the early 1990s was full of inaccuracies and untold stories. It seemed broadly to reproduce the interests of dominance in the stories about homelessness which were deemed newsworthy – it also reflected those interests when articles on mortgages, interest rates and house prices appeared on other sections of the paper. Whereas homelessness was 'news', housing articles were always part of the specialist journalism of finance, business and economics. This emphasised a definition of homeless as roofless but also defined home as investment, property and asset. Even though the drive to ownership during Thatcherism left many families in penury, the concept was rarely questioned in the specialist pages. Instead, there were serial debates on the battle between the banks and building societies for the home loan market – as in 'the new aggression in mortgage lending makes sense for the banks' balance sheets' (*Financial Times* 13.4.94) alongside concern with a drop in building society profits during the recession, which only 'grew by 53% in 1993 raising societies return on assets from 0.76 to 0.93 %' (*The Times* 13.4.94), and criticism that some lenders were maintaining 'miserly' higher interest rates – 'The great rate rip-off' (*ExpressMoney* 13.4.94).

This split in accounts between news/homelessness and financial pages/home-ownership is partly explained by the structural organisation of newspapers around story genre. One effect was to miss the link between the two phenomena which might have allowed a politically critical account to be told; another was a tendency towards homogeneity, with stories divided into news about the mad and bad or features on 'how to make the most of your money'. Not only did journalists adhere to the 'safe' stories that complied with the 'institutionalised force of news values' (Hartley 1982) but they organised news content to fit those values, so possibly impacting on popular/political understanding of issues and events. In order for homelessness to become newsworthy, it had to have a recognisable angle that could pitch it out of the features pages and onto the news pages. The complex, dry, legalistic and economic realities of Britain's housing problems were only foregrounded on the news pages if they could be translated to the personal, the dramatic and the negative, preferably all three – as in: 'When the beggars can be choosers ... Alan Grandison manages without qualifications to pull in an income of about £18000 per year. The trouble, alas, is that, Mr. Grandison is also a beggar' (*Daily Express* 9.5.94) and in the same paper on the same day: 'Dougy 16 will not go hungry ... we watched Dougy [readers are told he is an epileptic and a schizophrenic] make £14 in just 20 minutes.' Such stories were rarely contextualised in issues of unemployment, poverty, family collapse and the deconstruction of the welfare support system. If anything they were used to support even more stringent measures against those on the streets. *The Times* (4.1.94) reported 'scores of complaints' about 'fraudulent begging' leading to police action: 'About 40 beggars were arrested in the two month Operation Grail and future methods of coping with the problem are being considered.'

A kind of middle-classness of family life and values was evident in this reporting of the homeless and housing; a middle-classness that was commensurate with the political interest of the state and added a logic of experience and identity to the journalistic representations of home. Class ideology added to journalistic ideology directed selections and representations in the media towards the interests of those producing the news and creating the policy. This was not surprising. Tunstall described the profile of up-market and mid-market 1990s journalists as mostly men, university graduates and highly dependent on personal contacts, gossip and networking:

All of these things correlate with an elite education, followed by working and living in London. This is an extremely London oriented group, many of whom live in familiar inner-London locations from Islington to Fulham. (Tunstall 1996: 152)

He also claimed that 'from the 1979 General election onwards the national press was overwhelmingly partisan in supporting the Conservative party in general and Mrs Thatcher in particular' (Tunstall

1996: 240). As evidence, he cited Butler and Kavanagh (1992) who found a circulation split between the dailies at the 1992 election of 70 per cent Conservative and 27 per cent Labour.

Left in the shadows of that focus were the experiences of people like those whose case-histories were studied at the Yorkshire HAC: poor, regional, often unemployed or low-waged people whose relationships had collapsed – in the case of the single-parent families, mostly because of abandonment by the men involved. Yet, in all the newspaper reports on homelessness I read I found no critical reflection on such 'masculine' behaviour towards families. Rather, I found discursive accounts, which justified political interventions that supported the family, irrespective of the levels of masculine dysfunction associated with it (and protected by it). By focusing on single, young beggars and squatters or on single mothers, journalism was also, by omission, leaving intact 'normal' masculinity – mature, heterosexual and paternal. In terms of the ideologies dominating representations of homelessness the interest of patriarchy could be identified alongside those of political conservatism, journalistic professionalism and commercialism.

Paradoxically, Van Zoonen (1998) suggested that the feminisation of the news both in terms of journalism and the search for audience has led to more focus on the kind of human interest stories, emotion and sensation, within which homelessness is made newsworthy. She argued that such a shift has acknowledged space for a feminised journalism and the female audience but within the 'lower status space of market driven journalism' as opposed to the more elite tradition of objective journalistic investigation.

Homelessness news in the 1990s tended to be in the form of just such 'soft' news. In content, it barely addressed some of the most crucial questions around gender, family and housing. For Van Zoonen this would be explained as evidence of the existence of a 'general patriarchal scheme' within which 'most things women do and like are not valued very highly' (1998: 46). By way of explanation, she referred to her earlier research[7] that showed:

> Daily journalism, whether it is print or broadcasting is dominated by men; the higher up the hierarchy or the more prestigious a particular medium or section is, the less likely it is to find women ... regardless of difference in years of experience, education level and other socio-economic factors, women are paid less for their work. These inequalities were shown to stem from discriminatory

recruitment procedures and from discriminatory attitudes among decision-makers. (Van Zoonen 1998: 34)

Such a complexity of ideological orientation, political, commercial and gender, has significant implications for theorising the media. It certainly makes any model of the press as puppets of state propaganda seem woefully simplistic; they appear much more powerful than that or perhaps more diverse in their potential ideological power. This raises major issues about the nature of ideology, which also has implications for the debates on effects.

Ideologically there are three identifiable fields operating in news about homelessness: the policy initiatives around privatisation and the deconstruction of the nanny state of the governing Conservative Party seemed to be being served, as did the moral agenda round family values. The issues were being reformulated around news values in order to provide the kind 'shock-horror-probe' story linked to high cover sales and, through selections, evaluations and omissions, men's role in household collapse was not being addressed. This triad also seems to comply fairly closely with my interpretation of van Dijk's (1998) reconceptualisation of ideology as having three components: the social, the textual/discursive, and the cognitive. Journalists' cognition of their subjective identity is informed by their place within the major socio-cultural relations of class, race, gender, sexuality and age (but also within more minor and less stratified relations); cognition of their professional identity is informed by institutional practices and pressures. Of course these are not in everyday terms so neatly discreet: gender issues may be raised in the workplace and the feminist adage that the 'personal is political' is worth restating. Integrated, such knowledges inform journalists' selection, reformulation and production of news texts as discourse but also make it difficult to tease out the sources and causes of such ideologies. Moreover, the inclusion of the cognate agent in conceptualising ideology requires a model of ideology that is about probability in relation to the socio-political, subjective, experiential and discursive, none of which is necessarily static or necessarily dominant.

Such a multiplicit model of ideology also, necessarily, complicates any theory of effects in that media messages may deliver a range of ideologies, differently accessible according to differing discourse types and according to the identity of producer and consumer. Although such agents will create and read texts as individual 'minds', that individuality comprises their experience as members of particular social groups, within broader language and political communities. The shared experience of agents in discursive contexts may frame the meanings that can be generated. Conceptualising ideology in such a way recalls Hall's (1973) encoding/decoding model of media messages, which critiqued the rigidity of Marxist media theory for its inability to explain or support change, with a reformulation of producers and consumers as active constructors of meaning – though not necessarily the same one for the same text. In Hall's view most media messages would 'encode' dominant interests and values due to the mutuality of interests between journalists and other powerful social groups and institutions. However, although audiences would be able to understand such messages they need not necessarily accept them. For Hall the extent of match of experience/identity/values between producer and consumer supports different kinds of meaning creation amongst readers/viewers/listeners in terms of accepting/preferring the meaning offered, negotiating a partial fit with experience or resisting/rejecting the dominant view. So, effect may depend not just on producer and message but on interpretation – that in turn may relate to cognitive processes linked to identity, and even then interpretation does not necessarily lead to actions that may indicate 'effect'.

As work on the meaning potential of media texts has become more sophisticated, work on media effects has become less and less satisfactory – in fact, so unsatisfactory that I would advocate a shift away from effects research towards two forms of promotion: first, media education, to enable audiences to critically engage with meanings (Fairclough 1995)[8] and second, media ethics (Stevenson 1997)[9] to strive for and support quality and equality in media aesthetics and representations.

For Hall, the audiences are active interpreters/constructors of ideologies which are likely to reproduce dominant interests; van Dijk strengthens the role of 'people' even more by making cognition, 'mental representations', integral to ideology:

That is people are said to 'have' and share opinions, whether they express them in discourse or not, and both within and across specific contexts. That beliefs are socially acquired, constructed, changed and used (also) through discourse is obvious, but that does not make them discursive in the usual sense of 'being a property of discourse'. (van Dijk 1998: 31)

For van Dijk, close attention to the 'opinions' brought to news is essential to analysis. It informs his suggestion for 'how to do ideological analysis' and illuminates the process and findings of the study of representations of homelessness, albeit undertaken some four years before van Dijk's chapter was published. His suggestions were to: a) examine the context of the discourse; b) analyse the groups and power relations involved; c) seek out positive and negative judgements of Us and Them; d) spell out any presupposi-tions and implications; e) consider how form emphasises, or not, opinions (1998: 61). This neatly summarises the analysis in relation to homelessness news, which considered the political context, the identities and power relations of those involved, the denigration of the 'homeless' (and by implication the positive evaluation of the 'homed'), the identification of taken-for-granted ideas about gender relations and family, and the effect of news values in structuring opinion as 'truth'.

Yet it is Hall's much earlier model that clarifies the analysis of the case-studies in the Yorkshire HAC. The housing officers' experience of real homelessness seemed to have equipped them to negotiate the popular representations of homelessness, even resist them – cases for example of masculine dysfunction or violence were dealt with sym-pathetically and there was little evidence either in decision-making or annotations of the excesses and obfuscations of the journalistic accounts. Such findings support analysis that compares different discursive types around the same topic. The elicitation of different readings both throws light on issues of ideology and effect but also illuminates different 'real' interest and experiences out of synchrony or even in conflict. Such lack of fit or gaps make it possible to identify whose ideas are expressed where and with what potential – illuminating sites of the exercise of power and areas of resistance necessitating that exercise. Disjunctions between popularised accounts and real experience are a problem for government as they challenge the legitimacy of consensus and mark the limits of dominant hegemony, and the potential beginnings of dissent (Hall's resistance). When experience denies the information offered repeatedly and popularly, even members of dominant groups may be discomforted by perceived injustices and take sides with the oppressed – forcing the use of real power (state violence) to restore control or forcing the state to 'reform' sufficiently to reduce tension.

In the housing crisis of the 1990s the risk of dissent to legislative changes was too slight to prevent the consultation paper of 1994 eventually becoming law, curtailing the choices of even the most empathetic housing officer. The ideologies 'realised' through news about homelessness confirmed the legitimacy of the divide between Them and Us (even though, or perhaps because, many of Us were in 'negative equity') in terms not only of housing but implicitly of family norms and gender relations.

Comment

From 1994, Shelter maintained a running battle with the Conservative government over proposed changes in legislation affecting housing and homelessness. In September 1995 the charity organised 'barnstorming' campaigns to combat the plans laid out in the 1994 consultancy document,[10] which re-emerged in June 1995 as a white paper entitled 'Our Future Homes'. The campaign was featured by the *Guardian* in the Society section on Wednesday 13 September 1995 titled 'Gimme Shelter Again'. The photograph above appeared to be of a 1960s anti-homelessness march and was subtitled: 'Another peace and love style due for revival'. The campaign was unable to prevent the new housing laws being passed in July 1996. 'By April 1997, they were all in force, and although a new government was elected in May 1997 the laws have not been amended or repealed, although some new regulations have been issued' (Lukes 1999).

For the first time, the Housing Act was directed specifically at immigrants, as it requires applicants for homes to pass a 'habitual residency test'. The residency rules are now much more complex, making it difficult for local housing departments to be clear about the status of homeless clients. The definition of homelessness was brought much closer to rooflessness because in the act a person 'is defined as homeless if s/he has nowhere in the world where s/he has any right to live with the people who would normally form part of his/her household' (Lukes 1999). This provision particularly affected young people already penalised by exclusion from benefits until the age of 18 and yet increasing in numbers on the streets (Grant in the *Guardian* 15.2.97). Grant's piece is a strong critique of the 'glamorisation' of degradation – evident in films like *Trainspotting*, in the use of skeletal, dark-eyed models for 'heroin-chic' fashion shots and in a contemporary exhibition of photographs of young homeless removed from the street and 'posed against a white backdrop where, to some eyes, they became indistinguishable from a *Face* fashion shoot'. In the same article Chris Holmes, Director of Shelter, offers 'growing public awareness of the growth of sexual abuse' as an explanation for this rise of young homeless: 'Until the past ten years, people suffered in silence. Or, if they did say something no one believed them, so they stayed in intolerably oppressive and abusive home environments. Now they escape from it.' Housing legislation now seems to be designed to reinforce traditional family organisation – not just in terms of definitions of homeless, which forced young people back into difficult family circumstances, but also in relation to the redefined criterion of vulnerability.

Assessing an application as 'in priority need' requires a local authority to offer temporary accommodation; it also requires a check on eligibility that focuses on risk. Pregnancy, dependants, sexual abuse, racial harassment, violence, health and disaster may render applicants vulnerable, but definitions are contentious and councils are not obliged to accept them. Part of Shelter's campaign against these clauses in the new act included a focus on the implications for victims of domestic violence. Prior to the act local authorities had a duty to rehouse any women supplying evidence of fleeing violence, even if they were staying temporarily with friends or relatives. Since 1996 that duty has been only to provide temporary shelter to the actually roofless. The government's efforts at reducing the pressure on housing had the effect of reconstructing families in line with their broader 'back to basics' ideologies but at the price of forcing women to stay in abusive relationships or live on the streets with their children. Once the final two clauses of the changed act were applied to such women their position became even more impossible, as they could be deemed intentionally homeless or they might be forced to stay close to abusive partners under the requirement for a local connection, unless they could prove their claim of violence.

The relationship between such legislative changes and media accounts of homelessness, whether due to conspiracy, dumb compliance or the daily commercial and industrial constraints on journalism, was nonetheless convenient for the Conservatives. Portrayals of the homeless as outsiders/deviants and criminals inhibited public and political pressure to resolve the real issue of the lack of affordable housing. It also maintained as 'right' the Conservative-promoted norm of home-ownership as a valuable investment for family well-being, wealth and social status. This, despite the fact that overvaluation by building societies, huge mortgage loans, rising interest rates and rising unemployment were making a 'home of one's own' more a liability than an asset.

Promoting home-ownership usefully justified the gradual decimation of public housing, commensurate with the wholesale deconstruction of welfarism and the promotion of individual responsibility, both of which were central to the Thatcherite project. At the same time more implicit ideologies in news about homelessness supported another set of conservative values, explicit in the 'back to basics' campaign. By criminalising and/or labelling the homeless as morally deviant and/or mad they were set apart from the 'normal' as undeserving victims of their own personal failings. A further consequence of that was the concurrent, implicit legitimation and reproduction of traditional models of social organisation as desirable and correct. Homelessness in the press was often featured in relation to non-conforming femininity and family collapse – so promoting conformist femininity and the shoring up of the family. Men as abandoners, abusers, alcoholics and adulterers barely feature as relevant to homelessness.

Also largely missing was 'news' about the 'scandal' of empty housing, or the 'sensational' waste of tax-payers' money involved in housing the homeless in 'bed and breakfast' because much council housing had been sold.

6
Journalism, Justice, Gender and Violence

Sex and violence saturate contemporary popular culture in Britain. During the late 1980s and early 1990s stories linking sexual relations with extreme violence proliferated in the media. Popular films about serial killers and mad, bad women showed to packed houses whilst television soap operas thrived on domestic violence. Concurrently, the factual news repeatedly featured aggressive masculinity in reports of dangerous strangers alongside accounts of crimes involving women killing lovers or rivals. Popular films were often preoccupied with extreme interpersonal violence. Frequently, such violence was depicted as female, heterosexual and commonly directed against male suitors, lovers or spouses, as in the films *Fatal Attraction*, *Body of Evidence*, *Dirty Weekend* and *Black Widow*. In reality, women were (and are) most often at risk, at home, from men they know. And in 'real' life, women are rarely violent.

That apparent media emphasis on violent sexual relations occurred during a period of considerable tension over gender issues and concurred with a 'backlash' against feminism in favour of traditional models of gender organisation. Faludi (1992) described the language of the contemporary media as a culture machine working to 'try to push women back into their "acceptable" roles whether as Daddy's girl or fluttery romantic, active nester or passive love object' (1992: 16). In our culture, the traditional model of 'good' women infuses images and texts (Berger 1973; Heidensohn 1986; Young 1990). By convention, 'good' women should be pure, passive, caring, maternal, monogamous, house-proud, dependent, fragile and fair. Such are the qualities contemporary culture associates with ideal womanhood: qualities relating closely to the socio-economic needs of Victorian capital and patriarchy (Weeks 1981; Collier 1994). Women who do not conform to that model attract labels outside of the range available for 'good' women and are thereby defined as deviant, often mad or bad. In fact, Heidensohn argued that 'although men provide more menace to the basis of society, it is women who are instructed in how to behave' (1986: 106) throughout our culture. In such gendered discourses, femininity is tightly constrained whilst masculinity is hardly addressed.

The press is a significant contributor to such discourses. Violence has a particular salience for the press, and the press a particular salience for media analysts. Other common topics in the press discourse of violence, during the Thatcher government – such as the racial uprisings and strikes discussed in earlier chapters – occurred in public, between groups.[1] This chapter looks at the private, inter-personal and gendered crime reported as sex'n'violence in the British newspapers during the government of the UK's only woman Prime Minister.

Handbagged

By 1990, second-wave feminism had worked for over 20 years to empower women to resist subordination in social relations and organisation. Yet, such attempts were slow to achieve change. Women remained significantly disadvantaged in many areas, even after considerable legislation. For example, 'research evidence shows that despite the existence of sex discrimination law, in most professions women are still discriminated against at the point of recruitment, and in terms of career development' (Chapman 1991: 157). The 1960s and 1970s resistance to traditional models of sexual behaviour and gender relations appeared in the later 1980s and early 1990s as riddled with contradiction. Faludi described that contra-diction as grounded in two assertions, the second based on the false premise of the first:

> At last women have received their full citizenship papers. And yet ... [b]ehind this celebration of women's victory, behind the news, cheerfully and endlessly repeated, that the struggle for women's rights is won, another message flashes. You may be free and equal now it says to women but you have never been more miserable. (1992: 1)

Conservative socio-political history appears to have included a backlash in gender relations which Faludi argued was not a response to any genuine realisation of women's equality but a 'pre-emptive strike that stops women long before they reach the finishing line' (1992: 14). For Faludi the backlash was not a political conspiracy by men to keep women in their place but evidence of a cultural struggle for the re-evaluation of the meaning of gender in the interests of the still most powerful group, men. She identified the process in the discourses of politics, family, work, reproduction, film, fashion, masculinity and sexual relations and accused the media of being a 'backlash collaborator', supporting 'pro-family diatribes' and ignoring the facts of women's continued oppression. Institution-alised, mythologised and politicised patriarchal rhetoric was so powerful that it affected a woman's consciousness until she began 'to enforce the backlash too – on herself' (1992: 16). Faludi identified, on both sides of the Atlantic, the extent not only of represented dis-empowerment of women but realised disempowerment through violence, such that in the USA 'in the 1980s, almost half of all homeless women (the fastest growing segment of the homeless) were refugees of domestic violence' (1992: 8).[2]

For Faludi, such actual, threatened or symbolised violence towards women was indicative of tension and struggle in relations between the sexes. Male power was being actively challenged, and was responding on all levels. At the beginning of the last decade of the millennium, the normal legitimate, covert and subversive exercise of dominant power to win consensus to traditional gender norms and roles arguably shifted closer to the use of force to restore order. As with earlier struggles for racial and class authority, violence gained an 'extraordinarily salient position' (Chibnall 1977: 141) in influential, institutional gender discourses, such as the law and media.

For feminists, the slowness and paucity of change toward gender equality, despite new legislation, suggested that change was/is inhibited by cultural practices. Although feminist work continued on 'real' gender inequality and on 'real' sexual violence, particularly on women as victims of domestic violence (Dobash and Dobash 1992) or rape (Lees 1993, 1995), evidence of inhibitions to change drew feminists towards the cultural sphere and especially towards the media and language in the search for the means by which patriarchy was managing to absorb resistance in a consistent re-winning of power. Feminist criminologists, concerned both with apparent injustices to women criminals and the high incidences of violence against women, routinely commented that representations of women in the media were somehow contributory (Heidensohn 1986; Allen 1987; Carlen 1988; Young 1988; Smart 1989).

At the end of the millennium, any feminist project has to confront the fact that feminism has become an increasingly difficult term to use, to define or to adhere to. This too is arguably a legacy of media representations of women. However, for me 'feminism remains a pretty simple concept, despite repeated – and enormously effective – efforts to dress it up in greasepaint and turn its proponents into gargoyles' (Faludi 1992: 18). The media has contributed to such dressing up by constructing a complex threat from a relatively simple concept. For most feminists Mary Wollstonecraft's statement that she did not wish women to have power over men but over themselves would still be formative (see *A Vindication of the Rights of Women*, 1792). Yet, power, arguably grounded in symbolic, potential or actual violence, remains firmly associated with the male, in reality in our social world and in representations throughout our culture.

The Power to Represent

Violence, of all kinds, fits with news values. It also offers a good story – struggle, drama, problem, danger, heroes, villains, good, evil and resolution (Propp 1968) – with many of the requisites for fables and folk-tales. News values though are 'professional imperatives which act as implicit guides to the construction of news stories' (Chibnall 1977: 23) in the British press rather than the motifs of effective fiction. They relate closely to the fact that our contemporary newspapers are deeply and increasingly embedded in large capitalist organisations and arguably governed by the dominating ideological perspective and oriented within its hegemony (Hall 1972). Twenty years after Hall's article, media analysts continued to argue that the values of the press in Britain were likely to be commensurate with the interests of contemporary capitalism (Garnham 1990; McGuigan 1992). But interest was also growing, inspired by feminist media criticism, in the fact that the journalists who wrote and edited the news and often owned and/or controlled newspapers, remained, despite Equal Opportunities and Sex Discrimination laws, over-whelmingly male (Christmas 1997).

The high profile given to gendered violence by feminist pressures presented such a press with a potential dilemma. Journalists were and are drawn to reporting such crimes (sex and violence satisfy news value criteria, attract large audiences and boost sales) yet such reports inevitably give wide publicity to the violent collapse of and abuse within normal heterosexual relations. Violence between men and women can be construed as not only breaking the law but also the sanctity of heterosexual relations, which are central to patriarchal power (Foucault 1979; Collier 1994). Publicity linking heterosexual relations to the most extreme form of law-breaking presents a contradiction of interests for our press because whilst capitalist news values insist such crime makes good copy, patriarchal sexual values that 'normalise' stable, traditional, heterosexual relations are undermined by the existence of and representation of 'intimate killing'.

The means by which press accounts negotiated that 'conflict' illuminate the various shifts, collapses and reconstructions evident in real gender relations during the Conservative years, because although cultural forms are 'articulated through a very complex set of mediations to power' (McGuigan 1992: 178) there is ample empirical evidence in studies of the British media and social history to support:

> An assumption that a notion of ideological dominance in some form, however qualified by recognition of audience activity and popular pleasure, remains indispensable, and at least at the textual level, discernible. (McGuigan 1992: 178)

McGuigan defined ideology as referring 'to systematically distorted ideas motivated by oppressive power' and justified its use in media analysis on the grounds that 'if we cannot say that the *Sun* has told lies on behalf of oppressive power then we are in trouble' (1991: 180). I have tried to interrogate the media with sensitivity to that possibility but also to cultural populist arguments that in the consumption of cultural forms social subjects may find ways of 'expressing individuality and of participating in a "real world" that transcends hierarchies of power' (Curran and Seaton 1991: 126) evident in their production;[3] and to the liberal view that the variety of our newspapers (left-wing, right-wing, popular and quality) ensures a plurality of representations (Tunstall 1983). None of these positions is necessarily mutually exclusive.

Any concern with relations between representation and reality necessitates some close attention to issues of power, ideology and knowledge about the world. Harvey argued that 'the production and reproduction of power relations is central to the operations of any capitalist economy' (Harvey 1993: 21) and that differences such as those of gender and race which preceded capitalism have been, and continue to be, transformed according to the dynamics of capitalism.

Young recognised in the press discourse a tendency to 'closure in place of openness, unity in place of plurality' (1990: 106) as real events are transformed through journalistic practices and organisational imperatives into unambiguous and meaningful accounts for dissemination. Further, the 'potential power of the media to define reality makes it extremely important that we subject media representations to close, systematic and critical analysis' (Chibnall 1977: 22). So certainly any feminist commitment to challenging and seeking to change real inequality and injustice should be concerned with representations of women. Similarly, any challenge to the powerful (men) must also be aware of how they are represented as that relates to how they are treated in life and how *ipso facto* their power is articulated (Dyer 1993).

In general, in gender relations power is associated firmly with the male and masculinity (Hartsock 1987) and the most powerful male group usually is white, middle-class and heterosexual. Unless feminist work examines the representations of the powerful (men) they remain unaddressed, undescribed and so unchallengeable. Failing to address masculinity can consolidate power as essentially male and frustrate (with biology) political effort toward sexual equality. So although the goal of this chapter is primarily feminist and concerned with the socio-cultural position of women, the case-study I offer analyses representations of both men and women. The chapter discusses press coverage of conflict in relation to why gendered violence, and especially women who killed, were so redolent with news value for the British press in the early 1990s. Retrospectively it seems bizarre that feminist pressure had forced the recognition of widespread wife battering whilst concurrently Thatcherite ideology was reifying the family unit. The co-existence of such conflicting views of 'marriage' suggested a collapse of consensus and signified something of a crisis for hegemony. The nature of the reportage of gendered violence indicated ideological allegiances between the British press and conservatism, around patriarchal interests.

Sex'n'Violence in the News

Conflict metaphors underpin many everyday discourses, particularly sport, sexuality and politics[4] in British culture. Conflict delivers many of the components that constitute news values. It also satisfies narrative demands for villains and heroes, lost and found, good and evil. Sexuality adds frisson to conflict stories because we all know about it; it is the discourse which probably more than any other underwrites our identity but it is also the site of taboo, danger and moral dilemma (i.e. conflict).

During the Victorian period sex was reconstructed, discursively and legally, as legitimate only in the home, between husband and wife and for the purposes of reproduction. Foucault (1979) argued this 'repression' actually nurtured fascination with forbidden and risky sexualities. Sex became private and secret, which also made it a site of prurient curiosity that was served (though for men only) by an underground trade in pornography and prostitution. Concurrently, the Victorian press began to develop a 'softer more ticklish type of news' (Holland 1998: 18) that included features on the family, romance and domesticity. Softer news was more human, more personal, full of gossip and scandal and bordering on the titillating and entertaining rather than the 'hard facts'. Softer news was the stuff of the 'popular' press, now dependent on larger audiences, including women and the working classes, for advertising sales. Holland argued that it became 'sexualised' soft news during the 1970s when sex 'invaded the news columns and dominated the entertainment pages' (1998: 18) largely because women's feminist challenges to the male world had eroded the protective patronage that kept sex hidden and also because selling sex (licit or illicit) was/is always profitable. However, 'it was clear that the movement from feminisation to sexualisation in the pages of the downmarket tabloids had a political dimension' (Holland 1998: 19) because much of the depiction of sexuality was actually the depiction of provocatively posed women's bodies. Page three's naked pin-up in the *Sun* was seen by many, including MP Clare Short, as degrading and indicative not of women's greater freedom in the public sphere, but of misogyny and the 'backlash' against feminism. Sex sells papers by selling women.

Sex like crime satisfies news values so it is integral to the journalistic agenda. It is certainly meaningful, sustainable and consonant with audience experience. It fits within a long and broad set of cultural discourses from the pulpit to the playground, from purity to promiscuity and from peep-shows to *Playboy*. It has great importance for most people, in one way or another, and offers audiences cheap and legitimate access to representations of a hugely constitutive part of themselves. Sex news teases and titillates with stories of the rich, famous, deviant and dangerous but ultimately promotes both a conventional moral code and the law. We are reassured that we are normal and that to be 'abnormal' is risky – you risk denigration, danger, despair, prison and even death. Moreover, the media also sells us 'normal' 'good' sex usually by association with some product to buy that will make us more attractive: diets, fashion, cosmetics, exercise and even cosmetic surgery. Sex is very potent for the media because it sells twice: first the media text and second the products that it advertises. Add violence to sex and you have the journalists' newsworthy dream, intensifying the 'danger' of sex that in turn normalises and promotes 'normal' sex. So rape, assault and murder, most commonly by men of women, is reported in dramatic and titillating ways.

Benedict saw the sexualisation of the news as ending any genuine concern in the media with rape as a social problem. Instead there was a shift to reporting sex crime not as relating to broader gender norms and values (that is as a feminist issue) but as 'individual, bizarre or sensational case-histories' (Benedict 1992: 251), the norm prior to feminist interventions in sexuality. Incredulity characterised accounts of the crime of rape before second-wave feminists addressed it as a serious and gendered violent crime. Brownmiller published *Against Our Will* having changed her mind about rape during feminist discussions with friends in 1970. From writing about rape as a 'sex crime. The product of a diseased mind' (1975: 8) she came to apply a feminist critique to rape in order to look at 'male–female relations, at sex, at strength and at power' (1975: 9). Feminist concern with rape brought it out of the private and into the public violent/sex discourse. There are now rape crisis centres in most major cities (although many are currently threatened by the withdrawal of funding) and special police units to interview and advise rape victims. In theory, the campaigns of various feminist groups such as WAVAW (Women Against Violence Against Women) ensured that rape victims could not only resort to law but also expect sympathetic support.

In practice, the meanings attached to rape changed so little that in 1989 Sue Lees wrote: 'Rape trials are so biased towards the man that he will usually be acquitted. They are so cruel and humiliating for the woman that they amount to a second rape' (*New Statesman and Society* December 1989). Given such court procedures it is not surprising that although a 1982 WAR (Women Against Rape) survey indicated that one in six women reported having been raped and two thirds of rapes were committed by people known to the victim, 'only 8% of raped women, however had reported the assault to the police' (Segal 1990: 242). A popular women's magazine article on marital rape (*Bella* 2.6.90) suggested a further cultural constraint on women going to law; a woman 'forced to have sex by her husband faces a stark choice: breaking up the family or accepting violation as part of everyday life'. Perhaps worse, even where prosecutions for rape were brought, as few as 23 per cent led to conviction (Lees *New Statesman and Society* December 1989).

During a trial a rape victim had/has to 're-live the whole life threatening experience face to face with the man' (*New Statesman and Society*); have intimate details of her body and sexual history made public; and be publicly disbelieved in a way unheard of in a trial for burglary or non-sexual assault. The barrister, Helena Kennedy, suggested that failure both to bring to court, and to convict, has much to do with the white, male, middle-class profile of the courtroom whose values identify strongly with those of the men in the dock. Judicial comments in rape trials, such as these (quoted in a range of newspapers at the time), accompanied acquittals and suspended sentences:

- Women do not always mean no when they say no (Judge Wild 1982).
- It is the height of imprudence for any girl to hitchhike at night. She was, in the true sense, asking for it (Sir Melford Stevenson 1982).
- This is within the family and does not impinge on the public (Mr Justice Jupp 1987).

The news media in faithfully reporting the courtroom proceedings often actively reproduced the myth that 'women ask for it'. In the United States, there were several high-profile rape cases in the news in the early 1990s. They included the group sodomy of an undergraduate whom the newspapers reported as 'speaking flirtatiously ... engaging in sexual banter and using intimate body language' (Naomi Wolf, *Guardian* 7.8.91) with the accused. There was also the trial of William Kennedy Smith for rape, where, when four other women said that 'he raped them or tried to rape them', the press were 'suddenly on the alert about whether Smith would get a fair trial' (Naomi Wolf, *Guardian* 7.8.91).

As with cases of child abuse[5] the public discourse on rape was not a medium within which a critique of male sexuality was undertaken. It was no longer denied in the early 1990s but was explained as either criminal, the woman's fault or, as one judge said of a builder who raped a seven-year-old girl, 'one of the kinds of accidents which could happen to almost anyone'.

Sex and Violence and Feminism

Work on 'domestic' violence faced the same kind of resistance that was commonplace towards data about the frequency of rape. Yet surveys indicated that, 'of married women 28% had been hit by their husbands and 33% hit or threatened with physical violence. The proportion rises to 63% among women who are separated or divorced' (*Guardian* 25.2.90). Because many women did not leave violent men this was sometimes interpreted as collusion or masochism. But sometimes they could not leave. As in the case of rape centres, women's refuges were severely hit by funding cut-backs linked to the roll-back of welfarism. Also, the government was 'exerting a constant moral pressure on everyone at all costs to keep the family together' (*Guardian* 7.8.90) making it both actually and ideologically difficult for women to leave violent partners.

Although there was some recognition of the need to study masculinity and violence (Achilles Heel collective; Bradford University domestic violence project – 1990) efforts were embryonic and involved 'working at the cutting edge of men's sexism, misogyny and sadism to women. It is coalface dark with ignorance and social taboo, and no one is rushing to join them there' (Adam Jukes, Camden Men's Centre, *Guardian* 7.8.90). Least evident of all was any apparent recognition of wife-battering as a male problem by the law-courts. Sue Lees (1989) analysed press reports and process recordings of trials of domestic murder and found that men who killed their wives were consistently represented as having suffered severe provocation.

When women killed, even after suffering years of violence from sexual partners, the provocation plea was rarely possible because women, physically weaker, often premeditated the act in some way. The alternatives were trial for murder as in the cases of Thornton (1991) and Aluwahlia (1989), or manslaughter on the grounds of diminished responsibility as in Sainsbury (1991) and Aluwahlia on appeal (1993). Ann Jones pointed out that 'from one historical epoch to the next, the percentage of homicides caused by women remained the same' (1991: xv), at about 15 per cent in the United States. In 1989, in Britain, only 10 per cent (39 in number) of male homicide victims were killed by wives or lovers compared to 48 per cent (112 in number) (*Observer Magazine* 17.2.91) of women victims killed by male sexual partners. Women are rarely violent at all, yet those rare few who killed male partners in the early 1990s were the subject of considerable interest in the law and the media. It may be that such an agenda related to feminist pressure on the law and the media to recognise abusive male power.

Institutional discourses can be understood as playing a vital part in covert reproductions of power relations constituting and recon-stituting historically based power relations according to contemporary conditions (Lukes 1986; Fairclough 1989; Harvey 1989, 1993). Power relations between men and women are regularly symbolised in the public domain of the media. In the 1990s, sex and violence news often focused on the most extreme exercise of power, the ability to take life. Britain was at the apex of high Thatcherism and feminism was arguably the final frontier (after the containment of race and class resistances) in the campaign for a new consensus around conservatism. Exploring press accounts of men and women who killed spouses or lovers during the early 1990s was part of a project designed to investigate violence as a discourse of sexually appropriate behaviour, the part played in that by the British press and the relation of both to broader socio-political discourses.

News about Intimate Killing: Ideology About Gender

During this period the news media featured several high-profile cases of women who had killed husbands or lovers, while a campaign on behalf of battered women who kill posed many questions about the relationship between the representation of gender in the media, sexual violence and criminal justice. Some women, like Marion Kennedy, were brutally killed by husbands who found them not good enough women. Others, who tried to end unhappy relation-ships, like Arminda Perry or Rachel Maclean, were murdered to save alimony or mere pride. Several, such as Pam Sainsbury and Sara Thornton, refused to conform to their partners demands of them and, finally, refused to be beaten any longer, fought back and killed their abusers. One or two women, like Linda Calvey, transgressed gender boundaries to plan and carry out the murder of their male partner. Such sex'n'violence contained many of the requisite ingredients for the news. 'Crime is news because its treatment evokes threats to but also reaffirms the consensual morality of the society' (Hall *et al.* 1978: 66). Not only are intimate murders violent and deviant but they also allow journalists to generate the sexual innuendo and romantic drama for audiences with which they can 'tickle the public'. I analysed newspaper coverage of six cases of intimate killing: the perpetrators were Sara Thornton, Joseph McGrail, John Tanner, John Perry, Linda Calvey and Pam Sainsbury. The aim was to investigate whether the press was acting ideologically in reproducing traditional gender power relations in accounts of intimate killing and to assess the implications of any such process.

Sara Thornton (who served a life sentence for killing her brutal husband until a successful second appeal on the grounds of diminished responsibility in 1997) explained, 'I've finally decided I won't be bullied any more' (*Independent* 23.8.91). However, the newspaper reports referred to Sara's abortions, use of marijuana and dislike of underwear. Sara Thornton was, herself, acutely aware of being tried not only as a criminal but as a woman who was too liberal, too independent, too feminist.

The press accounts that I collected appeared not only to report cases of violent men and women differently but also indicated that the law seemed to work differently on behalf of men and women. Joseph McGrail 'killed the bullying, alcoholic woman he was living with [and] was given a two year suspended jail sentence'. McGrail 'finally cracked on Feb. 27 when he came home from work to find her drunk and demanding yet more drink' (*Daily Telegraph* 1.8.91). McGrail's reaction was described by prosecuting counsel as a 'sudden, temporary loss of control caused by provocation' (*Daily Telegraph* 1.8.91). He was offered twelve months' psychiatric supervision to help him 'overcome his feelings of remorse'. McGrail's common-law wife, Marion Kennedy, was not violent, only verbally abusive. The press barely covered the case at all but the accounts I read were uniformly uncritical of his action, and none mentioned his sex life or underwear.

The press reports of Rachel Maclean's murder in April 1991 immediately assumed the killer was a dangerous stranger. After her disappearance at the start of the Oxford summer term the *Sunday Telegraph* highlighted '[t]he danger beneath the dreaming spires' and described an Oxford where 'women undergraduates are nowadays loathe to walk alone at night across sinister Magdalen bridge' (28.4.91). All the assumptions were that Rachel had been the victim of a sinister stranger in a dangerous city, that a woman should not go out on her own. The police also succumbed to this theory because it took them over a week to find Rachel's body beneath the floor of her own bedroom. In December 1991, her boyfriend, John Tanner, was sentenced to life for murdering her. The press made much of Tanner and Maclean's passionate love affair with headlines such as 'Fatal Obsession' and persistent references to *crime passionnel* and Rachel's infidelity (entirely a lie to support Tanner's plea of provocation). Rachel was depicted as glamorous, worldly, secretive and dark. Less was written on Tanner's ability to sleep next to her body, write to the woman he had killed and take part in a reconstruction of the crime to try and cover his tracks. In general, even when men were the killers, journalists seemed to prefer to write about the role of women in intimate violence.

Another mode of explanation was to draw on fiction. Linda Calvey was presented as a fantasy femme fatale figure. Her nickname 'Black Widow' appeared regularly as a headline and she was described as a 'platinum blonde East-ender', who was passionate, cold-blooded and ruthless. In the *Daily Mirror* (13.11.91) she was a 'gangster's moll'. Such constructions moved the site of intimate killing into a scenario that offered explanations, through familiar myths, film noir and other fatal 'blonde' women such as Ruth Ellis and Myra Hindley.

In the Perry case, the press informed readers that the victim, Arminda, was promiscuous and had worked as a prostitute in the Philippines before the marriage. Perry blamed his act on the discovery of his wife's affair with a neighbour and told the court 'she was slashing at me with a knife and I hit her somewhere on the face with my fist. Then it all went rather blank' (*Daily Telegraph* 23.11.91). Yet his composure returned sufficiently for him to dismember her in 'an extremely orderly way' (*Independent* 21.11.91). John Perry had in fact decided to save the cost of alimony, £72.67 per week, which he would be liable for after the divorce she sought, by killing his wife. Two jurors were prepared to accept the plea of provocation on the grounds of her promiscuity, and the press focused on her foreignness and sexuality as if they were symptoms of her eventual murder.

When Pamela Sainsbury was in court for killing her husband, again it was the woman who received the full attention of the press.

The *Mirror* headlines referred to Sainsbury as if she was a dog. The text offered the headlines: 'MERCY FOR THE KILLER WHO BIT BACK' and 'WHIPPED AND FORCED TO EAT OUT OF A BOWL ON THE FLOOR'. Sainsbury was so disturbed by her husband's violence that after killing him she kept his head 'to reassure herself he was not suddenly going to come through the door' (*Daily Mirror* 4.12.91). Little information was presented about the history of such fear.

Such press accounts of intimate killing appeared to support the unease of feminist criminologists about gender representation in accounts of crime in the media. But I wanted to find a way of showing that news is not merely subjectively/intuitively prejudicial against women in reports of sex'n'violence,[6] but that it is systematically prejudicial, in ways which may impact not only on justice for women but on their everyday lives and sense of self.

All the news reports analysed here were published between April 1991 and December 1991. This made the socio-historical context of the cases consistent and the variables of my cases were as far as possible controlled with the exception of the gender of the participants: my perpetrators were all white, heterosexual, working and mature. Mindful of Trew's (1979) interest in the effect of press political ideology on meaning, I took an article on each case from the *Guardian* or *Independent*, the *Daily Telegraph* or *The Times*, the *Mirror* and the *Sun* or *Today*. This should have produced 24 articles in total from four differing daily press sources, i.e. left-wing quality, right-wing quality, left-wing popular and right-wing popular. The titles and sources for the articles selected/found are as listed in Appendix Table 1.[7]

The kind of content I analysed is illustrated by this sample transcript from the *Daily Mirror* coverage of the Pamela Sainsbury case.

Mercy for the Killer who Bit Back

Cruel husband treated her just like a dog. Battered wife Pamela Sainsbury walked free from court yesterday after a judge heard how she strangled and butchered the madman who treated her like a dog. Blonde Pam sawed up the body of her sadistic common-law husband and dumped it in a hedge near her home. She kept the severed head in a garden shed not as a grisly trophy but for reassurance that he was dead. She was let off with two years probation after admitting manslaughter on the grounds of diminished responsibility. Mr Justice Auld heard how the gentle and intelligent wife suffered years of violence at the hands of the burly strongman Sainsbury. (*Daily Mirror* 4.12.91)

The press production context provides such material daily, at low cost by lay (i.e. not criminological) writers for lay (i.e. the general public) readers from many different backgrounds to be read once only amongst articles of many different kinds; volume, pervasion, repetition and comprehensibility are reasons enough for analysts to pay attention to the press. But what I wanted to investigate was whether or not the press was acting ideologically in a systematic way to the disadvantage of women, within criminal justice but also more broadly.

Men and women who kill lovers or spouses are taking part in the most extreme form of gender conflict. Conflict is newsworthy but threatening. In the earlier chapter on racial conflict I used Trew's (1979) methodological focus on transactive syntax to analyse news articles about race. This approach focused on syntactic constructs that frame meanings towards interpretation of causality, which allows for the resolution of the problem through dealing, symbolically, with the cause. Transactive clauses include an agent, process and patient, so providing a structural form which predisposes attribution of responsibility or blame. Simply, such clauses construct someone or something acting on someone or something. I was wary of the problem of focusing on structure at the expense of content (Pateman 1984) but I was concerned also that much commentary on gender representation had been largely unsupported by systematic work, making it intuitive, subjective and difficult to apply generally or reliably. Therefore I decided to analyse news about intimate killing by looking systematically at the representation of blame, which I isolated from the text by identifying agency and action as evidenced by transactive clauses.

The sample articles contained high proportions of attributive/ transactive clauses. In accounts of men who killed it was 57.8 per cent of all verb clauses, almost identical to the overall rate of the incidence of transaction in the quality press samples. In accounts of women who killed it was 63.4 per cent, matching the overall rate for transaction in the popular press. The higher incidence of transaction for female cases and popular articles might indicate greater tendencies to seek causes in accounts of women's violence than in accounts of men's, and a greater tendency to resolve conflict in the popular papers. Certainly the British press in the early 1990s was engaged in an exercise of syntactic attribution, which was likely to cognitively predispose readers to seek out an agent of blame in accounts of intimate killing (Tajfel and Fraser 1978). Next I examined the terms that occupied the agent position and the nature of the action ascribed to that agent.

In news about intimate killing, causal agents could be identified fairly easily as lexical forms, for example 'blonde Pam', but it was impossible to assign that phrase even to the group female without the cultural knowledge that 'Pam' is a female name. If the causal agent were 'blonde Sam' even that assignment would be impossible without taking account of the modifier 'blonde', an adjective rarely used to describe grown men (although it may be used correctly to describe the hair colour of a grown man) but commonly used as a direct label for a woman, and sometimes nominalised to be used alone. No one in Western culture would, for example, assume the clause 'blonde killed lover' referred to a male murderer of a female victim. Yet, without a mapping of the incidence of such structures, arguments that the press is actively engaged in ideological repro-duction are necessarily reduced in authority. It may be limited in potential, but structural analysis as part of discourse analysis nonetheless places interpretation specifically. It makes more legitimate generic claims for the existence of ideology by grounding assertions in recognisable forms both intratextually and intertextu-ally. Grounding such an integration in a systematic account of text makes it possible to address criticisms made of other discourse work for its 'failure to specify detailed mechanisms of change' (Fairclough on Foucault 1992: 212).

Evaluating Blame

Retaining a structural model in order to locate and circumscribe more qualitative work, I developed a means of evaluating the selections of words for the causal agent in transactive clauses which related to componential analysis.[8] In explanations for intimate killing, the terms for those deemed responsible, according to the syntactic structures, could be assessed in relation to the qualities which legitimate and reproduce British society (Chibnall 1977). I used Chibnall's grid (detailed in Chapter 1) to assign legitimate/positive or illegitimate/negative values to the lexical selections for agent-process-patient. Ideally, for the purposes of researching ideology, the grid provided criteria for evaluating existing and emergent forms of behaviour in relation to the concepts and values which form the stock of common-sense knowledge about the British way of life (Chibnall 1977). Using the grid added rigour to meaning identification by matching interpretative common-sense understanding to a value scale.

I produced a list of the incidence of agency and the patient (the doer and the done to) affected by the action and identified agents as belonging to specific accounting categories. As suggested by the texts these were: male perpetrator/male victim, female perpetrator/female victim, the law, family/friends, medicine and other (to include any lexes I couldn't assign to the most frequently occurring group/agents). I produced models of the incidence of agency, and also a value assignment for agency in terms of the legal discourse of deviant behaviour so, for example, 'killer' connotes negative evaluation in law. Patient phrases were used to help with the evaluation. Exemplars of the value assignment process for the *Daily Mirror* report on Pam Sainsbury are included in Appendix Table 2.

The results of the same analysis of all the news reports was that all the papers offered more positive labels for male perpetrators (mp+) than for female (fp+) and more negative labels for female perpetrators (fp–) than male (mp–). Male (mv–) and female victims (fv–) attracted similar patterns of negative labelling (even though the men were each violent and criminal to some extent). The popular press offered accounts that focused on castigation of men and women agents, whilst the quality press veered towards accounts of the role of law; surprisingly even more often when the perpetrator was male despite the contemporary concern over women's treatment in the criminal justice system. Whether male or female, the killers were deemed syntactically/semantically responsible and denigrated for their acts, as well as holding the agent place most frequently in the actional text. Perhaps significant was the way that both victims (the battering man and innocent woman) were also denigrated in the text, whilst the law was rarely attributable with negative evaluation. The difference between male and female cases seemed fairly minimal. In a world of equal relations and factual accounts of extreme violence where other variables have been held fairly stable this might have been the expected profile of agency – although even in such a world there would be some curiosity about the more positive account of male killing of women, the more negative account of women victims of killing and the greater incidence of positive legal syntactic agency in the male texts. Figure 3 (the Appendix) shows the patterns of incidence clearly.

Such apparent equality in syntactic structures, denotative categories and evaluation in terms of the law was at first unnerving given the context of these articles, which were all published about trials of intimate killing during profuse debates about gender inequity in the criminal justice system. They were even more unnerving when it was considered that two of the women perpetrators suffered a history of violence and abuse from their partners and the third claimed to be in fear for her life from the man whose mistress she was. Such experience and claims did not feature in the male cases, where only Joseph McGrail claimed provocation from verbal abuse (nagging) which 'tried his patience'. Moreover, the victims were also denigrated in these reports, not only the battering men but even Rachel Maclean and Arminda Perry whose crime was that their lovers were jealous of them. There was virtually no positive account in these texts of women who killed in fear of their lives and yet there was such an account identifiable for men who suffered hurt pride and stretched patience. Further, the women victims were denigrated virtually as frequently as men whose history of assault eventually led to their partners' refusal to take any more.

Once the discussion of meaning was informed by the context of the events – the social relations and historical conditions – the paucity of the straightforward top-level reading according to British legal values was revealed. In both sets of cases the law as agent was overwhelmingly represented as positive. The assessment of the values of agents' actions in the articles invited various interpretations. The first was that the law and the media were offering accounts of male and female crime that were very similarly structured and evaluated because in legal terms they were very similar crimes, given that my variables of relationship, race, time and sentence are reasonably well established. So androcentric is the law that it was gender-blind even with regard to the fact that most criminals are men let alone to any concern with women criminals. Simply, the legal discourse of the early 1990s assumed criminals were male: it could not differentiate between men and women who kill. The law took no account of women's lower status, disadvantaged economic position, lack of physical strength or subordinate sexual role. The law as representative of the state seemed to support male power over women even in the 1990s after 20 years of second-wave feminism, perhaps relating to the influence of highly traditional political and policy perspectives on gender from a government elected on a law and order mandate.

The second interpretation was that analysing the legal discourse alone could not deliver sufficient meanings to analyse accounts of men and women who kill, and relate them to broader gender relations, because it doesn't make space for women nor identify men as masculine, only criminal. Other sites of meaning had to be explored for evidence, in accounts of intimate killing, of differentiated values that might relate to men's and women's unequal social relations. Without attention to the gender discourse there seemed to be nothing very significant at all to question in the evaluations presented by the legal accounts of men and women who kill. Yet, such accounts had to resolve conflict not just between law and crime but also between men and women. Although they had to castigate the crimes so as to promote social stability and moral order, they also had to restore the norms of gender relations, decimated for those involved and decimated symbolically for those reading the press, by the crimes. Somehow patriarchy needed to differentiate between the men and women involved so as to promote and restore the gender norms of masculine/dominant and feminine/subordinate, and the gender values of strong, aggressive males and frail, passive females.

Julia Kristeva (1988) argued that the sexual base of difference between men and women is translated to gendered social relations through the symbolic exchange of power, meaning and language. Somehow these accounts of men and women who transgressed that social/sexual contract negotiated the gendered contradiction of women who kill men, and legitimated the criminality of men who kill women, in order to restore gender order. Young (1990) identified the invocation of sexuality in press accounts of Greenham Common as foreclosing debates on the actual issues of nuclear weapons. Such an invocation was also identifiable in accounts of intimate killing where sexual innuendo foreclosed discussions of injustice and oppression.

Alongside sexualisation, two other interpretative arenas were evident in the genderising of these accounts. First, the medicalisation and/or psychiatrisation of behaviour is part of the technology of power described by Foucault (1967) as informing both the discourse of law and that of sexual behaviour. Such invocations support a view of bad women as also mad women, 'lacking any control over their own lives' (Heidensohn 1987: 99). Yet when used in mitigation of male violence, male insanity may be interpreted as the result of bad women's behaviour, as in John Tanner's complaint that Rachel Maclean was 'a dark being' who destroyed his life and caused the fit of fury during which he killed her (*Daily Mirror* 3.12.91).

Second, given the contemporary debates on women's position in the social world, at work, in the family and in leisure, and the backlash to women's efforts to secure a more equal part in these, I was interested to see whether such social issues featured in the press articles on intimate killing. I was curious in terms of Faludi's claim that the media were actively engaged in denigrating strong, independent, career women as miserable or materialistic bitches and in doing so point an 'accusatory finger at feminism' (1992: 17) for having failed women.

To explore these discourses of gender rather than legality, I drew up a similar grid table to that developed by Chibnall but to evaluate the lexical selections made for gendered nouns in accounts of intimate killing rather than British values (see Table 6.1). For the remit of violence and gender I could then interpret descriptions in polar terms as either positive or negative both in terms of common-sense norms of law-abidingness and/or gender qualities (Smart 1989). So 'distraught mother hurled her two baby sons to their death' (*Sun* November 1988) could be judged as doubly negative in that the agent (mother) has acted both illegally (murder) and against normal expectations of the female role of mother (nurturing). The value judgements inherent in the grids were a subjective guide, based on my own experience and perception of the conventional, traditional models of male and female attributes and roles.

The values cover areas of sexual role, social role and subjective/psychological identity. The range of terms available to label women was (is) much greater, and many more could be inferred.

For the analysis, all terms relating to attributes of women according to biological sex (motherhood, sexual activity, physical type) were accounted for under the sexuality discourse. For men, gendered labelling was (is) less readily accessible and there was a paucity of male-negative labels, so I retained criminality, as very often the only discursive context for male violence. Some social activities attracted similar positive/negative labels in common-sense terms for either sex, drunkenness, for example, but in practice a drunken women is more severely castigated than a drunken man, who may even be admired for his capacity for alcohol. Any conflict over valuation in such areas was resolved either through the wider text, or if necessary through intertextual comparison of the relevant case. In assigning value I referred to other lexes in the immediate syntactic context for explication. For example 'Blonde Pam killed' was adjudged to be negative not only as already evaluated (in the last section) in breaking the law but also through the association of blonde with a specific denigratory female sexual stereotype. 'Husband who murdered his Filipino wife' was adjudged negative in the legal discourse but positive as a gender label; in contrast 'unemployed man who murdered' would be labelled negative on both counts.

Table 6.1 Gender Value Grids: Guide to Dominant Model

male positive	male negative	female positive	female negative
heterosexual	homosexual	heterosexual	lesbian
virile	impotent	wife	single woman
working	unemployed	maternal	non-maternal
strong	weak	passive	aggressive
aggressive	passive	dependent	independent
mature	immature	monogamous	promiscuous
husband		natural	artificial
single man		frail	powerful
father		slender	gross
lover/boyfriend		married mother	single mother
sober	drunk	sober	drunk

As before, Appendix Table 3 depicts examples of sites of meaning and the interpreted value judgement for the Sainsbury *Daily Mirror* article. Proper names provided an interesting example of the process because male proper names were always used in full or with the surname only. Women were very frequently referred to by their Christian names, whether victims or killers. I felt this was significant and adjudged it as treating the women referred to as not meriting the use of a full name and/or title so excluding them from respectability or adulthood (i.e. in accord with dominant requirements of femininity sex–). Men on the other hand were usually called by their surname, sometimes full name but never by their first name alone.

The remaining articles were analysed similarly. The resulting statistics of value judgement in the sexual, social, psychological as well as criminal discourses are depicted in Figure 4 (see Appendix). The result for victims and perpetrators were amalgamated to offer a purview of gendered discourses in articles. The statistics used are the percentage of all sex-agent labels.

The graph in Figure 4 shows considerable differences, qualitative-value and quantitative-volume, in accounts of men and women involved in intimate killing. Not only were the women negated more than men as law-breakers and nearly as much as victims, as shown in the analysis of value in the law discourse, but they were then further negated in second orders of discursive production as women. In terms of their various gender roles: sexual (wife/lover/mother/attractive); social (housewife/work/leisure); and psychological (caring/stable/intelligence) women attracted more labelling and more negative value than men in the press accounts. In contrast, the majority of negative evaluation of male killing falls within the law discourse, that is they were negated as criminal rather than poor husbands, devious lovers or social misfits.

Overall 37 per cent of labels for women in press accounts of intimate killing attracted negative labels in the gendered discourses of sexuality, social life and psychology; similar negative male labels accounted for 15.7 per cent of all gendered labels. Only 9.8 per cent of female labels were positive compared to 13 per cent of labels for male protagonists. Yet, where the only available accounting discourse was the law some 15.6 per cent of male labels were simply criminal whilst only 8.9 per cent of female labels could be evaluated solely within that discourse. Finally, agency itself was assigned more frequently to women, whether perpetrators or victims: 44.3 per cent of the lexes in the place of causal agents in news about intimate killing were male labels, 55.7 per cent were female labels. This was strange given the equalising of cases and sources but suggests that blame was syntactically directed toward women more often than men, even though these cases included three women victims and two battered women.

To summarise, identifying, consistently, numerous instances of transactivity in press texts clearly suggested such texts were engaged in accounts that ascribed responsibility to agents for actions. As such, they were actively ideological in that such structures inherently support the idea that events have identifiable causes. In terms of meaning, syntax in the press might be understood best as operating ideologically at a macro knowledge level, supporting a positivist and determinist view of the world. Transactivity encourages readers to seek resolutions for conflict as if there are straightforward linear relations between agents, actions and consequences specific to the event reported. Cultural knowledge, social relations, orders of discourse and institutional profiles provided the journalist writing news about intimate killing with a repertoire of labels for actors in these crime narratives. Such labels bear values and meanings, which transpose themselves onto those men and women involved in sex'n'violence and perhaps operate beyond the text to broader social gender norms and values through the readers. It is worth remembering that 'readers' include judges and juries in relation to Carlen's comment that 'women who go to prison are sentenced not according to the seriousness of their crime but primarily according to the courts assessment of them as wives, mothers and daughters' (1988: 10).

In total, terms used to label women in crimes of intimate killing were more frequent, more often negative and more likely to offer up that negative meaning in more than one discourse, with the second discourse most often that of sexuality. Sexual and social reference to men in these accounts attracted nearly as many positive value judgements as negative. It seemed that issues of women's violence, criminality, power, strength, injustice, rejection of marriage and action on their own behalf were foreclosed in accounts of intimate killing. In their place was a framework of explanation which explored women's deviance in terms of the gender discourses of appropriate feminine behaviour. In contrast, in the male accounts, violence was accounted for primarily as breaking the law rather than as breaking any taboos of masculinity. Thus, the press accounts managed to perpetuate the legitimacy of male violence in gendered terms (by not mentioning it) whilst also castigating it in legal terms. The accounts thus resolved the ideological contradiction of restoring both law and order and patriarchal power. In contrast, women were depicted as breaking the law, or causing men to break the law, because they had broken taboos of female behaviour.

Comment

Accounts of intimate violent crime from the British press in the 1990s neglected the evidence that such crime was largely masculine and offered little critique of violence as associated with masculinity. Yet, when the same press accounted for the women in these cases, especially their sexual roles, the focus was on gender. Given the crucial place of gender relations in maintaining existing power relations, in both the private and public sphere, it was not surprising to find evidence of a struggle to reassert the interests of patriarchy in these accounts because if women's actions persistently overturned gender stereotypes 'the whole bloody system would collapse' (delegate Forensic psychiatry conference London 1990). The most significant pointer to this process of censure and foreclosure in late Thatcherism was the way in which the press accounts selected negative labels for women involved in killing, either as victims or perpetrators, from the sexual and social discourses, whilst male negative labels tended to be drawn from the criminal discourse.

This kind of systematic approach to language-use is valuable on several levels: it supports a theory of the press as actively engaged in reproducing the state's interests (through the law discourse) and patriarchal ideology (through the gender discourse); it suggests that such a process may have an effect on audiences in that accounts are simple, attributional and repetitive; it grounds interpretation in structures making easier the identification of foci and contexts and it offers a clear template for similar work on other topic themes or discourse types. Any attempt to describe and explain correlations between media accounts and social relations can, I think, be strengthened by such rigorous and explicit attention to language. Such close, formal examination makes it possible to argue that during late Thatcherism the British news was systematically complicit with conservatism in relation to gender via the vehicle of sex'n'violence stories.

Syntax and signification acted as vehicles for news values and con-temporary ideological discourses and 'sold' a calling to consensus around patriarchal interests disguised as news about sex'n'violence. The sales pitch was that women were to blame for both their own and men's violence because they were deviating from conservative femininity. The articles analysed consistently linked both female violence and male violence to non-traditional femininity. The net effect was to promote marriage, monogamy, maternity and moderation as safe, normal and responsible for women. In contrast, feminists, femmes fatale, foreigners and feckless women drive men to badness and themselves to madness.

However, the methodology used in this analysis also indicated the limit of a focus on structural forms in work on texts. Without theorising ideology as working in different discourses but ostensibly in the same syntactic forms it would have been very difficult to elicit evidence to support feminist claims that women involved in crime were being judged not just in relation to the law but also in relation to patriarchal values. Being able to elicit different stories as effectively being told in the same text informed and continues to inform the way I analyse news.[9] For example, in the news coverage of environmental protest in 1997,[10] the liberal middle-class *Observer* Sunday newspaper had serious columnist Nicci Gerrard use the unforgettable headline 'Tunnel of Love: for Denise and Grandpappy the earth moved under Manchester airport' (15.6.97) to introduce a couple's subterranean romance. As in the case of news about intimate killing, the sexual discourse shifted the meaning away from the challenges to dominance, presented in this case by Green politics, rather than feminism. The call to the 'normal' was evident in news about tunnels. It was worked through in accounts of conflict and the body (violence and sex), woven around and behind the issues of environmental politics, which actually impelled both the 'real' events and the media 'representations'.

Explaining violence was a central concern during Thatcherism because violence was the antithesis of the 'law and order' mandate of government and of course its justification. Violence is commonly perceived as a male norm: part of the masculine profile and a natural tendency which is held in check through civilised man's self-control (and traditional woman's softening effect) until provoked or unleashed. Some radical feminist work has taken this position, immutably aligning violence with the male sex (Dworkin 1981), with all men potential aggressors (Stanko 1985). Segal criticised this explanation, suggesting it 'puts 19th century biologism back in the saddle, cloaked in a spurious sociological rhetoric' (1990: 260).

Men's proclivity for aggression, however theorised, even if not enacted through actual physical violence, serves to maintain and re-enforce their dominance over women socially and sexually. Social dominance requires no exercised violence, other than the maintenance through power and control of resources in such a way as to limit or preclude access to them by women. Sexual dominance is described as achieved particularly through the production and consumption of images consistently denigrating women (Dworkin 1981); images that Stanko (1985) maintained legitimate sexual intimidations ranging from unsolicited touching to flashing. Commonplace misogyny (real or represented) supports all men's power to violate. Segal claimed all men are 'part of the culture and climate of misogyny which permits violence against women to occur with very little protest from men' (1990: 241) and 'women are right to see our society as riddled with the cultural expression of contempt for them as the subordinate sex' (1990: 253). The newspaper reports of intimate killing went further than contempt because the representations of women in these cases criminalised the perpetrators for going against the law and then blamed both perpetrators and victims for going against the grain of normal femininity.

The newspapers I analysed show little evidence of plurality in the British press of the Conservative period, at least in relation to patriarchy, but the possibility of a critical 'feminist' reading does at least counter too strong a model of patriarchal propaganda. However, this is not enough because as Hartsock (1987) insisted, when the various minority experiences have been described and when the significance of these experiences as a ground for critique of the dominant institutions and ideologies of society is better recognised, we will at least have the tools to begin to construct an account of the world sensitive to the realities of race and gender as well as class. To paraphrase Marx, the point is to change the world, not simply to redescribe ourselves or reinterpret the world again – and there the problem begins.

7
Straightening Out Sex

This chapter moves to another site of conservative reconstruction, the call to straight sex. In Western culture sexuality, both real and represented, has become increasingly riddled with ambivalent and discontinuous knowledge since the 'liberating' 1960s. Previously secret, illicit or unacknowledged desires and practices have become part of public discussion, prompting many debates on sexual acts and identities. The accepted truths that hid and made deviant anything other than mature, heterosexual, monogamous, marital, reproductive sex have given way to:

> A veritable explosion of discourse – talk about sex, television and radio programmes, sermons and legislation, novels, stories and magazine features, medical and counselling advice, essays and articles, learned theses and research programmes, as well as new sexual practices (e.g. safe sex) and the pornography industry. (Hall 1997: 50)

Sexual liberation, polygamy, bisexuality, gay parenting, control of reproduction provide titillating material for commercial popular cultural forms but still provoke fierce denigration in formal and factual discourses such as the law and the news media. (Sharon Stone's lack of knickers in *Basic Instinct* attracted huge audiences to the film, alongside calls for censorship, whilst Sara Thornton's admittance that she 'doesn't always wear knickers' contributed to a media and legal construction of her as a feminist husband killer (see Chapter 6).

Different sexualities are provocative and profitable: they sell sex, literally and metaphorically, in a range of commercial contexts and sex sells products through advertising and association. 'Publicity increasingly uses sexuality to sell any product or service ... To be able to buy is the same thing as being sexually desirable' (Berger 1973: 144). Yet, sexuality is also about both the subjective self and social reproduction. Whilst the market may tolerate any amount of sexual outlets and variations, Western social organisation has tended to recognise as legitimate only the model of sexual organisation that served the needs of social organisation and reproduction. From the Victorian period, the family had been the mainstay of both patriarchy and capital (Collier 1994) but, from the swinging sixties, affluence, contraception and the media generated what Seidman (1992) called a culture of eroticism that was rapidly transformed into a multi-billion dollar business. Yet, that erotic culture was very much at odds with the traditional morality of conservatism and Christian fundamentalism that launched a backlash against sexual liberation during the 1980s. The Reagan administration in the USA and the Thatcher government in the UK both had ruling authority by dint of the voting power of the moral right. On both sides of the Atlantic, sex was made a political issue as 'the powerful moral lobby increased its media visibility' (McNair 1996: 20) through consistent challenges to deviating sexuality. This chapter considers how and with what implications the British news media made sexual issues 'visible' during the Conservative years.

Body Talk

At the centre of that sexual profusion and confusion was, and is, the body: the body in relation to pleasure and personal freedom; the body as essential for the labour that underpins social production; and the body as necessary for the sexual reproduction that supplies that labour. The body is therefore a site over which a range of different areas of social organisation construct meanings and strive to intervene. The body is tempted by diverse products though commerce, disciplined by chemicals in psychiatric medicine, controlled by incarceration within the criminal justice system, constrained through morality and excited by desire (Foucault 1967, 1975, 1979). The complexity of ideas and practices working on the body, and its importance in socio-economic relations, make it a site of struggle and conflict, which in turn makes determinist models of ideology, whereby the 'ideas of the ruling class become the ruling ideas', seem over simplistic and crude.

Foucault expanded such class-stratified concepts of language, power and ideology (Volosinov 1929) into a more subtle concept of power exercising in the farthest reaches of human relations. Foucault suggested that power permeates all social life. Power 'traverses and produces things, it induces pleasure, forms of knowledge, produces discourse' (Foucault in Hall, 1997: 50). Discourse is not in this context meant as simply linguistic, but includes the practices that inform and reproduce meanings regularly in particular contexts. Discourses are shared within historical periods – they are the means by which we make sense of the world; they are what we know. Inversely, what we know about the world depends on discourse. Concepts such as madness, badness and sexiness relate to the discourses within which those concepts are shared and maintained.

When a discourse has a specifically identifiable source, site, authority and set of values – such as medicine, the law or the church – and offers systematic consistency, it becomes institutionalised. Such discourses permeate society through the media and education and also within personal and familial interactions. Redolent with authority and repeated regularly, these readily assume the appearance of truth. Those truths inform sexuality, sanity and legitimacy and are transformed into a technology of power in the public domain through institutions in Foucault's (1975) terms.

Social institutions were likened by Foucault to watchtowers overlooking the landscape of humanity, each responsible in symbiosis with one another for articulating behaviours, within practices. Foucault theorised the social subject as always potentially powerful but also subject to our 'whole territory of social narratives' (Inglis 1990: 107) Moreover, the 'exercise of power has always been formulated in terms of law' (Foucault 1975: 87) that disguises power through 'devious and subtle mechanisms' as prohibition of the abnormal. Prohibitions that exist in:

> Manifold relationships of force that take shape and come into play in the machinery of production, in families, limited groups and institutions, are the basis for wide-ranging effects of cleavage that run through the social body as a whole. (Foucault 1975: 94)

As an example Foucault described the nineteenth-century embour-geoisment of sexuality, which promoted the family as the factor of sexuality through prohibition of alternatives and promotion of family norms. It negated child sexuality, denigrated 'frigid' and 'nymphomanic' women as hysterics, made reproduction a social behaviour and psychiatrised alternative sexualities. Through this construction of sexuality developed control of the body by legislation, medicalisation, psychiatrisation and education (recently evident in reproductive technologies, Section 28 on homosexuality, AIDS education and child-abuser therapy). Commensurate value judgements accompanied this construction. Therefore, Foucault's theory explains how Heidensohn (1985) could claim that our cultural heritage can be reduced to two themes of good and bad women, both traceable back to Victorian models of appropriate femininity. It also provides a framework that enables an analysis of meanings around sexuality.

For Foucault, the exercise of power through the law and prohibition is subtle. It can change over time but may also operate variably in any given historical epoch, or in particular contexts. The anti-repressive struggle of gays and women, the demise of sexual alliances for life, the appearance of sex-aid shops, the sale of contraception have achieved change that Foucault described as 'nothing more, but nothing less – and its importance is undeniable – than a tactical shift and reversal in the deployment of sexuality' (1979: 131). But that discursive practice reconstructs and refracts in accordance with power, so that with sexuality the paradox is that the mechanisms of prohibition are enforced sufficiently laxly to allow a multiplication and proliferation of pleasure which generates a sexual marketplace for countless economic interests and supports a range of differing micro-power relations in private and personal situations. As a result the sexual discourse maintains public control over sexuality through prohibitive authorities whilst within consumerism it promises and excites an 'explosion of unorthodox sexualities' (Foucault 1979: 49). The duality of the most powerful is accommodated: patriarchy retains control over processes of reproduction and the subordination of women[1] whilst capitalism makes space, sometimes illicit but nonetheless profitable, for the commercial exploitation of sex from prostitution to advertising.

Prostitution: Sex for Sale

Prostitution was high on the agenda of the media, the state and therefore the public during the Conservative governments. On the one hand it was being driven off the streets by vigilantes in Birmingham, on the other it informed popular moral fables in films like *Pretty Woman*, where the whore who learns how to be respectable gets her guy. However different, the media messages were promoting similar models of positive feminine sexuality, by negating the sale of sex, negation that is reinforced in the UK by the law.

Yet, although prostitution has a long history, it has a relatively brief history of illegality. Until the nineteenth century legislation about prostitution was more concerned with the brothel than the prostitute, as in The Disorderly Houses Act 1751 and The Brothel Act 1755. Although much of the European continent transformed the focus on the brothel into a licensing system, Britain shifted more puritanically into attempting to stop prostitution altogether. Although arguably driven by morality, the excuse for tightening controls was disease, with prostitutes defined as dangerously infectious. The Contagious Diseases Act 1864 was purported to protect men, soldiers and sailors especially, from sexually transmitted illness. Women who were seen talking to military men in a public place could be forcibly examined and then imprisoned if venereally diseased (Perkins 1991). Men's role in spreading disease, from woman to woman (and of course, but never acknowledged in the nineteenth century, from man to man), in Britain and the empire was initially ignored so, by the time the act was repealed in 1886 after feminist campaigning, there was a widespread, popular association of female promiscuity/prostitution with disease. This legitimated a different set of legislation aimed at closing down prostitution by targeting the premises used and raising the age of consent to 16 years for girls.

The term 'common prostitute' used in the 1864 act remains in the statutes and applies to any woman who on two or more occasions has been cautioned by police for soliciting on the streets. Yet the illegality of brothel-keeping either places women on the street or in the dangerous position of being at home alone with clients. A prostitute cannot easily live with another woman, which might constitute a brothel, nor with a man, who would then run the risk of being charged with living off immoral earnings (Macleod 1982). So prostitutes are isolated, as if morally and physically contagious. Men have stepped into this space, to exploit and control prostitution by acting as agents and protectors – pimps or ponces – with the net effect that men sell women to other men with neither kind of man particularly inhibited by the law (Kennedy 1992).

Smart (1989) argued that whilst purporting to protect women, much existing legislation around sexuality actively reproduced existing gender power relations, by recognising men as sexual aggressors but viewing this as a natural tendency, normally latent but provoked by deviant femininity. The Parliamentary Expenditure Committee (1978–79) appeared to tackle this inequity with vigour, recognising feminist arguments that women should have the right to control their own bodies and suggesting that laws on prostitution contradicted the Sex Discrimination Act (1975). From 1985 The Sexual Offences Act introduced two clauses to enable the prosecution of men who kerb-crawled or persistently solicited, yet in 1996 the programme *Sex off the Streets* (Granada 20.3.96) reported that in Stamford Hill, London, the previous year, police had arrested 500 punters and 1,000 prostitutes – at half a client each this does not make prostitution seem very profitable. This anomaly was partly explained later in the programme when the presenter reported that some prostitutes might be arrested 40 or 50 times a year and then be back on the streets after paying small fines. The law seemed unable to control prostitution, it merely made sure it was as dangerous for women as possible and as profitable/affordable as possible for men, whether pimps or punters. It also reinforced stereotypes of prostitutes as dirty, diseased and illicit by forcing the activity onto the street and outside of 'normal' sexual encounters.

Reform is common elsewhere in the world. Even Melbourne in Australia licensed alcohol-free brothels from 1986. This freed women from criminal charges, allowed them to work co-operatively, improved heath and safety, destigmatised clients and contributed considerable amounts of revenue to the tax collector. Yet, in the UK the All Parliamentary Group on Prostitution remained split in 1995 between decriminalisation and increased legislation – the Conservative government took the view that the law was sufficient.

Sex remained on the streets where vigilante residents added to the difficulties faced by the women involved. The *Observer* (4.2.96) reported that in Birmingham 'people power cleaned the streets', using the metaphor of dirt to describe prostitution. The picket against prostitution 'forged a community spirit where previously there was just a fragmented and despairing population'. Prostitution was cleared out of a previously 'red-light' area by a process of shaming and naming, using surveillance cameras and telling drug pushers to 'move on'.

Prostitution is paid promiscuity but women who have sex with many different men, outside of marriage, outside of the home and family, for purposes other than reproduction are also stigmatised even when money does not change hands. In fact, the probable real objection to prostitution is not the selling of sex but the availability of it for non-monogamous pleasure. To be promiscuous is to act outside of the regulatory frameworks that shape women's sexuality.

Promiscuity was used to challenge those frameworks rebelliously in the sexual liberation of the 1960s – though retrospectively it is possible to see how that approach merely 'justified a cavalier predatory approach to sexual relationships which offered few apparent benefits to young women' (McNair 1996: 12). Nor did it change very much – women's promiscuity was, years later, used to explain both rape and murder. It was the basis of the provocation plea in the case where John Perry killed his wife, cut her up, cooked her and fed her to the family cat (November 1991).[2] Medically, female promiscuity continued to be associated in the press with disease: HIV/AIDs (*The Times* 21.10.90, 16.2.92), cervical cancer (*Woman's Hour* 17.3.88) and herpes (*Guardian* 14.2.92) – see Elleschild 1994.

Dangerous sexuality continues to be associated with promiscuous women (paid for or not). It is linked symbolically to disease, deviance and death. It contrasts neatly with 'safe sexuality' and promotes that by default – maintaining as right monogamy and the heterosexual family. Such values are readily sustained by the particular nature of sexual inequality between men and women, the specificity of which 'can too easily be lost in discussion of other categories of inequality less subject to taboo, such of those of power and gender. Men's sex-right is central to contracts, from marriage to prostitution' (Holland 1998: 26).

It seems unlikely that attitudes to women's promiscuity will change as long as women remain materially and socially subordinate to men because such behaviour is too readily labelled as deviant or criminal, leading to either cultural or legal/welfare controls. The means to decriminalise prostitution were there throughout the Conservative governments' terms of office but were not taken up. To recognise that women might be promiscuous, be paid for it and be neither criminal nor deviant was and is anathema to the moral right because that would mean admitting that for many men (and women) family, marriage and monogamy were/are either undesirable or insufficient. Decriminalising prostitution would be the beginning of recognising promiscuity as neither criminal nor deviant but normal and legitimate. Such an admittance would undermine irrevocably the familial ideology, deeply embedded in Victorian patriarchy and puritanism that underpins conservatism. It would do so by freeing women economically, legally and culturally from an exploitative relationship with male sexual power, both in marriage/monogamy and in prostitution/promiscuity.

Sectioning Homosexuality

The Victorian legacy of prudery towards promiscuity similarly affected attitudes to and representations of homosexuality a century later. As existing heterosexual boundaries were confirmed by Thatcherism, homosexuality was subjected to a real and symbolic attempt to drive it back into the closet. The effort was to secure and strengthen familial heterosex's place at the top of the sexual hierarchy by silencing other sexual formations:

> Heterosexuality secures its self-identity, and shores up its ontological boundaries, by protecting itself from what it sees as the continual, predatory encroachment of its contaminated other, homosexuality. (Fuss 1991: 3)

During the 1980s and early 1990s that 'contamination' was HIV/AIDS and it paralleled the 'contagion' that informed the Contagious Diseases Act a hundred years previously. The panic over HIV/AIDS in Britain initially focused very much on those perceived as risks – gays and intravenous drug-users. As Young (1996) pointed out, risk was associated with how a person could be labelled rather than whether or not they engaged in high-risk practices. Disease was used as it had been a century previously to divide sexuality into good and bad – then it had been monogamous/promiscuous, now it was heterosexual/homosexual. The association of the spread of HIV/AIDS with promiscuity added to the binary split, doubly damning gay men as not heterosexual, not monogamous. HIV/AIDS became represented as the awful viral result of 'unorthodox deregulated desire' (Watney 1988: 60).

Again, the liberals of the 1960s and 1970s were blamed for the social ills of the 1980s (see Chapter 2 on race). Fear of HIV/AIDS made it complex and controversial to promote sexual liberation, despite the growing need to combat the manipulation of people's fears and anxieties. This left space for the right who stuck doggedly to their task of opposing it (Segal 1994: 311). The conservative Reagan/ Thatcher context of the 1980s was always likely to support a climate of moral rectitude. HIV/AIDS legitimated an assault on both promiscuity and homosexuality, which reasserted repeatedly that safe sex was monogamous heterosex despite the highly effective campaigns by the gay communities for safer sex and the relatively low risk of infection through any heterosexual sex. The process of shoring up traditional sexuality was underpinned by the law and culturally mediated via discourses of health and family well-being, which sometimes masked the moral fable being offered – only traditional, familial sexuality is good.

In 1988, Section 28 of the Local Government Act was explicitly anti-queer.[3] It made it illegal for any local authority to promote gay identity and for state schools to 'teach acceptance of pretended family relationships'. Section 28 was a backlash against those homosexual men and lesbians who, since the raid on a gay dancing club, the Stonewall Inn in Manhattan in 1969, had presented as a sub-culture resisting and challenging the heterosexual status quo. These challenges manifested as pressure groups in the public sphere and prompted re-examinations of private relationships. There was a call to introduce more positive representations of gay lifestyle and identity, to counter old prejudices and make it easier for gay people to be open about their sexuality, linking to the liberal struggles for tackling racial and sexual discrimination in the 1970s.

In the UK, many Labour-controlled councils introduced anti-homophobic strategies and information, which remained in place after the election of the Thatcher government in 1979. These were anathema to a political party that believed it 'could only get to the roots of crime and much else besides by concentrating on strength-ening the traditional family' (Thatcher 1995: 628). Department of Education circulars stressed the importance of 'stable married life and the responsibilities of parenthood' (no. 11 1987), and right-wing academics made the link between family and home-ownership (see Chapter 5), neatly supporting one Tory philosophy with another.

Section 28 revealed not just the fear of the other in terms of its implications for family, and thus for capital and patriarchy, but also the idea that gayness was not 'natural' but cultural and as such could be taught and learnt much as a political doctrine might be propa-gandised. Another set of binary oppositions natural/cultural was added to the denigrative discourse within which gay sex is compre-hended. The idea that gayness could be learnt shored up another cluster of legislative debates around the age of homosexual consent. The notion that being gay was just an adolescent phase inhibited the reduction of the age of consensual homosex from 21 to 18 and continues to inhibit its reduction to 16, the same age as heterosex – as in, 'Lords oppose Equality again' (<www.outrage.cygnet.co.uk> 16.5.99). The logic offered was that access to positive representations of gayness in childhood might increase the numbers of practising homosexuals (*Hansard* 18.12.86).[4] This is the same attitude that informs calls for censorship and assumes that the media have the power to affect identity and behaviour, as strongly claimed by the Viewers and Listeners Association. What was at issue in Section 28 was not the act of gay sex but the publicising of it. It was literally sectioned away from sight by the legislation because of the fear of effects. Like HIV/AIDS, and perhaps by the constant association with it, homosexuality was viewed as contagious.

Acceptance of an effects/contagion model meant that not only might publicity have resulted in more homosexuality per se but in the legitimation of that publicly. The fear seems to have been that once identity and personal practices were accepted it would not be long before lifestyle followed and it was the idea of the pretended family that most horrified the right, because 'that could undermine the basis of our society' (Rhodes Boyson in *Hansard* 8.5.87). The press seemed to concur, with frequent and damning accounts of lesbian parenting, turkey-baster conceptions and confused kids with either two mums or two dads added to their other anti 'other' family diatribes, which also focused on single-parent mums jumping the housing queues and bringing up delinquents.[5]

TV journalists agreed. BBC2 asked *Who Killed the Family?* (31.10.95) and concluded that it was feminism and free-love under the banner 'wedlock is deadlock'. On the programme, Janet Daley equated family life with civil order and Melanie Phillips warned that if the family dies there may be no 'tomorrow'. The power of these normalising discourses is their familiarity: family matters to us all; it informs our sense of self through experience and culture – to challenge it is in some senses to doubt who we are in the world.

Those gays who adhered to a traditional model of monogamy and children found themselves depicted as part of the problem of the collapse of 'normal' families; those who challenged 'normal' sexual organisation fared as badly if not worse. Drawing on Foucault's (1979) work on the body as a site for disciplinary practices and discourses, active in constructing normal and deviant behaviours, some highly politicised members of the gay community sought to deconstruct the sexual hierarchies by focusing on the body, and the binary oppositions within which it becomes meaningful. The goal was to destabilise heterosex and to throw the values and knowledges underpinning it into confusion.

Parody, mimicry, gay erotica, political lesbianism and a strategy of disruptive excess (Irigaray 1985 in Segal 1994: 191) were seen as ways of thwarting the power of straight sex. But, as gays sought self-consciously to perform a reordering of gender through the cosmeticised, girly, blonde femme and the butch, black, denim-clad dyke, a lack of attention to further differentiating factors, like race and class, often perpetuated other stratifying stereotypes. Many gays were

> Too far out in the icy seas of economic and social disadvantage, much too endangered by the contaminating poisons of media and interpersonal hostility, to swim back on a lifeline of subversive performance. (Segal 1994: 207)

Inversion and subversion were other possible means of resistance, perhaps most stridently though sado-masochism as a challenge to the gentleness of 'vanilla' sex. S&M split the lesbian community. Radical feminists saw the associated violence as continuing the misogynistic oppression and degradation of women. S&M lesbians on the other hand saw the practice as a challenge to authority, 'deliberate, premeditated erotic blasphemy' (Pat Califia the *Guardian* 28.11.92). Such 'perversion' linked to the gay community became another icon of the collapse of the domestic, familial and orderly and exacerbated the right-wing onslaught against queer lifestyle.

In 1987 the Obscene Publications Squad began to investigate the sado-masochistic practices of a group of gay men who in private enjoyed 'genital torture with nails, canes, scalpels and electric wires' (*Guardian* 28.11.92). Their preferred practices were uncovered only because they video-taped sessions, a practice that contradicted the privacy requirement of the 1967 Sexual Offences Act. None complained, none knew they were breaking any law and none needed medical attention. Yet, eleven men were sentenced for up to four and half years in 1990 in the 'Spanner' Case, which became 'a barometric reading of the boiling turbulence of sexual politics' (*Guardian* 28.11.92). It was about what consenting adults should be allowed to do at home and the conclusion was that they should not be allowed to inflict pain. Kellan Farshea, who ran a support group for the convicted men, commented that 'it's a strange kind of liberal democracy we live in when consensual pleasure is put in the dock and sent to prison' (*Guardian* 28.11.92). A series of appeals reduced and partly overturned the original decision through reference to the European Convention of Human Rights but the cultural damage had been done, with homosexuality tried and found wanting.

Mary Whitehouse, of the right-wing pro-censorship Viewers and Listeners Association, dubbed Superintendent Hames of the Obscene Publications Squad a 'kindred spirit in the fight against filth' (*Guardian* 28.11.92). When gay activities challenged straight tradition in ways that also challenged the courts, they were easily labelled criminal. However, it is worth mentioning that neither heterosexual nor lesbian S&M faced these kinds of powerful cultural and criminal justice constraints. Instead they were treated as a 'joke' or just another example of lipstick lesbian chic.

The Conservative heterosexual agenda was well served by the law and media during Thatcherism, with HIV/AIDS or the courts the threat should people stray from the straight path. Much of the discussion about sex, outside the family, was that it should be inside – however, sex inside the family was also a significant problem for the Tories as it became increasingly obvious that physical and sexual child abuse was a major social problem.

Keeping it in the Family

In 1885, the Criminal Law Amendment Act had raised the age of consent for girls from 13 to 16, officially recognising childhood as a sexless zone and giving the law more authority to intervene in sexual and family matters by constructing the family as the proper and safe place for young women until the age of consent. Childhood was constructed as innocent, subject to parental control, supervised by medicine and educated by the state, making marriage and family pivotal sites of social/sexual control (Wykes 1998).

In 1985, Thatcher had great regard for the Victorians and in the face of what she claimed were social ills caused by the breakdown of the family she set about reconstituting the stability of the family. She introduced the Child Support Agency to force fathers to pay for their children after divorce – so relieving the burden on the state, refused to make divorce a quick, no-fault process and resisted pressure to provide tax relief for child care to encourage women to stay home with their children (see Thatcher 1995). Such pro-family political discourses were mirrored in the media where traditionalism explained problem families in terms of unconventional sexual organisation (Wykes 1998). By the late 1980s it was clear that many families were sites of terrible abuse, and that had probably always been the case, yet there was little popular discussion of the family as a problem. Rather, press accounts seemed to support Faludi's (1992) claim that the media was a 'backlash collaborator', reporting sexual abuse and deviancy in ways that reinforced traditional gender roles and family organisation.

The Cleveland child abuse cases of 1987 suggested the most extreme of gender role transgressions – the buggery by heterosexual fathers/father substitutes of their children, although on no occasion that I could discover was that fact voiced by the media, except by the radical journalist Bea Campbell in *Unofficial Secrets* (1988). Campbell found that of the 121 children diagnosed by Dr Marietta Higgs and Dr Geoffrey Wyatt as sexually abused, only 26 were returned to their parents as wrongly diagnosed:

> All the rest were children whose alleged abuser left the environment, or whose parents agreed to protective plans with social services or who were removed from their homes. Contrary to the media myth that most cases were cleared by the courts, most of the children became the subjects of some form of state support or protection. (Campbell 1988: 1)

The average age of these children was under 7 years and 17 lived in households where the father or other male 'had already been convicted of sexual offences' (Campbell 1988: 2). Yet media and political ire was not directed against the men who violated these children – instead it fell on the doctors and social workers who had dared to reveal the violation. In the media coverage of Cleveland, discussion raged over the weakness of a previously uncontroversial anal-dilation diagnosis, over-enthusiastic social workers, feminist man-haters, unprotective mothers, fantasising children and the rights of parents. Conspicuous by its absence was the kind of literal, accusatory headline that might be expected from the *Sun*: EVIL DAD BUGGERS HIS BABY.

The treatment of the sexual abuse of Cleveland children in public texts seemed to involve filtering the actual issues through a particular set of criteria, which selected out of the newsworthy material the systematic violation by men (in the father role) of the children for whom they were responsible. Paternal, male heterosexuals as child rapists never made the news. In its place was a whole critique of liberal intervention (Stuart Bell MP, quoted in *Woman*, 23.7.88, 'Child Abuse – One Family's Nightmare') into the rights and privacies of family life. That critique sought to re-establish the rectitude and sanctity of traditional family roles rather than challenge them in the interest of abused children, as suggested by the medical and social evidence.

After Cleveland, there were other clusterings of evidence of large-scale child sexual abuse, in Nottingham and Orkney, investigated by other social and medical workers, but the debate on male hetero-sexuality and paternity as threatening to children remained closed. In its place developed a strange and complex discussion attributing such abuse to satanic practices, black magic and ritual. The *Guardian* (21.8.91) went to some length to discuss ritual abuse but only mentioned in passing the conviction for child abuse of the father of three of the children whom police and social workers removed to a place of safety after dawn raids in the Orkney islands. Although in concordance with news values, which demand repeated events become more extreme in order to remain newsworthy (Galtung and Ruge 1965), this example of shift in blame illustrates a certain reciprocity of interests at work in the processing of news and the reproduction of dominance.

Instead of the description of the dangerousness of families and fathers in the media there seemed to be a strategy of deflection. This was perhaps never clearer than in the coverage of the West case in 1995. Fred and Rose West had systematically raped, sexually tortured and killed some of their own children and other young women who were lured to their house in Gloucester. During February 1994, police had disinterred the parts of twelve different bodies in the house and surrounding countryside. When Fred West hung himself, whilst waiting trial, all the attention of the news media focused on Rose. During the period of her trial in October and November 1995, every denigratory term applicable to a woman was probably applied to Rose by journalists covering the case. She was described variously in the news as: depraved, lesbian, aggressive, violent, menacing, bisexual, likes black men, likes oral sex, kinky, seductive, a prostitute, over-sexed, a child abuser, nymphomaniac, sordid, monster, she had a four-poster bed with the word c**t (*sic*) carved on the headboard, posed topless, exhibitionist, never wore any knickers, liked sex toys, incestuous, who shed tears in silence, no sobs, no sound at all. At puberty she developed, allegedly, an obsession for sex and 'Fred confided, "When Rose was pregnant her lesbian tendencies were at their strongest. I had to go out and get her a girl. She gets urges that have to be satisfied"' (*Sun* 3.11.95).

Such a commentary links to the bio-explanations for women's violence found in accounts of so-called pre-menstrual and post-puerperal killing and maintains a model of femininity always close to mad (Young 1988). In the same accounting vein, the *Daily Mail* paralleled the case with Hindley with the information that 'Rose West and Myra Hindley have formed a macabre friendship in jail ... the two most evil women in Britain, both openly bisexual – have been seen holding hands in Durham prison' (23.11.95)

There was so little attention paid to Fred in the news that it was almost as if he was excluded from blame. His role as a father and husband who raped and killed was barely addressed, nor was his collection of home-made pornographic videos, his role as Rose's pimp or his previous convictions. Despite many police visits to the West's house in the years leading up to the discovery of the murders, and copious records of the children at hospitals and social services, the family was left intact. The veneer of the traditional family had actually hidden years of terrible sexual violence; still, the role of the family in perpetuating that violence was never on the journalistic agenda. Instead, blame was heaped on the liberal social services and Rose's deviant femininity. Fred was 'only the undertaker' (*Sun* 23.11.95).

The lack of attention to Fred as abuser and pornographer secured other male abuse by perpetuating the myth of home, fathers and family as safe. Heterosexual, paternal masculinity was left intact by news about the Wests, as was the lucrative business of prostitution and pornography that Fred ran. Yet, the contemporary climate was one of vigorous official concern about pornography and especially child pornography and paedophilia.

Pornography and the Mass Media

Debates about pornography move the struggle over sex from real practices to represented ones. Yet, there seems to be more moral uproar about depictions of sex than about actual sex, despite levels of sexual and violent abuse of women and children in their own homes that most of us would find shocking (Stanko 1990). There are several possible, and not unconnected, reasons for this: first is the deep psychological need to explain crisis, discover a cause and blame something (Eiser 1978); second, the media is the source of information for most of us about events we cannot witness, so to learn about abusive sex from the media implicates it by association – it is the media that brings sexual deviance to our attention so we tend to blame the medium/messenger (McLuhan 1964); third is a societal inability or unwillingness to deal with the family and male sexuality as a problem (Wykes 1998); and fourth, there are interests being supported by a focus on representation rather than reality.

The association of pornography with sexual deviance and abuse makes two assumptions: that pornography is depraved material and that it has an effect. Neither of these is by any means demonstrable. Pornography defies definition, at least in any way that would gain universal acceptance of what should or should not be regulated or banned. The dictionary offers literature about prostitutes as a literal denotation, which would include the press coverage of much of the West case and exclude images of sexual activity involving animals or children unless a prostitute was involved. McNair suggested three historical examples as informing a better definition: Aretino, a sixteenth-century poet, added images to sexually explicit sonnets that challenged contemporary norms; in the eighteenth century the Marquis de Sade added pain to the range of pleasurable sexual depictions and in Britain *Fanny Hill* had little story or political agenda and 'pursued the aim of sexual arousal alone' (1996: 42–3). For me, a very basic working definition might be sexually explicit material, intended to arouse and depicting sex other than for the purposes of reproduction – in other words the depiction of sex for pleasure. The first two aspects of this definition are commonly part of attempted definitions; the last is less usual.

The first stumbling block is the word explicit and arguments about it have informed divisions of pornography into hard-core (explicit) and soft-core (implicit) in the UK but in the United States hard-core only applies to sex acts other than vaginal and oral penetration. This in itself exposes the anomalies of definition because oral sex remains illegal in several American states (as revealed in the debates around the Clinton–Lewinsky affair) and identical material could be illegal in the UK and legal in the US. The second problem is intentionality or the demonstration that material is deliberately and solely produced to arouse. There are two issues: the first is why that should matter, and the second how do you demonstrate it?

The only reason it might matter is if being 'turned on' was in any sense a threat to self or others. The fear of rampant sexuality goes straight back to the Victorians and their anxiety about what Foucault called the great untamed, sex. The association of sexuality with disease, danger, crime, damnation, castration[6] and the 'other' has left a legacy of sexual fear to accompany the taboo of sex. In this sense, the British attitude to sex is a little like their attitude to drugs – if you try a joint you will end up a junkie. But sex like drugs can be a pleasure and therein lies the problem for the moral conservatives.

Even if it were possible to argue that anyone being sexually aroused is a problem for most people most of the time, the second problem is how do you prove intention. Sexual excitement depends on such a large range of variables that any one product cannot be assured of affecting all members of any audience similarly. Moreover, sometimes arousal is an important part of the message, for example adverts for condoms importantly stress the pleasurability of 'safer sex' and have been accused of being pornographic. Also, it seems to me ridiculous to express dismay at high rates of teenage pregnancy in the UK when most sex education stresses the relationship between sex, love and reproduction (whilst denying contraception to school girls) rather than sex, pleasure, responsibility and self-worth. Why not arouse them, tell them they are amazing, and then tell them how to be safe from pregnancy and disease?[27] And anyway intention does not matter unless sexual arousal does.

My suspicion is that the only definition that it is feasible to use to describe porn is my last and the reason it appears so infrequently is that it exposes the censorious as conservative, heterosexual, patriarchal, Christian fundamentalists. Really, what is subject to most objection is erotica because material depicting other acts such as 'real' violent sex as opposed to consensual adult S&M and 'real' child sex (not computer generated) are already subject to the law. Such things do not need to be censored because display could already lead to prosecution of the producers, and if they can't be traced they can't be prosecuted either for depiction or enaction. The argument about the content of material is largely irrelevant if no laws are broken in production. If laws are broken, it is already illegal. So what would be gained by more laws? It only becomes relevant if harmful effects can be demonstrated amongst audiences and it is assumptions about effects that inform efforts to censor sexual imagery.

Effects and Ethics

The most strident voices of objection to the media proliferation of sex have one common assumption, which is that the media have a profound effect on behaviour. Each new medium has been subject to a similar tirade: newspapers, the music hall, cartoons, photography, film, radio, pop music, television, video, computer games and the Internet.

The beginnings of public discussions of sexuality came out of the study of sex within the sciences in the early twentieth century. Sex became a site of concern in relation to health and social wellbeing through the pioneering studies of Sigmund Freud, Havelock Ellis, Alfred Kinsey and Marie Stopes. But these discussions were respectable publicly only through their association with knowledge institutions and even then Stopes's books on sexual relations were 'sufficiently controversial to be denounced as pornography' (McNair 1996: 10) – sex as entertainment remained largely private, illegal or at least illicit, but increasingly profitable.

The debate over effects has grown steadily since the 1960s, impelled by the growth of the media, sexual freedom and increased spending power. In Britain, the first significant marker of substantial change was the liberalising 1959 Obscene Publications Act that lifted the ban on a range of texts on the premise that they were art not pornography. Soon 'popular culture became sexualised to an unprecedented extent' (McNair 1996: 11) in response to the freed-up marketplace and growing consumer demand. Television in particular took sexual imagery off the bookshelves and backstreet cinemas and into people's homes.

From the 1970s, feminism presented significant challenges to traditional sexual relationships and practices, expanding definitions and practices. In 1979, the Home Office Committee on Obscenity and Film Censorship further liberalised controls on sexual material. The 1980s highlighted gay sexuality, initially as a challenge to heterosexual norms and then in relation to AIDS and safe sex, and then in the late 1980s and 1990s, issues of children and sexuality featured high on the moral and media agenda. For each shift media critics identified a range of concerns over the effects of publicising 'deviant' practices as in the representation of promiscuity, depiction of rape, celebration of homosexuality and eroticisation of children. Two clear groupings, radical feminists and the moral right, emerged as being in favour of controls on sex in the media, though for very different reasons.

Others disagreed. Liberal feminists viewed sexual imagery as needing reform to cater for women's taste and sexuality not as something requiring censorship (Segal 1994). Marxist feminists saw little point in trying to change a product in a marketplace dominated by the interests of patriarchy and capital without addressing the power structure supporting it, but many felt any censorship would support the power of the state and chose a liberal view. Others felt an assault on patriarchy might help destabilise the power hierarchy and so aligned with the radical group.

The radical view focused on patriarchy and argued that male sexuality is intrinsically oppressive of women, with pornography the symbolic expression of male sexual violence. Such symbolism is seen as culturally representing as normal, women as subordinate to men, so bolstering up real gender inequalities. This view extends the definition of pornography to include any imagery that can be interpreted as degrading, commodifying, objectifying and injuring women or that associates women's pain with pleasure or dehumanises women in any way. Dworkin (1991) viewed pornography as any medium that uses sex to depict male power over women and called for censorship.

Equally censorious on the grounds of effects but for different reasons were and are the moral conservatives. During the 1980s this group was epitomised by Mary Whitehouse and Lord Longford, who argued that the right place for sex was between married couples for the purposes of reproducing a family. The view was Victorian and Judeo-Christian and the assumption was that depictions of sex in any other context than marital was likely to badly affect family values specifically and the moral order more generally. Ironically, the moral right and radical feminists found themselves interpreting the messages of pornography completely differently – the former saw a threat to the patriarchal family and the latter saw the production of patriarchal power – and yet both groups came to the same conclusion to use the law to prevent its circulation. In a sense their differences of opinion about the meaning of pornography illustrated precisely the impossibility of any universally interpreted meaning and associated effect.

The Conservative Party Manifesto for 1992 claimed 'we have the toughest anti-pornography laws in Europe and we intend to keep it that way'. Their alignment, it might be unnecessary to add, was with the moral right not the radical feminists, and it resulted from decades of media effects research that was broadly inconclusive. In 1989 an all-party group of MPs requested a review of the research into the effects of pornography because of concerns over the prolif- eration of video material, telephone sex lines and cable or satellite

TV sex like *Red Hot Dutch*. These were matched against an apparent rise in the reported numbers of rapes and incidences of domestic violence and child abuse with the assumption of a causal relationship. Yet, in a Channel 4 programme about the review academics Howitt and Cumberbatch, who undertook the review, of the relevant research, found little evidence to support such a theory. Their conclusion was that the 'evidence was not clear cut and was any way based on the results of laboratory experiments which were not reflected in the field' (*Dispatches* Channel 4 3.11.92). Nonetheless the documentary also featured radical feminist Catherine Itzen who claimed that 'pornography conditions male arousal to violence towards women'; a report on the US Attorney General's Commission on Pornography 1986, which claimed evidence that sexual violence did stimulate aggression; comments by convicted paedophiles that they used porn to 'warm up' child victims; and an interview with a woman who claimed to have been forced as a child to participate in pornographic film-making and blamed the pornography market for her experience. The programme therefore represented a model of pornography that linked sex to violence and/or to children in a harm model, despite the Howitt and Cumberbatch academic findings that Chris Patten MP accepted.

The only novel part of the programme was also misrepresented to appear to support those associations. Katherine Mahoney talked of the Canadian Supreme Court's decision to ban pornography that depicted torture, abuse or degradation not on the grounds of effect but on the grounds of prejudicial representations of women in an egalitarian, multi-cultural and democratic society. This decision is much the same as the one that led to the banning of racist material under the 1986 Public Order Act (see Chapter 2) but there has been no argument that I know of simply saying that regardless of effect, misogynistic representations are not ethical in a democracy. Perhaps because such a ban would leave in place a whole array of texts depicting pleasurable, consensual, legal sex that would be unacceptable to the moral right whose authority continues to dominate our culture, sexual practices and policies.

The effect of the angst and moral panic over pornography that drifted through the Conservative period was constantly to conflate sex with violence – partly because this was the only arena where any kind of effect had been arguable. Constantly reiterated, this redefined all pornography as about violent sex, making it more difficult for the liberal view, in any sense, to argue in its favour. Most recently that definition has been shifted again as work on violence and effects has also failed to deliver the evidence (Barker and Petley 1997). Now definitions increasingly link sex not just to violence but to children and the paedophile has been made the bogey man of our age – the dangerous stranger who lures away children with sweets and promises.

Comment

The effort to control and contain forms of sexuality, and the representation of those forms that are anti-pathetic to traditional marriage and family – prostitution, promiscuity, homosexuality, sexual experiment for pleasure – was commensurate with the political agenda of the Conservatives during the Thatcher/Major years. A very British model of family was invoked as a motif of continuity at a time of profound social change. The deconstruction of the welfare state and dismantling of major working-class communities impelled people back within their own homes and increased their dependence on family. The family, the centre of middle-class life for a century, had to be presented as desirable enough to compensate for other losses amongst social groups more used to work and community cohesion and identity. The reduced role of organised religion in Britain also had left something of a moral void, so simply preaching Christian family values from pulpits and in educational leaflets was never going to reach the masses the way it had during the previous drive to family in the Victorian period.

Clear ideological assaults towards family were the push to normalise home-ownership (see Chapter 5), which gave people a purported material stake in family life, and fear of crime, especially sexual crime against women and children, which gave people an illusion of safety in the home and family. However, describing a violent society required careful handling to deflect blame from the state, which is, after all, responsible for law and order and Margaret Thatcher had been elected on a law and order mandate. The Conservatives and their electorate, the moral right, therefore had understandable reasons for blaming the media for sex crime and violence – despite the problems of definition and effects. They were also quick to provide the solution: control the media and support the traditional family and its values, 'for the stability of the family is a condition for social order' (Thatcher 1995: 630).

> Conservative forces have mobilised, consistently, for battle against abortion, against homosexuality, against divorce, against sex education, against 'pornography', in short against any change that would promote women's or gay men's sexual autonomy by transforming the order of gender. They have been particularly active in Britain since the mid eighties. (Segal 1994: 311–12)

And the chosen site for action was the mass media.

Social psychological theory for the deflection of blame softens slightly the image of conspiratorial plotting in smoke-filled rooms, though the Conservatives did have their think tanks such as the Adam Smith Institute working on social issues. The deep psychological need to explain crisis in a way that is self-exonerating has been well documented (Eiser 1978; Husband 1984). The poverty, unemployment, greed, interventionist policing and individualism of the 1980s were all part of the strategy of reconstruction with which Conservatives identified and benefited. A scapegoat was needed, and the rapid growth and popularity of both broadcast and other media forms, alongside a history of popular and political concerns with effects traceable back to the Frankfurt school's work on propaganda in the 1930s, presented an ideal solution.

Sex and violence characterised much popular fictional media output, and the news values that make factual events newsworthy, so it was a slight shift to blame the media for the 'real' existence of sex and violence, and to present censorship and traditional family values (the antithesis of pornography) as solutions to the moral crisis responsible for crime.

The impetus diverted attention from real issues to represented ones and from economic problems to moral ones. Petley pointed out the 'us and them' attitude informing calls to censor the media. First was the simple 'we are right and they are wrong' perspective, which shaped the Reithian view that the BBC should trickle down culture to the masses; second was a model of the mass audience as more vulnerable to suggestion than the educated elite; and third was a:

> Thread of class dislike and fear ... No one should be in the least surprised therefore, given the prevalence of such attitudes that the

prospect of unregulated, uncensored videos being freely available to the British public at the start of the 1980s was greeted with such horror and dismay from certain quarters, and that draconian censorship was soon imposed. (Petley 1997: 93)

The implications of this focus on family and media were profound and are ongoing.

8
News Cultures

From 1979 to 1997 Britain was governed by the Conservative Party, led by Margaret Thatcher for the first thirteen years and John Major for the last five. During that period, the broad social arenas of class, race and gender were frequently the foci for political and cultural interventions. The 1980s witnessed the cultural construction of ethnic and working class politics as criminal (or terrorist) and the 1990s shored up the traditional moral order in the area of sexual politics. This book has attempted to relate news about crime and deviance to the discursive shifts generated by Thatcherism informing consensus, centralisation and conservatism in Britain at the millennium.

The construction of news simultaneously constructs for audiences a framework of interpretation as it presents the 'facts'. Once presented in the terms of discourses of deviancy, social practices readily achieve the values commensurate with criminal justice – innocent and guilty, good and evil, sane and mad – making any other accounting paradigm difficult. Crime news is about moments of immediate crisis, extreme conflict and resolution; its hold on the news media contains major conditions such as poverty, racism and patriarchy within those parameters. Consequently, because they were reported in the crime genre of journalism, many endemic, fundamental and profound social issues were rendered either invisible or inconsequential in popular, public discourses at the end of the twentieth century.

Political messages were not merely generated directly by the government via the mass media in a neat propagandist way – in fact Fairclough pointed out that the genre of political discourse does not fit well with media genres – 'a source of constant difficulty and tension for politicians' (1995: 184). Rather, the match between news values, the new political discourses and cultural values was good enough for meanings appropriate to the Conservative agenda to be represented within a range of news topics reported as crime and deviance. In retrospect it is possible to identify a mutuality in terms of practices, values and meanings within the power elite in the UK in the late twentieth century that informed a symbiosis of media and state in producing a publicity of control (Chibnall 1977; Erickson *et al.* 1987) through the medium of conflict journalism.

Reportage

News-making is the business of journalism. Journalists are narrators, they relate stories. Simply, the etymology of 'story' can be linked to history and the role of journalists is often described as writing the first draft of history. Stories may well relate to facts or fictions and there is a curiosity in the way that a word so often used by children to describe a lie also describes a journalistic article. The curiosity is of course that in everyday use a story often has connotations of embellishment, gossip and aggrandisement of the facts, yet:

> The journalist takes a different view. He or she collects facts, reports them objectively, and the newspaper presents them fairly and without bias, in language which is designed to be unambiguous, undistorting and agreeable to readers. This professional ethos is common to all news media, Press, radio and television and it is certainly what any journalist claims in any general statement on the matter. (Fowler 1991: 1)

So journalists represent events for audiences, and most would claim to try to do so objectively and truthfully in line with the ethical guidelines of their profession, their codes of practice. However, journalism is a very specific form of communication, because unlike interpersonal communication it depends on selection of information. In Herman and Chomsky's (1988) terms it filters events, reducing the 'cacophony of information flows' (Stevenson 1995: 157 on Baudrillard) in order to construct a manageable quota of news. News is not the first draft of history but a chosen slice of history. The selection of stories is not arbitrary but highly systemised and conventionalised by conditions external to the story, as well as integral. Audiences do not/cannot access all the news, there is only the news that journalists present to us. Macro factors such as money and power place a set of external filters (Herman and Chomsky 1988) on events, but external controls may also be pragmatic constituents such as time, cost, expertise, publication space and also news agenda and access (Dearing and Rogers 1996). News is therefore highly structured not only by non-textual motives but also by narrative motifs.

Many of the attributes of news values are paralleled/replicated in models of fictional narrative form (Propp 1968). In texts there are narrative devices 'used to convey information to readers, either directly or indirectly' (Berger 1997: 44); in news values there are techniques that inform the selection and representation of events in texts. It is also worth noting that for Berger much of the process of writing narrative is unconscious functionality, 'often writers can't explain why they used this word rather than that one' (1997: 4).

News-making is not only highly structured by narrative form but also within economic, political, social and cultural boundaries. This book has attempted to focus more on the cultural because it has tended to be least considered in work on the factual media (though it is often foregrounded in fictional media research) and yet it is the cultural product of the media that is the most prolific source of evidence of the political, economic and social context. Journalists produce cultural records in language and claim objectivity but language itself is not value free. Words, sentences, narratives are laden with inferences prompting meaning; inferences that can work alongside or rather under cover of the formal text. Meanings are vehicled by form but 'they may be substantially independent of linguistic units they may indeed coincide ... but occasionally not systematically' (Barthes 1977: 91).

Most journalists are not reflexive about the process of selecting and representing news. It is simply the art and craft of their work. Their claim to independence, objectivity and impartiality is a necessary delusion of a profession that justifiably imagines itself to be prey to propagandists, spin-doctors and image-makers. But objectivity is a dangerous delusion, which supports a mythic communication ideal that sustains journalism as disinterested when in fact: 'Journalism, regardless of the integrity of individual journalists and editors, is always a selective, partial account of a reality, which can never be known in its entirety by anyone' (McNair 1994: 34).

But it is not a partial selection made by outsiders with a panoramic purview but by insiders shaped by specific cultural places, identities and experiences. Practically, journalists share the same concepts and values as their audiences; they are audiences too. The relationship between author and reader/viewer/listener is reciprocal and symbiotic: an implicit agreement about what matters based on convention, interdependence and repetition rather than on any secret knowledge conferred only on a preferred few. 'The categories by which we make sense of our world in consciousness are culturally

specific' and so 'news and journalism, in short, are social constructions' (McNair 1994: 33).

British News at the End of the Twentieth Century[1]

News is culture and during Thatcherism, conservatism – loaded with
national heritage and moral fable – was the old cultural mainstream
that underpinned the new agenda of enterprise and individualism.
In 1997, Franklin argued that British journalism, in its quest for
profit, had largely abandoned its ideals for newszak and infotainment. Ian Jack is a rarity – a journalist willing to acknowledge and
comment on this shift:

> Today a spectre haunts the editorial floor – the spectre of the
> reader's boredom, the viewer's lassitude. If customers are to stay
> with the product, they need or are thought to need, a diet of
> surprise, pace, cuts-to-the-chase, playfulness, provocation, drama,
> 'human interest' ... One effect has been to demote 'straight'
> reporting, the kind which relies on accurate information for its
> value and interest. (Ian Jack in the *Guardian* 8.8.98)

This can be partly explained by the structural constraints and
values applicable to journalism as professional practice but also
relates to broader cultural sensibilities and developments. First, the
deep resonance of particular narrative forms, metaphor and myth
and second, the exponential growth of the mass media and
concurrent collapse of boundaries between media products, both of
which relate to technology. Boundaries between fact and fiction,
newspaper and cyber-space are dissolving, not fragmenting in the
post-modern but leaking and penetrating. The collapse of old
structures was evident throughout the 1980s from industrialisation
via the welfare state to the Berlin Wall. The emergent new order
claimed to be free of history, master-narratives and even society
itself, which was deemed by Thatcher to be just a collection of
individuals.

The power of Thatcherism was its potential to promote the
freedom of the individual though a persuasive appeal to the popular
consumer whilst maintaining an 'authoritarian commitment to
strengthening the state in certain respects (defence; law and order;
control over money supply; control over trades unions)' (Fairclough

1989: 177). Twin discourses dominated the period: conspicuous consumption and display and traditional Britishness and morality. These were evidence of the government's desperate need to forge a way forward in the era of economic collapse, signalled by the end of industrial power, and the need to promote the populist back-to-basics conservatism, which was the source of its electoral strength.

Late twentieth-century Britain was certainly depicted in the news as experiencing considerable turmoil; however, as I hope this book shows, the reporting of that turmoil systematically offered symbolic resolutions conducive to the interests of dominance (but not through the direct use of political rhetoric) particularly in relation to conservative morality, which characterised Thatcherism and provided a familiar context into which to interject a new right politics. The construction of a crime model of cultural difference facilitated the call to consensus around conservatism by creating a climate of anxiety. To combine Williams and Wordsworth the structure of popular feeling during the Thatcher/Major years was the result of a ministry of fear. News narratives in late twentieth-century Britain provided a cultural context within which black politics, trades unionism, working-class leisure, rebellious youth, gay sexuality and feminism could be constructed as generally deviant, disturbing and dangerous. The resolution was implicitly familial, patriarchal, white, middle class and heterosexual – politically conservative in a context where Conservative politics were radical.

Sex and Violence

In contemporary Britain, sex and violence are perhaps the most commonly repeated, the most familiar, accounting genres or paradigms. For the audience this textual familiarity offers recognition leading to cognition and then to re-presentation for a further audience.[2] Conflict makes news. If there is little real conflict then conflict metaphors are used to exaggerate the struggle and define the disparate positions.[3]

Conflict delivers news values. It is dramatic and unusual but part of a continuum of knowledge about our 'violent society', so understood as negative and illegitimate. Few of us experience violence but we know it is bad, we feel at risk and because it is rare, we are curious about it. We also have a fund of violence references to bring to bear on any new instance because our culture is so steeped in conflict.

Conflict also provides journalists with the context to demonstrate their professional commitment to objectivity in that it always involves more than one point of view or set of practices. Two sides or more of a conflict story should be told or at least appear to be told. Working through differences offers much potential for story-telling as journalists label up the various components as villains and heroes, lost and found, good and evil. Some conflict news offers immediate resolution; other news runs as a serial – always deferring the happy ending to tomorrow's edition, or next week's or next year, but hinting at and anticipating its arrival so we buy tomorrow's paper.

Sexuality adds piquancy to news because it allows journalists and audiences to peek behind the bedroom door – firmly closed by the Victorians but creating in the closure a legacy of prurience and repression that nurtures a continuing fascination with the taboo. That fascination is played on in advertising – sex sells but in doing so it tells us we are not sexy until we buy that product – our sexual identities are sold to us but always deferred to the next purchase.

For journalists 'deviant' sex stories satisfy news values and offer audiences, largely deprived of access to representations of a hugely constitutive part of themselves, a glimpse of the forbidden. Sex is secret so journalists can also draw on their investigative identity to 'expose' the truth of sexual lives. Prurience is legitimated in the public interest. When sexual deviance becomes criminal or violent it is doubly news valuable as the personal, secret and illicit gains drama, rarity and negativity. Sex'n'violence allows for the mobilisation of all the old morality plays in the media and we can be reassured of our normality through dire warnings of what happens to those who stray from the straight and narrow path. Curiosity is served but, in resolution, Hall's consensual calm is restored.

For Thatcherism here were discourses – sex and violence – that in tandem could excite conspicuous consumption and centralise the individual sexual subject (rather different from the politics, citizenship and the public sphere of the nineteenth-century radical press) whilst simultaneously restoring traditional family values. Sex sells everywhere and anything whilst crime and deviance provide a stage for moral diatribe and the legitimacy of state control. Yet, because such narratives and myths appear to be common-sense truths they fit with audience expectations – so their origins and roles tend to be unquestioned.

Journalists buy into these discourses just as audiences do because they are our means of identifying ourselves in terms of history and community. The media does not create but merely recycles representations. The process of generating them, rendering them conventional, recording them and conserving them is lost. That process is conditioned by power. Journalists don't generate new ideas but recycle existing expressions, which are normally already steeped in the interests and values of dominance. This happens because the exercise of power is necessary to make meanings conventional (Foucault's 1979 normalisation process), the powerful have greater access to the knowledge of recording (for Derrida 1968 writing is violence) and those with power have the authority to confer legitimacy, reverence and conservation (Williams's 1961 selective tradition).

Contemporary models of power emphasise not just its class-based/economic authority but other dominant norms such as heterosexuality, whiteness, patriarchy and maturity. Powerful subjects may be multiplicitly empowered, subordinate subjects variously disenfranchised – and power itself may be greater or lesser depending on contexts. Our subjectivity is a complex integration of identifying aspects of the self, with aspects foregrounded depending on context despite the fact that each of us appears as recognisable physiological forms.

Texts are similar. Language appears as a familiar known form but meaning is more nebulous. Overt dominant meanings may also disguise powerful other stories, as in the case of news about 'intimate killing' in Chapter 6, or promote one set of interpretations to the exclusion of others, as in the news about the tunnelers discussed in Chapter 4. A text may appear at the top level to be telling one story whilst also working ideologically at another. The difficulty is in demonstrating the process rather than merely theorising it and doing so in a way that offers evidence of the media's symbolic significance.

Media, Meaning, Method

It seems to me that media theories which claim that audiences are told what to think, or even simply what to think about, are no longer adequate or viable in increasingly (in form and message) mass-mediated societies of culturally diverse, literate and educated audiences. Rather, I think the news media offer audiences ways of thinking: 'ways of seeing' (Berger 1973) the world.

The analysis of text reveals the evidence of that, linking the social, the cultural and the individual in a way that 'effects' work on audience or political economy approaches to institutions cannot. Moreover, in an increasingly complex world of global audiences, multiplying media products and international communications conglomerates text is also mappable, empirical evidence albeit demandingly complex for the analyst in both form and interpretation. Even single words have meaning/s according to their place in classes of like terms (paradigmatic), and meanings according to their place in sentences (syntagmatic). Work has shown that familiar patterns of syntax[4] – like transactivity and relationality – relate closely to psychological theories of attribution and association (Barthes 1957, 1977; Eiser 1978). In *Image, Music, Text*, Barthes offered the argument that 'without wanting to strain the phylogenetic hypothesis, it may be significant that it is at the same moment that the little human "invents" at once sentence, narrative and the Oedipus' (1977: 124). Barthes saw the relationship between language, knowledge and subjectivity as operating:

> At a higher level than the language of the linguists. Discourse has its units, its rules, its grammar: beyond the sentence and though consisting solely of sentences, it must naturally form the object of a second linguistics. (1977: 83)

Similarly, Levi-Strauss (1958) claimed that the same logical patterns operate in myth as in science and, like science, myths function as explanations, often for a custom or tradition. For Levi-Strauss the repetition, diachronic and synchronic, of myth provides a cognitive/cultural framework for interpreting the world – knowledge. This is reinforced by its structuring in narratives, which Propp (1968) demonstrates are systems, drawing from a pool of frequently present constituents (villain-hero-lack-search-struggle-resolution-happiness) organised into a logical story. News contains these familiar and formal elements.

News matters because it purports to tell us the truth about the world beyond our immediate experience. Crime matters because it generates the moral boundaries within which state and subject are oriented – it marks the normal from the deviant. The state requires popular cultural authority to legislate and the populace learns most about real crime in their community from the news. This book brings together those three aspects – news, crime and culture – in order to explore their relationship to and role within the nation state during 18 years of Conservative government.

Part of that process necessarily involved exploring methods with which to elicit meanings. Meanings that I theorised would frequently, in the conflict discourses around crime, violence and deviance, present as commensurate with what Fairclough called the 'Thatcherite political discourse' ... 'a new articulation of elements of traditional conservatism, neo-liberalism and political populism' (Fairclough 1995: 179). In other words, crime would be seen to be resolved by family morality and law and order; individuals not society would be responsible for conflict and 'we' ordinary British people would be bound in to sharing the same common-sense values. As this book has shown: 'The body of crime is continually being reconfigured as feminine, young, black, homosexual, maternal and so on' (Young 1996: 19), reasserting the legitimacy of the masculine, mature, white, heterosexual, paternal, and so on.

Fairclough saw Margaret Thatcher as part of a process of 'the engineering of discursive practices to achieve institutional objectives' (1995: 180). The resultant rhetoric was 'lifeworld': calculated, quotable, memorable and media-focused. It offered a means of making sense of the world that was common sense rather than political and so fitted well with news values, but it was also a middle-class kind of sense that journalists themselves identified with. Add to that mix the Thatcher government's direct interference in the media: the courting of Rupert Murdoch, the banning of IRA 'voices', the breaking of the print unions and the warning to the tabloids that they were 'drinking in the last chance saloon' (Stephenson and Bromley 1998) and it seemed reasonable to anticipate that there would be some evidence of mutuality of interests between the news media and political discourses during the Conservative era, particularly if conflict appeared to threaten the stability or legitimacy of that mutuality.

Criminalised Cultures

In terms of race, the perceived threat of black disorder in the early 1980s was transformed into a perception of black criminality. My analysis showed a consistent use of stereotypes and metaphors that legitimated the institutionalisation of racism in policing and the law. It also showed the way in which the popular press systematically used syntax that allowed for the attribution of blame and that blame for conflict was normally directed at black agents. The legacy for the millennium is arguably a disaffected but disempowered black youth, increasingly criminalised inner-city communities and a continual policing problem.

Retrospecting on the race riots of the early 1980s, Margaret Thatcher commented: 'The rioters were invariably young men whose high animal spirits, usually kept in check by a whole range of social constraints had on these occasions been unleashed to wreak havoc' (1995: 146). Her analysis of the cause was that, 'welfare arrangements encouraged dependence and discouraged a sense of responsibility, and television undermined common moral values'. She offered the same explanation for football hooligans. At the millennium the sport has been spring-cleaned and is now (mostly) a massive global leisure market.

Tessa Keswick recalls that during Thatcherism there were dragons for the Tories to slay – racial tension was certainly one, and disruptive working-class practices in leisure and industry, another. 'The trades unions required two election victories to vanquish' (*Guardian* 20.4.99). The mining communities and cultures were also vanquished – re-emerging, sometimes, as theme parks. The web site for Caphouse Colliery Museum offers the delights of going 'down 140 metres underground with a local miner to experience authentic workings and discover mining conditions from the early days through to the present' and 'The National Coal Mining Museum is a great place for parties ... With plenty of vegetarian choice' (<clanvis.com/coalmine> 11.5.99). At £5.75 for an adult, it is much cheaper than football and you can experience the thrill of an underground treasure hunt – fun for all the family, except perhaps truculent teenagers.

Youth though is very much on the agenda for New Labour in 2000 but not the kind of youth politics demonstrated by the eco-warriors. Instead, Labour proposes lessons in citizenship in the national curriculum and the Political Service Initiative aims to encourage employers to involve staff in workplace democracies. There are some 14 million people aged from 18 to 34 in Britain of whom very few play any active political role. Changing that may be crucial if the Labour government expects the kind of lifespan of the last Conservative government. The bid for youth may require some careful attention to the political implications of criminalising anyone found using recreational drugs, especially if they are the educated sons and daughters of middle-class liberal Britain. Much of the bid for youth is narrowly directed, leaving out 'people on the edge, the ethnic minorities and the young unemployed' (*Guardian* 29.1.98). 'Everyone is desperate to woo the elusive youth – but only those who will get degrees and credit cards' (*Guardian* 17.5.99). Channel 4 is seeking to reconnect with the young audience – sport coverage will be funky and hip; large wealthy audiences produce big advertising contracts. Graduates receive postal promotions, enticing them to banks, stores and credit cards, unrequested through the letterbox. Fine for some, but as Decca Aitkenhead offered, 'God help the ones with bleaker prospects' (*Guardian* 17.5.99) such as the one in twenty who experience homelessness and 'sleep in public toilets, sometimes under motorway bridges – but rarely in the public view' (*Guardian* 22.5.99).

The legacy of the Conservatives' treatment of homelessness for the millennium, not just amongst the young, is that for many there will be 'no room in the inn'. Shelter's web site 'Changing Minds' offers facts about contemporary homelessness:

- In 1997, 32,770 homes were repossessed in the United Kingdom.
- At the end of 1997, nearly 236,900 home-owners were in mortgage arrears of three months or more.
- During 1997, a total of 165,790 households were officially recognised as homeless by local authorities ... Shelter estimates this represents approximately 400,000 people ... It does not include most of the 41,000 people who are living in hostels or squats or the 78,000 couples or lone parents living in shared accommodation who are unable to afford to set up a home of their own. (Shelter 1999 <www.shelter.org.uk>)

Currently the plight of these people seems not to be very newsworthy; nor or perhaps because of that has Blair's Labour government been quick to institute any reforms in the now punitive housing legislation. However, 'people' are agents of ideology; journalists are people too and editors are powerful journalists. Roy Greenslade recently interviewed one such powerful journalist. In spring 1998 Rosie Boycott took over as editor of the *Daily Express*. The paper is now very different from the time when, as Boycott says, it was trying to drive the homeless off the streets. It is struggling for readers and under-funded but it is different and so is its editor. 'Different from her rival editors in manner, philosophy, and most significantly, as we shall see, by virtue of her gender' (*Guardian* 19.4.99). Greenslade's piece is patronising and pessimistic probably because Boycott informs him that 'Fleet Street is a blokes' world. They love waving their willies around. It's scary.' But difference in cognition supports difference, even dissent, in ideas, which alongside editorial power might support other forms of news, alternative selections of events as newsworthy and opinions from another perspective. Such a possibility in journalism matters because:

> How social groups are treated in cultural representation is part and parcel of how they are treated in life ... poverty, harassment, self-hate and discrimination (in housing, jobs, educational opportunity and so on) are shored up and instituted in representation. (Dyer 1993: 1)

In terms of gender roles and representations, misogyny and disparaging images continue but with even less opposition from women themselves than was evident during the 1970s and 1980s. Feminism seemed much clearer before Thatcherism than it does today. Certainly, there have been some scant gains for women that make some of the early battles seem won. 'In the UK now as many women as men are entering the professions such as medicine and law. Girls are doing better than boys at school' (Nicci Gerrard 'What's a Girl to Think' *Guardian* 11.4.99). Yet, a recent survey of university staff found women consistently paid less than their male counterparts.

Contemporary feminists seem more concerned nowadays with celebrating the clitoris (Natalie Angier), arguing against social reforms that support mothers (Eleanor Burkett) or defending 'fuck-me' shoes (Suzanne Moore). Recent research that showed people use media stereotypes to describe violent women as 'assertive go-getters like the career woman in *Working Girl*' and 'bitter and twisted revenge seekers' (*Guardian* 9.4.99) has gone uncriticised despite the links it claims between disparaging media representations and popular attitudes to women. Feminism seems to have been reduced to either a reformist struggle for parity with aggressive, macho, pathetic men or a debate over whether it is acceptable to wear lipstick. In April 1999 most of the newspapers carried discussions about whether women should shave their armpits after actress Julia Roberts appeared 'hairy' at the opening of her film *Notting Hill*.

Meanwhile the increase in sexual offences for 1997/98 'included an 11.1% rise in rape ... the number of recorded rapes has risen by 165% in the last ten years' (HOSB 22/98: 7). In real numbers 6,530 women reported that they had been raped in Britain in that year. Simultaneously, girls are starving and vomiting themselves into waifs[5] similar to the 'supermodels' who 'grace' the catwalks and magazines. Bright young women are 'committing suicide in refractory doses', as Johnson *et al.* explain the effect of anorexia nervosa (1998: 1). So much, at the millennium, for Mary Wollstonecraft's 200-year-old feminist ideal of women having power over themselves.

It is curious that representations that depict women as frail, boyish or pre-pubescent are used consistently in advertising[6] but are damned as child pornography in other arenas. Images of provocative children and women are used to sell products with very little objection from the right[7] (Hartley 1998). Yet, the promotion of straight sex during the Tory years mobilised a popular push towards censorship by labelling pornography as dangerous through specific association of it with sexual violence and child abuse and through the maintenance of the effects paradigm. The focus on child porn is a particularly useful one for the moral right as it was/is the one area of sexual activity that even the most liberal-minded citizen would be unwilling to defend. Once legislation can be secured to ban one type of pornography, the mechanisms are in place for further censorship.

The existence of a strong censorship lobby, despite the lack of substantial evidence of effects, is a considerable and worrying achievement in relation to freedom of expression and cultural and political democracy. The same process has created associations between non-traditional sexualities and moral decay or crime that have legitimated the hardening of regulations over our sexual lives. And by default they have shored up the Victorian model of heterosexual family, preferred by the Conservative Party and moral conservatives.

Perhaps worse than anything though is what has not been done in consequence of the overwhelming focus on represented sex. The site of most sexual and violent crime against women and children, the home and family, has been left unqueried, and the perpetrators of the great majority of those crimes, heterosexual and paternal men who know their victims, have been left unblamed. This despite the fact that male behaviour as a major problem for families was nowhere more evident than within the ranks of Tory MPs themselves, many of whom had two families. Just before the last election, the *Mirror* (3.4.97) announced ironically 'Major's Happy Family' with pictures of eight MPs involved in sex scandals.

The extent of the ideological diversion was made evident to me when I re-read McIntosh's 'Introduction to an issue: family secrets as public drama'. She complained that the media had very rapidly tired of reporting child abuse but was optimistic for work on the family and households within Britain where the problem was centred, because of feminist initiatives at local level. She notes, though, that:

> The wider world of child prostitution, the international traffic in children, sex tourism and child pornography (all coolly yet chillingly, discussed by Judith Ennew 1986) may be numerically smaller, but it provides the context and surely some of the imagery and motivation for domestic sexual abuse. (1988: 13–14)

Now at the millennium this wider world rather than British families is the centre of British concern. The National Criminal Intelligence Centre <www.ncis.co.uk/> tracks paedophile activities on the Net and maintains an intelligence database of sex offenders sanctioned by the Sex Offenders Act 1997, and the newly formed Internet Content Rating Association at <www.internetwatch.org.uk/> invites users to inform them of pornographic sites. Yet, children and women are most at risk at home from men they know. Perhaps at the millennium less academic, legal and policy time and money should be spent blaming the media and debating effects and more should be directed towards improving and empowering the lives of women and children to resist abuse and denigration, and on educating men (and all of us) to be responsible for and manage their sexuality and violence.

News, Criminology and Culture

This failure properly to deal with significant crime whilst criminalising other areas of socio-cultural life and identity like drug use and blackness relates to the chapter on criminological crises that outlined the criticisms and failings that are part of the project of understanding, preventing and containing crime. Crime is not static: what was criminal last year may not be next; what is criminal in the UK may not be in the US; what would be theft for one group of people amounts to creative accountancy for another. What has become clear to me during the writing of this book is that much of what we understand to be crime is simply what the media report as crime news, and that much of what is written in the media represents not universal truth but relative values.

Criminology has been in long-term dispute as to what crime actually is and has increasingly turned to other disciplines in order to try to make sense of the phenomena which underwrites its own. Scientism, androcentricity, middle-classness, maturity, whiteness and heterosexuality have gradually been exposed as the invisible criteria for knowledge legitimacy in the discipline, not least by feminist criminological work. But recognising, problematising and deconstructing those old disciplinary informants (not just within criminology) has raised other issues for epistemology in that post-modern and post-structural approaches, by querying the power-maintaining structural meta-discourses, have theoretically devolved power. Yet, in practice stratifying and often oppressive power is evident everywhere in the ongoing inequalities of our daily experiences – many of which are based on difference/deviance. If determining models of the world were too crude to explain change and contradiction then capillarised cultural relativism is too ephemeral an interpretative tool to 'produce a comprehensive account of contemporary culture and the forces shaping it' (Murdock 1997: 181).

Using crime as a value concept rather than a truth, and as a research tool rather than research goal, helped to bridge that structural/interpretative gap. Analysing the dissemination of different criminalities through the news media at different periods and in different news outlets over a time of some ideological consistency allowed for comprehensiveness in my account of the forces shaping culture. It also meant that although the ideological consistency of conservatism was in many ways a party political discourse, looking for evidence of its impact in another discourse (that is I did not analyse party political news – see Fairclough 1995) revealed a much more complex, subtle and multiplicit generation of meanings and values than straight political rhetoric.

What I found was a range of dominating perspectives – middle-class, white, masculine, heterosexual and mature – that could not have been identified by a theoretical adherence to political economic

determinism. On the other hand, abandoning any notion of ideologically structured discourses in favour of some pluralistic
post-modern model of mediated meanings played out equally
between producer and consumer of texts would require wilfully
ignoring the volume and range of representations of powerful
interests in crime news. That range indicates the need for a much
broader model of power than economic, but a model that remains
nonetheless hierarchical and middle-class – however, that concept of
middle-classness also must shift away from the merely economic
measure to include norms and values around gender, race, sexuality
and family. Politics too needs to be interpreted more broadly than
party ideology – the personal, private and popular are also political.
With such a conceptual review it becomes possible to argue that the
interests and values of conservatism were readily and systematically
supported by the language of crime and conflict news that I analyse
in this book. And that has implications for theorising the media,
crime, politics and culture. Language is evidence, however corrupted,
incomplete and complex and the language of crime news media is
mass-mediated evidence of events that the great majority of any
audience do not personally experience so:

> Crime news may serve as a focus for the articulation of shared
> morality and communal sentiments. A chance not simply to speak
> *to* the community but to speak for the community, against all that
> the criminal outsider represents, to delineate the shape of the
> threat, to advocate a response, to eulogise on conformity to
> established norms and values, and to warn of the consequences
> of deviance. In short, crime news provides a chance for a
> newspaper to appropriate the moral conscience of its readership.
> (Chibnall 1977: x–xi)

Concluding Notes

In Western culture, which pivots more and more around sophisticated, mass-mediated information transmitted to a highly
media-literate audience[8] unlikely to be wholly innocent of the
machinations of the media, I would argue that particular benefits
are gained from media analysis that pays close, systematic attention
to language as opposed to attempting ethnographic work on the
practices of journalists (increasingly plural and/or inaccessible),

theorising the role of media institutions (increasingly diverse and/or impenetrable) or demonstrating effects on audiences (always fraught but increasingly impossible with fractured but global viewers of integrated, cyber-time systems). Language is at least empirical data with a specificity of form. For Fairclough, language is a social barometer in that 'representations, relations and identities are always simultaneously at issue in a text' 1995: 17).

Identifying in any media text choices between available discourses that benefit, legitimate or seek consensus for the ideas and identities of the particular social group/s producing the text makes it reasonable to claim ideological bias. When such analysis links discursive choices to the cultural values (or political and economic values) of already powerful social groups, and presents them in familiar and satisfying narrative forms, then the exercise of power over meaning is made evident. The importance of analysing news in this way is that it can reveal that even in accounts which are not overtly denigratory or exclusive, which may even appear laudatory and pervasive, the interests of the subjects of the accounts may not necessarily be being served. As quoted earlier (p. 27), Chibnall suggested that, 'it is much easier for most readers to reject the open, substantive (factual) content of newspaper accounts than the more latent and implicit interpretative schema in which the content is embedded' (1977: 45).

Like Chibnall I do not believe the news media tells us literally what to think or simply what to think about, but rather how to think. Journalism offers us a method for eliciting knowledge and informing values, similar to that once provided by organised religion. Journalists/priests are increasingly the major providers of moral judgements and ethical guidelines. Du Bois (1986) claimed that discourses gain power when ritualised and rendered mysterious. Most of us read the same paper, listen to the same radio station, watch the same TV news, day in and day out. Few of us have any access to the events being reported or the processes by which the news is made. We can only trust the word of a journalist,[9] with a feel for story, just as once we would have trusted the word of a priest when he urged us to have faith in God (O'Sullivan et al. 1994).

Disputing the news is not a straightforward matter, any more than disputing the church once was, partly because access to contradictory evidence is beyond our experience, partly because authority is intimidating and partly because mass-mediated knowledge is the currency of our culture. Moreover, not only has the instructional ritual remained similar in structure and role but the old religious paradigms of good and evil still underpin the modern media discourses albeit 'represented in a form that post-modern viewers can understand: detective stories, murder mysteries, real-life crime constructions' (Osborne 1995: 36). Post-modern media culture blends fact and fiction seamlessly across time, text and space but the narratives follow familiar patterns – normal is good, deviating from normal is bad. These constituents are evident throughout factual and fictional media. Deviation prompts moral instruction, especially if it threatens the stability of normality. Whereas once the priest would have given a sermon on hell and damnation now a journalist may warn us of the dire consequences of stepping off the straight and narrow path. Their role as guardians and tutors means it is inevitable that journalists should prefer and audiences should seek guidance on issues of morality. So it is no surprise that reports of sexual deviance, crime and violence are popular with both producers and consumers of the media.

Fairclough (1995) notes Bourdieu's stress on the importance of communication between politicians and publics and notes a lack of emphasis on the media in Bourdieu's own accounts of political discourse. Fairclough's own study of mediatised Thatcherite discourse addresses that lack. He argued that the

> [p]ower of political discourse depends on its capacity to constitute and mobilise those social forces that are capable of carrying into reality its promises of a new reality, in its very formulation of this reality. (Fairclough 1995: 182)

I hope that this book has shown something of how that power works by bleeding out of the narrow party-ideological political paradigm to work subversively through Fairclough's 'lifeworld' political discourses of work, community, sex, leisure, family and identity, all represented in news about crime and conflict.

Some 14 million national newspapers are sold daily in the UK (*Guardian* 13.5.98); sex'n'violence sell. Crime is newsworthy, news is representation, representations are culture and our culture is pervaded with crime and resolution in text and context. News texts:

> Provide a familiar discourse, based on common sense and precedent that makes the world plausible. The sense of plausibility provides a structure of reassurance, a tool for acknowledging the familiar and silencing alternatives. (Erickson *et al.* 1991: 357)

Journalists have become entrapped in a cycle of reportage that is a major part of the art and craft of news-making. The logic of the crime and deviance discourses to journalism are their fit with our history of moral narratives and authoritative voices. At a production level our cultural records, fictive and factual, are increasingly blended and borrowed. We have a symbolic history that equips us to produce, interpret and evaluate such stories. Everyday, several times a day, the news is our guidance, our conscience and our redemption; sometimes familiarity should breed contempt or at least criticism because, 'Let's face it: Thatcher's legacy is Blair's Britain' (*Guardian* 20.5.99).

Notes

Chapter 1

1. In May 1994, a BBC2 MORI poll, in the aftermath of the Bulger case, found that over 80 per cent of respondents felt violence amongst youngsters under 16 had increased.

2. There is much research on fear of crime (Gottfredson 1984; Shapland and Vagg 1988) and it frequently indicates women's greater level of fear (Radford 1987; Stanko 1990), which conflicts with the statistics for reported crime produced by the Home Office annually that show men are at greater risk of violence, especially from strangers (see note 13).

3. See notes 5 and 6.

4. Tuchman (1978) and Butcher (1974) are included in Cohen and Young (1973–82) but both articles focus on the lack of representation or stereotyping of women in the media rather than on women as deviant or even not-deviant in comparison with men. The issue of crime as gendered is not engaged.

5. NACRO briefings No. 26,33,91 1989 showed only 1,758 women were in prison in 1987: 387 for violence against the person; 316 women were serving sentences of three years or more.

6. The same reports show a male prison population of 48,507 (40,755 white); 8,731 men were serving sentences of four years or more.

7. See Young (1988) on the coverage of the suffragettes and Wykes (1998) on the West case.

8. See Wilczynski (1995: 175) on infanticide.

9. Interestingly this approach is constant – the Ripper in 1984 and Fred West in 1996 were both deemed deranged through a head injury. In his book on the Wests journalist Howard Sounes (1996) argued that West was changed by a head injury caused by a motorcycling accident – see Wykes (1998).

10. Parallel to the early interventions in gender and crime of writers like Carol Smart was criticism of criminological work on race – central to this was the work of Hall *et al.* (1978). See Chapter 2 for a more detailed account.

11. See Foucault (1967, 1975, 1979, 1980).

12. Jacques Lacan (1976) revised Freudian theory in his own explanation of the development of the individual. He argued that language is the pivot between the unconscious and the conscious, and the means by which children negotiate becoming subjects. For Lacan: 'the unconscious is neither primordial nor instinctual; what it knows about the elementary is no more than the elements of the signifier' (quoted in Harland 1987: 34). The impulse toward meaning derives from desire. Desire for reunification with the mother coincides with sexual drives and this coincidence invests the phallus, real and symbolic, with the power for

resolutions of desire. The sexual subject is developed according to lack of, or fear of, loss of the phallus. The lack felt by the child as it senses its difference and separateness is causal of the acquisition of language and so the subject. As the conscious 'other' is constructed so the dialectic with the unconscious self is more and more conducted through language which positions the 'other' in the social fabric. So, Lacan argued, the unconscious is more and more structured according to language. The conscious subject is a function of language in use.

13. Contrary to popular myth few of us experience crime in any very significant way; very few indeed experience violent crime outside of our own homes. We may well witness, however, many representations of violence, factual and fictional, that bear little resemblance to the 'real' incidence and nature of crime. In consequence, *the fear of crime* (so readily attributed to women) is often a misplaced fear of violence to the person from strangers. In murder cases women are less likely to be killed than men (9 per million per year versus 14 per million for men) but nearly half of women victims are killed by husbands and lovers – only about 10 per cent by strangers; in contrast only 6 per cent of men are killed by spouses and some 37 per cent by strangers (*Guardian* 1.1.90). It is curious that it is women who are advised to take care on the streets.

14. This is not to say that the fictional media are not implicated in the construction of *interests, values, norms and deviancies*, it is only to emphasise that the factual media purport to tell the truth whereas the fictional require the audience to suspend disbelief.

15. It is worth recalling though that before the BBC existed, bawdy titillation and grotesque, morbid detail where the commonplace of Victorian newspapers. Accounts for example of Jack the Ripper in the 1880s were infinitely more salacious than the equivalent accounts of the Yorkshire Ripper in the 1980s.

16. Such claims by media analysts are generally refuted by editors who struggle to provide a facsimile of truth-telling and objectivity. Occasionally such interventions in the news are blindingly clear. In 1998, Rupert Murdoch's *The Times* found the story that Murdoch's publishing company HarperCollins was refusing to publish Chris Patten's book on Hong Kong (lest it damage Murdoch's media interest in China) not worthy of report until lambasted by the remainder of the press for kowtowing to Murdoch's agenda.

17. The bracketed inclusions may help to clarify the original terms used by Galtung and Ruge. Chibnall (1977: 23) offers a clear and simpler model reduced to eight points.

18. This discussion was developed for a chapter I wrote on environmental protest – Wykes (1999).

19. This pair of values may well not figure on any millennial list. Rationality seems to me to be rapidly giving way to emotionality, evidenced by the public outpourings over the death of Princess Diana in August 1997 – worse, reason is increasingly being associated with a kind of unfeeling right-wing elitism leaving the left to wallow in Weber's 'merely felt'.

Chapter 2

1. See Chapter 3 on class conflict and Chapter 4 on riotous youth.
2. For a discussion of Cohen's theory of moral panics and the media, see Chapter 4 on youth.
3. The use of the American context was not only inappropriate to Britain but also a distortion of racial violence in the US. White America remains a violent gun-toting culture most recently epitomised by the shooting of school children by their peers (male) in Littleton, Colorado in 1999, the sixth such shooting in the US since 1997. Liberal efforts to contain gun-ownership and at least to raise the age of gun-ownership to 21 continue to be opposed and within days of the shootings the National Rifle Association held its annual meeting in nearby Denver and reasserted the right to bear guns (*Observer* 6.6.99).
4. The original and full text appeared as Wykes (1999).
5. Pilger dropped out of the *News on Sunday* project as it foundered on lack of collective consensus, pressure to conform to the conventional journalistic processes and practices and the need to generate advertising revenue.
6. Transactive clauses involve actions as in 'the boy threw the ball' where the boy is the noun-agent, threw is an active verb and ball is the recipient of the action or patient.
7. I developed such a value grid to explore gendered violence, which is described in Chapter 6.
8. An example would be the term anorak, which means literally a hooded, waterproof coat but stereotypically refers to someone who is very enthusiastic about computers. The origins of the association are a mystery to me but a student insists it relates to the fact that trainspotters are stereotyped as anti-social people, obsessed with something pointless and boring. They tend to wear anoraks as trainspotting is a cold, wet, outdoor activity, unlike computing in context if arguably similar in content.
9. More material on the Lawrence case is available on-line. Try <www.homeoffice.gov.UK> and <www.guardianunlimited.co.uk>
10. My belief that this is the case has been systematically reinforced by the war in Kosovo in 1999 during which we have been reminded many times that the Albanians are people 'like us' or 'Europeans' or 'professional' people – to the extent that a student remarked that the easiest way for the West to deal with the Balkans would be to rename them Rwanda or East Timor, so they would be 'other' and therefore lesser, making the humanitarian argument for engagement in the war untenable.
11. See table 3.1, Total Arrests by Ethnic Appearance 1996/97 in HMSO (1999).
12. See Appendix 2 in HMSO (1999).
13. See table 2.1, Searches Under the Police and Criminal Evidence Act 1984 in HMSO (1999).
14. See table 4.1, Ethnicity of Homicide Victims by Ethnicity of Principal 1996/97 in HMSO (1999).

Chapter 3

1. Marsh assumed crowds were largely male, at least if they were rowdy. The largely female rowdy crowd – Beatlemania for example – has not as far as I know either been considered troublesome or subjected to study.
2. This project was funded by the ESRC (grant no. G00232311) to study mining communities in the aftermath of the 1984–85 strike. A follow-up study looked at the way communities and individuals coped with the systematic closure of the pits.
3. It is curious that this is barely referred to in Thatcher's (1995) memoirs – perhaps she forgot.
4. Even now football matches between Leeds and Nottingham may include the Leeds fans calling Notts supporters 'scabs'.
5. Police also frequently taunted miners about the enormous levels of overtime and unsociable hours' earnings the strike was allowing them to claim. Some even thanked the miners for striking as it was going to pay for their holiday of a lifetime.
6. Earlier events at Maltby in June had provided a template for controlling whole communities through arrest, isolation and curfew.
7. Critcher pointed out that many of today's familiar issues such as the 'expanded transfer markets, declining attendance and defensive football' (1979: 220) are not new and that change has always been part of the game.
8. It is worth noting that until 1998 when post-Blair the devolution process for Scotland and Wales was well under way, there was a tendency to lump together all football fans overseas as British. In 1998 the use of English and Scottish discriminated between groups.
9. Police organisations claimed to have identified a Mafia-like system in football in *The Policing of Football Hooliganism*, Home Office (1990, 1991)

Chapter 4

1. I visited San Francisco in May 1999 to find the streets of Haight-Ashbury, where the Summer of Love originated, shabby, tawdry, empty and tourist-centred. Grubby shops sold hippy souvenirs whilst homeless people and glazed-eyed youths, with strange dogs, lolled on the benches of the Golden Gate Park. It wasn't much of a legacy from all that promise and protest 35 years ago.
2. Christine Griffin's (1993) *Representations of Youth* is very full and interesting on discourses within which youth is constructed but barely addresses the media, apart from a few paragraphs on youth TV (pp. 196–7).
3. I have not dealt with those here because they have been documented fully and extremely well in Young (1990).
4. This is described and explained in Chapter 1.
5. This is a nickname for the young upper-middle classes who shop and socialise around London's expensive Sloane Square.
6. Liverpool was also held to blame by the *Sun* for the Hillsborough football disaster which killed 96 fans in 1989 – see Chapter 3. Of all British cities

it is perhaps the only one with an utterly distinct set of identifying discourses and stereotypes, often deviant in some way from the 'mainland'.

7. The full analysis of this material is published as Wykes (1999).
8. See note 7.
9. Greenpeace's storming of the Shell oil platform to prevent it being dumped in the North Sea in 1996.

Chapter 5

1. This was the case in Westminster City Council's district. Tory voters were sold their properties at reduced rates as sitting tenants in an act of 'improper and disgraceful gerrymandering' (*Independent on Sunday* 16.1.94). The then Leader of the Council Dame Shirley Porter currently lives in Israel and was technically liable for some £27 million surcharge to cover council money 'lost' in the homes for votes scandal. In May 1999 she was cleared of liability but Westminster Council's district auditor launched an immediate appeal.
2. This project produced an information booklet for Shelter in 1996 – Wykes and Woodcock (1996).
3. Much of this chapter relates to the Leeds research but it is also informed by an ongoing interest in the area. I continue to maintain a cuttings file on housing and homelessness and use the topic to teach students about journalism, discourse and representation.
4. A content analysis of the quality press from 1992 to 1996 showed that homelessness stories peaked in December and dropped sharply during the warmer months. Harvarde K. (1997) 'How the Homeless Are Portrayed by the British Press', BA Journalism dissertation, unpublished.
5. I drew on Pauline Neale's notes about the single homeless cases to describe the 'real' issues as elicited by the Leeds study.
6. Phrases in inverted commas indicate where the housing officer has used the legislative instructions in Section 64 of the Housing Act 1985 to come to a decision.
7. Van Zoonen (1994).
8. Fairclough suggested that 'it is essential for effective citizenship that people should be critically aware of culture, discourse and language, including the discourse and language of the media' (1995: 201).
9. '[W]hat are the media for? ... to reduce morality to the individual level is often to engage in the worst kind of moralism', Stevenson (1997: 62–85)
10. Department of the Environment (1994) 'Access to Local Authority and Housing Association Tenancies; a Consultation paper'.

Chapter 6

1. There were also gendered group activities, most notably the peace camps at Greenham common. I have not dealt with those here because they have been documented fully and extremely well in Young (1990).

2. See the discussion on homeless women in Chapter 5, in particular the news focus on 'single mothers' in the early 1990s when the real evidence was that women were left homeless through male violence and/or dysfunction.

3. See Chapter 5 for an example of this. Housing Officers seemed able to deal with their clients without being unduly influenced by the newspapers' descriptions of the homeless as beggars, scroungers and teenage mothers.

4. In *Metaphors We Live* (1980) Lakoff and Johnson go so far as to suggest that conflict is our dominant cultural metaphor, effectively underwriting all our institutions and relations. This seems an over-claim until they suggest how different our experiences and understandings might be if the dominant sense-making metaphor was dance.

5. Child abuse is discussed in Chapter 7 on sex under the section on family because most of it takes place within families and the perpetrator is usually the father or surrogate father.

6. A full account of the interpretative work on these articles is in Wykes (1995a). An early and partial account, with some incomplete quantification from a pilot analysis, appeared in Wykes (1995b).

7. There are only 21 instead of the ideal 24. I was unable to trace a tabloid article on the McGrail case (and the quality papers only wrote very brief pieces) nor was the Sara Thornton appeal covered by the right-wing popular press. The articles provide 10,200 words of widely disseminated, cultural documentation about white, comfortably-off men and women who killed 'affectional' partners. There are 9 articles from the popular press, 12 from the quality press, 11 from left-wing newspapers, 10 from right-wing, 11 accounts of female cases and 10 of male cases.

8. In componential analysis, Leech (1981) suggested that female is understood as plus adult minus male, girl is minus male and minus adult. It is not insignificant that the measurement norms/positives tend to correspond to the dominant group identity of linguistic scientists, much as Lacanian phallocentricity corresponds to the dominant group identity of psychoanalysts.

9. See Wykes (1998 and 1999).

10. The news about Green youth is discussed in Chapter 4.

Chapter 7

1. Foucault's later views moved from concern with social institutions and language to a 'post-structural' focus on specific, local and variable realisations of us as social subjects. Feminists, critical of Foucault, argued that such theory allowed for the hypothetical deconstruction of oppressive power and celebration of equal human potential without recognising the evidence of real stratification, systematically reproduced in language, and without offering any means of real equal reconstruction. His celebration of difference and the power of micro-politics, whilst enthusing and legitimating individual and small out-group beliefs and practices, supported parochial pleasures and identities rather than

providing an 'attack upon the central forms of capitalist exploitation and repression' (Harvey 1989: 46).

2. This is discussed in Chapter 6 on journalism, justice, gender and violence.

3. I owe thanks for an excellent essay discussion of the discursive role of Section 28 to Paul Curry, MPhil student at Cambridge's Institute of Criminology in 1996.

4. No such debates were or are held about lesbianism where Queen Victoria's alleged refusal to believe it exists seems to have protected gay women from much of the harsh legislation applied to men or maybe it is simply evidence of how little women's activities are foregrounded in the public sphere. Lesbianism does become an issue for the media and state when the possibility of men-free families is raised.

5. See the discussion on homelessness in Chapter 5 that reveals how few single mums were/are not married, and on delinquent youth in Chapter 4.

6. The classic Freudian Oedipal complex (Freud 1912).

7. In Sheffield, Jo Adams tries to do just this on the notorious Manor Estate with her Girl Power training pack developed at the Sheffield Centre for HIV and Sexual Health (*Guardian* 17.5.99).

Chapter 8

1. Some of the ideas in this chapter were presented as a conference paper (1998) 'Crime news as cultural narrative: journalism and conservatism in late 20th century Britain' at the Sixth Conference of the International Society for the Study of European Ideas, 16–21 August 1998, Haifa, Israel.

2. Erickson *et al.* (1991) showed in work in the United States that 'deviance' stories occupy between 45.3 per cent and 71.5 per cent of all broadcast and print news.

3. See Lakoff and Johnson (1980) who suggested that conflict is our dominant cultural metaphor, also Ricoeur (1978).

4. Other work has shown that the press prefers transactive clauses and an attributive style (Wykes 1995a and b; Trew 1979) predisposing the interpretation of agency and blame, and a preference for short words and simple sentences enabling comprehension.

5. In Britain, recent research on 37,500 school children, by Dr David Regis in the Exeter School's Health Education Unit, found 60 per cent of 14- and 15-year-olds felt overweight even though they were actually average and below weight. Dr Regis commented, 'more effort was needed to stop teenage girls becoming obsessed with trying to emulate waif-like models' (*Daily Mail* 27.10.98).

6. The most well-known example is the advertisement for Calvin Klein underwear and in 1993 *Harpers and Queen* offered a fashion spread of 'schoolgirls' in knickers and vests that was subtitled 'kittenish waifs'.

7. Except when those images are associated with drugs as in the fashion for 'heroin chic' which drew President Clinton's attention and condemnation (*New York Times* 21.5.97).

8. Obviously there are major issues around audience not dealt with in this chapter. Fairclough (1995) agrees that mediated discourse 'can usefully be regarded as a domain of cultural hegemony' but that 'consumption/reception of media discourse raises a number of issues' (pp. 198–9). He suggests that 'it is essential for effective citizenship that people should be critically aware of culture, discourse and language, including the discourse and language of the media' (p. 201). I agree and would argue that this would be a more useful way forward for academics as analysts and teachers, rather than continuing to pursue the mythical holy grail of effects.

9. Carey (1987) argued that a cultural tendency to replace religion with journalism explained why the latter was so profoundly taken up with the subject of death, in its various forms, of murder, massacre, accident, natural catastrophe and warfare.

Appendix

Table 1: Selected Cases and Accounts

1	Sains1dm Pamela Sainsbury popular 14.12.91 left – *Daily Mirror*
2	Perry2dt John Perry quality 27.11.91 right – *Daily Telegraph*
3	Sains3t Pamela Sainsbury quality 14.12.91 right – *Times*
4	Tann4dm John Tanner popular 3.12.91 left – *Daily Mirror*
5	Calv5g Linda Calvey quality 13.11.91 left – *Guardian*
6	Mcg6dt Joseph Mcgrail quality 1.8.91 right – *Daily Telegraph*
7	Calv7sun Linda Calvey popular 13.11.91 right – *Sun*
8	Perry8in John Perry quality 27.11.91 left – *Independent*
9	Tann9tm John Tanner quality 6.12.91 right – *Times*
10	Tann10sun John Tanner popular 6.12.91 right – *Sun*
11	Tho11gdn Sara Thornton quality 30.7.91 left – *Guardian*
12	Tho12dm Sara Thornton popular 14.8.91 left – *Daily Mirror*
13	Tann13gdn John Tanner quality 6.12.91 left – *Guardian*
14	Mcg14gdn Joseph Mcgrail quality 1.8.91 left – *Guardian*
15	Calv5dm Linda Calvey popular 13.11.91 left – *Daily Mirror*
16	Perry16sun John Perry popular 22.11.91 right – *Sun*
17	Sains17sun Pamela popular 14.12.91 Sainsbury right – *Sun*
18	Perry18dm John Perry popular 22.11.91 left – *Daily Mirror*
19	Tho19dt Sara Thornton quality 30.7.91 right – *Daily Telegraph*
20	Sains20gdn Pamela Sainsbury quality 14.12.91 left – *Guardian*
21	Calv21t Linda Calvey quality 13.11.91 right – *Times*

Note: The abbreviations as in Sains1dm are my labels for the articles e.g. Sainsbury 1 *Daily Mirror*.

Table 2: Exemplars of Value Assessment Process

Clause	Agent	Process	Value Label	Patient
Ta	xxxx (court)	(give) mercy	l +	killer
Ta	who (killer)	bit back	fp –	(xxxx) husband
Ta	Cruel husband	treated	mv –	Her like a dog
Ta	she	strangled	fp –	xxxx (madman)
Ta	xxxx (she)	butchered	fp –	madman
Ta	Blonde Pam	sawed	fp –	body

Key: Ta = transactive/active voice   mp = male perpetrator
Tp = transactive/passive voice   mv = male victim
fp = female perpetrator   fv = female victim
l = law   m = medicine
? = other   xxxx = term in other clause
+ = positive   – = negative

Table 3: Gender Evaluation Process

Male	Value	Female	Value
cruel husband	sex –	killer	crim –
madman	psych –	dog	sex –
Burly strongman	sex +	Wife Pamela battered	sex –
madman	psych –	dog	sex –
Sainsbury slept	sex +	she kept head at home	psych –
Fit runner	sex +	she pleaded diminished responsibility	psych –
		intelligent wife	sex +

Key: sex = sexual discourse   soc = social discourse   + = positive
        crim = legal discourse   psych = psychological discourse   – = negative

Note: Interpretations of value depended heavily on cultural knowledge, for example that
the term 'dog' is not just non-human but is also a derogatory slang term for a woman.

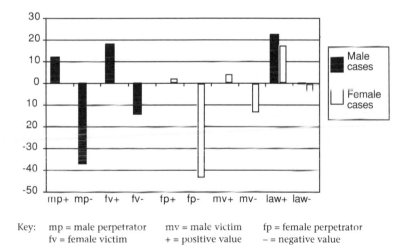

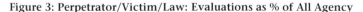

Key: mp = male perpetrator   mv = male victim   fp = female perpetrator
        fv = female victim   + = positive value   – = negative value

Figure 3: Perpetrator/Victim/Law: Evaluations as % of All Agency

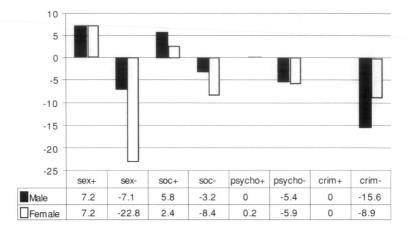

	sex+	sex-	soc+	soc-	psycho+	psycho-	crim+	crim-
■Male	7.2	-7.1	5.8	-3.2	0	-5.4	0	-15.6
☐Female	7.2	-22.8	2.4	-8.4	0.2	-5.9	0	-8.9

Figure 4: Explanation Type and Value: Gendered Discourses

Bibliography

Adler, F. (1975) *Sisters in Crime: The Rise of the New Female Criminal*, New York, McGraw Hill.

Adler, F. ed. (1981) *The Incidence of Female Criminality in the Contemporary World*, New York, New York University Press.

Allen, H. (1987) *Justice Unbalanced*, Milton Keynes, Open University Press.

Althusser, L. (1971) 'Ideology and state apparatus' in Storey, J. ed. (1994) *Cultural Theory and Popular Culture*, Hemel Hempstead, Harvester Wheatsheaf.

Althusser, L. (1977) 'Marxism and humanism' in *For Marx*, London, Verso.

Anderson, A. (1997) *Media, Culture and the Environment*, London, UCL Press.

Anderson, L.B. (1986) 'Evidentials, paths of change and mental maps: typologically irregular assymetries' in Chafe, W. and Nichols, J. eds, *Evidentiality: The Linguistic Coding of Epistemology*, Westport CT, Ablex Publishing.

Armstrong, G. (1998) *Football Hooliganism: Knowing the Score*, New York, Oxford University Press.

Arnold, M. (1869) 'Culture and anarchy' in Storey, J. ed. (1994) *Cultural Theory and Popular Culture*, Hemel Hempstead, Harvester Wheatsheaf.

Bacon, W. and Lansdowne R. (1982) 'Women who kill husbands: the battered wife on trial' in O'Donnell, C. and Craney, J. eds, *Family Violence in Australia*, Cheshire, Longman.

Bailey, R. (1977) *The Homeless and Empty Houses*, Harmondsworth, Penguin.

Barker, M. and Petley, J. eds (1997) *Ill Effects*, London, Routledge.

Barthes, R. (1957) *Mythologies*, London, Paladin.

Barthes, R. (1977) *Image, Music Text*, London, Fontana.

Baudrillard, J. (1983) 'Simulations semiotext' in Belsey, C. and Moore, J. eds (1989) *The Feminist Reader*, London, Macmillan.

Bell, A. and Garrett, P. eds (1998) *Approaches to Media Discourse*, Oxford, Blackwell.

Benedict, H. (1992) *Virgin or Vamp: How the Press Covers Sex Crimes*, New York and Oxford, Oxford University Press.

Bennett, T. ed. (1981a) *Culture, Ideology and Social Process*, Buckingham, Open University Press.

Bennett, T. (1981b) *Popular Culture Themes and Issues*, OU 203, Buckingham, Open University Press.

Berger, A.A. (1997) *Narratives in Popular Culture, Media and Everyday Life*, London, Sage.

Berger, J. (1973) *Ways of Seeing*, Harmondsworth, Penguin.

Booth, A. (1989) *Raising the Roof on Housing Myths*, Leeds, Shelter.

Box, S. (1983) *Power, Crime and Mystification*, London, Tavistock.

Brownmiller, S. (1975) *Against Our Will*, Harmondsworth, Penguin.

Butcher, H. (1974) 'Images of women in the media' in Cohen, S. and Young, J. (1982) *The Manufacture of News: Deviance, Social Problems and the Mass Media*, London, Constable.

Butler, D. and Kavanagh, D. (1992) *The British General Election of 1992*, Basingstoke, Macmillan.

Cain, M. (1990) 'Towards transgression: new directions in feminist criminology' in *International Journal of Sociology of Law*, 18 (1).

Cameron, D. (1985) *Feminism and Linguistic Theory*, Basingstoke, Macmillan.

Cameron, D. ed. (1990) *The Feminist Critique of Language*, London, Routledge.

Cameron, D. and Fraser E. (1987) *The Lust to Kill*, Cambridge, Polity Press.

Campbell, A. (1984) *Girls in the Gang*, New York, Basil Blackwell.

Campbell, A. and Gibbs, J. eds (1986) *Violent Transactions*, Oxford, Blackwell.

Campbell, B. (1988) *Unofficial Secrets*, London, Virago.

Campbell, B. (1991) 'Kings of the road' in *Marxism Today*, December.

Campbell, B. (1993) *Goliath*, London, Methuen.

Caputi, J. (1987) *The Age of Sex Crime*, Bowling Green OH, Bowling Green University Popular Press.

Carey, J. (1987) *The Faber Book of Reportage*, London, Faber.

Carlen, P. (1983) *Women's Imprisonment*, London, Routledge and Kegan Paul.

Carlen, P. (1985) *Criminal Women*, Cambridge, Polity Press.

Carlen, P. (1987) *The Cultural Construction of Sexuality*, London, Tavistock.

Carlen, P. (1988) *Women Crime and Poverty*, Milton Keynes, Open University Press.

Carlen, P. and Worrall, A. eds (1987) *Gender, Crime and Justice*, Milton Keynes, Open University Press.

Carter, C., Branston, G. and Allan, S. eds (1998) *News, Gender and Power*, London, Routledge.

CCCS (1982) *The Empire Strikes Back: Race and Racism in 70s Britain*, London, Hutchinson.

Chafe, W. and Nichols, J. eds (1986) *Evidentiality: The Linguistic Coding of Epistemology* Westport CT, Ablex Publishing.

Chapman, T. (1991) 'Gender and graduate under-employment' in Cross, M. and Payne, G., *Work and the Enterprise Culture*, London, Falmer.

Chibnall, S. (1977) *Law and Order News*, London, Tavistock.

Chomsky, N. (1989) *Necessary Illusions*, London, Pluto Press.

Christmas, L. (1997) *Chaps of Both Sexes*, Devizes, BT Forum.

Cixous, H. (1989) 'Sorties: out and out: attacks/ways out/forays' in Belsey, C. and Moore, J. eds, *The Feminist Reader*, London, Macmillan.

<clanvis.com/coalmine 11.5.99> at <http://www.clanvis.com/coalmine/colam1t/htm>.

Clark, K. (1992) 'The linguistics of blame: representations of women in the *Sun*'s reporting of crimes of sexual violence' in Toolan, M. ed., *Language, Text and Context: Essays in Stylistics*, London, Routledge.

Clarke, J. (1979) *Working Class Culture*, London, Hutchinson.

Cohen, B. (1963) *The Press and Foreign Policy*, Princeton NJ, Princeton University Press.

Cohen, S. ed. (1971) *Images of Deviance*, Harmondsworth, Penguin.

Cohen, S. (1973) *Folk Devils and Moral Panics*, London, Macgibbon and Kee.

Cohen, S. and Young, J. (1973) *The Manufacture of News: Deviance, Social Problems and the Mass Media* (1982 edition), London, Constable.

Collier, R. (1994) 'Waiting 'til father gets home: family values and the reconstruction of fatherhood in law' in *Socio-legal Studies*, 1995.

Connell, R. (1987) *Gender and Power*, Cambridge, Polity Press.

Cook, P. (1985) *The Cinema Book*, London, BFI.

Cook, T. (1979) *Vagrancy: Some New Perspectives*, London, Academic Press.

Coulter, J., Miller, S. and Walker, M. eds (1984) *State of Siege: Politics and Policing in the Coalfields*, London, Canary Press.

Cowell, D., Jones, T. and Young, J. (1982) *Policing the Riots*, London, Junction Books.

Critcher, C. (1979) 'Football since the war' in Clarke, J., *Working Class Culture*, London Hutchinson.

Cumberbatch, G. *et al.* (1986) *Television and the Miners' Strike*, London, Broadcasting Research Unit.

Cumberbatch, M. (1998) 'The Windrush years: the real story' in *Africa Centred Review*, Issue 2 June/July 1998, University of Sheffield DACE.

Cunningham, H. (1980) *Leisure in the Industrial Revolution, c.1780–c.1880*, London, Croom Helm.

Curran, J. (1990) 'The new revisionism in mass communication research: a reappraisal' in *European Journal of Communication*, 5 (2), 3 June.

Curran, J. and Seaton, J. (1991) *Power Without Responsibility*, London, Routledge.

Curry, P. (1996) 'Evaluate contemporary legislation and policy relating to deviant/different sexual practices. Referring closely to homosexuality', Cambridge, unpub. MPhil essay.

Dearing, J.W. and Rogers, E.M. (1996) *Agenda Setting*, London, Sage.

Derrida, J. (1968) 'From différance' in Easthope, A. and McGowan, K. eds (1992), *A Critical and Cultural Theory Reader*, Buckingham, Open University Press.

Derrida, J. (1976) *Of Grammatology* (trans. Spivak), London, Johns Hopkins University Press.

Dobash, R. and Dobash, R. (1992) *Women, Violence and Social Change*, London, Routledge.

Douglas, M. (1992) *Risk and Blame: Essays in Cultural Theory*, London, Routledge.

Downes, D. and Rock, P. (1988) *Understanding Deviance*, Oxford, Oxford University Press.

Du Bois, J.W. (1986) 'Self evidence and ritual speech' in Chafe, W. and Nichols, J. eds, *Evidentiality: The Linguistic Coding of Epistemology*, Westport CT, Ablex Publishing.

Dunning, E. (1982) 'The social roots of football hooliganism' in *Leisure Studies*, 1 (2).

Dunning, E., Murphy, P. and Williams, J. (1986) 'Spectator violence at football matches' in *British Journal of Sociology*, 37 (2).

Dworkin, A. (1981) *Pornography: Men Possessing Women*, London, Women's Press.

Dworkin, A. (1991) 'Against the male flood: censorship, pornography and equality' in Baird, R. and Rosenbaum, S. eds, *Pornography: Private Right or Public Menace*, Loughton, Essex, Prometheus Books.

Dyer, R. (1993) *A Matter of Images*, London, Routledge.

Dyer, R. (1997) *White*, London, Routledge.

Easthope, A. and McGowan, K. eds (1992) *A Critical and Cultural Studies Reader*, Buckingham, Open University Press.

Edwards, S. (1987) *Policing Domestic Violence*, New York, Sage.

Edwards, S. (1989) 'Policing domestic violence', paper presented at BSA conference 1989.

Edwards, S. (1990) 'Battered women who kill', *New Law Journal*, 5.

Eiser, J.R. (1978) 'Inter personal attributions' in Tajfel, H. and Fraser, C. eds, *Introducing Social Psychology*, Harmondsworth, Penguin.

Eldridge, J. (1995) *GUMG Vol. 1 News Content, Language and Visuals*, London, Routledge.

Eliot, T.S. (1938) *The Four Quartets*, London, Faber.

Ellischild, L. (1994) 'Bad girls and excessive women: the social construction of promiscuity', paper presented at BSA conference 1994.

Erickson, R.V., Banacek, P.M. and Chan, B.L. (1987) *Visualizing Deviance*, Milton Keynes, Open University Press.

Erickson, R.V., Banacek, P.M. and Chan, B.L. (1991*) Representing Order: Crime, Law and Justice in the News Media*, Milton Keynes, Open University Press.

Evans, K. (1998) *Copse: The Cartoon Book of Tree Protesting*, London, Orange Dog Productions.

Fairclough, N. (1989) *Language and Power*, London, Routledge.

Fairclough, N. (1992) 'Discourse and text: linguistic inter textual analysis within discourse analysis' in *Discourse and Society*, 3 (2).

Fairclough, N. (1995) *Media Discourse*, London, Edward Arnold.

Faludi, B. (1992) *Backlash: The Undeclared War Against Women*, London, Chatto & Windus.

Ferguson. A. (1968) 'Why Cathy has still not come home', *The Times*, 11.11.68.

Fine, B. and Millar, R. eds (1985) *Policing the Miners' Strike*, London, Lawrence and Wishart.

Foucault, M. (1967) *Madness and Civilisation*, London, Random House.

Foucault, M. (1975) *Discipline and Punish*, London, Allen Lane.

Foucault, M. (1979) *The History of Sexuality Vol. 1*, London, Penguin.

Foucault, M. (1980) *Power/Knowledge: Selected Interviews and Other Writings* (1972) New York, Pantheon.

Fowler, R. (1991) *Language in the News*, London, Routledge.

Fowler, R., Hodge, R., Kress, G. and Trew, T. (1979) *Language and Control*, London, Routledge and Kegan Paul.

Franklin, B. (1997) *Newzak and Newspapers*, London, Routledge.

Fraser, N. and Nicholson, L. (1988) 'Social criticism without philosophy: an encounter between eminism and post modernism' in Nicholson, J. ed. (1990) *Feminism/Post Modernism*, London, Routledge.

Freud, S. (1912) 'On the universal tendency to debasement in the sphere of love' in Easthope, A. and McGowan, K. eds (1992) *A Critical and Cultural Studies Reader*, Buckingham, Open University Press.

Freud, S. (1954) *The Interpretation of Dreams* (1900), London, Allen and Unwin.

Frieden, B. (1963) *The Feminine Mystique*, New York, Dell.

Fryer, P. (1984) *Staying Power: The History of Black People in Britain*, London, Pluto Press.

Fuss, D. (1991) 'Inside/out' in Fuss, D. ed. *Inside/Out*, New York, Routledge.

Galtung, J. and Ruge, M. (1965) 'Structuring and selecting news' in Cohen, S. and Young, J. (1982) *The Manufacture of News: Deviance, Social Problems and the Mass Media*, London, Constable.

Garnham, N. (1990) *Capitalism and Communication*, London, Sage.

Garratt, S. (1999) *Adventures in Wonderland*, London, Headline.

Gibbens, T.C.N. (1981) 'Female crime in England and Wales' in Adler, F. ed., *Female Criminality in the Contemporary World*, New York, New York University Press.

Gilroy, P. (1987) *There Ain't No Black in the Union Jack*, London, Hutchinson.

Glasgow University Media Group (1976) *Bad News*, London, Routledge.

Glasgow University Media Group (1980) *More Bad News*, London, Routledge and Kegan Paul.

Glasgow University Media Group (1982) *Really Bad News*, Glasgow Readers and Writers.

Glasgow University Media Group (1985) *War and Peace News*, Milton Keynes, Open University Press.

GLC (1984) *Policing London*, Police Committee Support Unit No. 13, July/August 1984.

Gledhill, C. (1978) 'Klute 1: a contemporary film noir and feminist criticism' in Kaplan, A., *Women in Film Noir*, London, BFI.

Glendenning, M. (1992) 'Is sport's writing as sick as parrot' in *British Journalism Review*, 3 (4).

Glover, D. (1984) *The Sociology of the Mass Media*, Ormskirk, Causeway Press.

Golding, P. and Middleton, S. (1982) *Images of Welfare: Press and Public Attitudes to Poverty*, Oxford, Blackwell.

Gottfredson, M. (1984) *Victims of Crime: The Dimensions of Risk*, London, HMSO.

Gramsci, A. (1971a) 'Hegemony, intellectuals and the state' from A Selection from Prison Notebooks in Storey, J. ed. (1994) *Cultural Theory and Popular Culture*, Hemel Hempstead, Harvester Wheatsheaf.

Gramsci, A. (1971b) *Selections from the Prison Notebooks*, New York, International University Press.

Grant, L. (1997) 'Romance of the road', *Guardian*, 15.2.97.

Griffin, C. (1993) *Representations of Youth: The Study of Youth and Adolescence in Britain and America*, Cambridge, Polity Press.

Griffin, C. and Littlemore, S. 'Law failing homeless people' at *Latest News* http://www.Shelter.org.uk/news/releas33.asp.

Grossberg, L. (1986) 'The deconstruction of youth' in Storey, J. ed. (1994) *Cultural Theory and Popular Culture*, Hemel Hempstead, Harvester Wheatsheaf.

Gunter, B. (1987a) *Poor Reception: Misunderstanding and Forgetting Broadcast News*, Hillsdale NJ, Lawrence Erlbaum.

Gunter, B. (1987b) *Television and the Fear of Crime*, London, Sage.

Gunter, B. and McAleer, J. (1997) *Children and Television*, London, Routledge.

Gurevitch, M., Bennett, T., Curran, J. and Woollacott, J. eds (1982) *Culture, Society and the Media*, London, Methuen.

Gurevitch, M. and Woollacott, J. eds (1977) *Mass Communication and Society*, London, Open University Press.

Hall, S. (1970) 'A world at one with itself' in Cohen S., and Young, J. eds (1982) *The Manufacture of News: Deviance, Social Problems and the Mass Media*, London, Constable.

Hall, S. (1972) 'External influences on broadcasting', stencilled occasional paper no. 4, CCCS, University of Birmingham.

Hall, S. (1973) 'Encoding/decoding' in Hall, S., Hobson, D., Lowe, A. and Willis, P. eds (1980) *Culture, Media, Language*, London, Hutchinson.

Hall, S. (1979) 'The treatment of football hooliganism in the press' in Ingham, R. ed., *Football Hooliganism: The Wider Context*, London, Inter action Imprint.

Hall, S. (1982a) 'The rediscovery of ideology' in Gurevitch, M., Bennett, T., Curran, J. and Woollacott, J. eds, *Culture, Society and the Media*, London, Methuen.

Hall, S. (1982b) 'The determination of news photographs' in Cohen, S. and Young, J. eds (1982) *The Manufacture of News: Deviance, Social Problems and the Mass Media*, London, Constable.

Hall, S. ed. (1997) *Representations: Cultural Representations and Signifying Practices*, London, Sage.

Hall, S., Critcher, C., Jefferson, T. and Clarke, J. eds (1978) *Policing the Crisis: Mugging, the State, Law and Order*, Basingstoke, Macmillan.

Hall, S., Hobson, D., Lowe, A. and Willis, P. eds (1980) *Culture, Media, Language*, London, Hutchinson.

Hall, S. and Jefferson, T. eds (1983) *Resistance Through Ritual: Youth Sub-culture in Post-war Britain*, London, Hutchinson.

Halloran, J., Elliot, P. and Murdock, G. (1970) *Demonstrations and Communication: A Case Study*, London, Penguin.

Hanmer, J., Radford, J. and Stanko, B. (1989) *Women, Policing and Male Violence*, London, Routledge.

Harding, S. (1983) 'The language of Thatcherism', occasional paper, Sheffield City Polytechnic.

Harland, R. (1987) *Superstructuralism*, London, Routledge.

Hartley, J. (1982) *Understanding News*, London, Methuen.

Hartley, J. (1996) *Popular Reality*, London, Edward Arnold.

Hartley, J. (1998) 'Juvenation: news, girls and power' in Carter, C., Branston, G. and Allan, S. eds, *News, Gender and Power*, London, Routledge.

Hartley, P. and Williams, N. eds (1990) *Technology in Human Communication*, London, Pinter.

Hartman, P. and Husband, C. (1971) 'The mass media and racial conflict' in Cohen, S. and Young, J. eds (1982) *The Manufacture of News: Deviance, Social Problems and the Mass Media*, London, Constable.

Hartsock, N. (1987) 'Foucault on power: a theory for women?' in Nicholson, L. ed. (1990) *Feminism/Post Modernism*, London, Routledge.

Harvey, D. (1989) *The Condition of Post Modernity*, Oxford, Blackwell.

Harvey, D. (1993) 'From space to place and back again: reflections on the condition of postmodernity' in Bird, J., Curtis, B., Putnam, T., Robertson, G. and Tickner, L. eds, *Mapping the Futures, Local Cultures, Global Change*, London, Routledge.

Hawkes, T. (1972) *Metaphor*, London, Methuen.

Hawkes, T. (1977) *Structuralism and Semiotics*, London, Methuen.

Hearn, J. (1986) *The Gender of Oppression: Men, Masculinity and the Critique of Marxism*, Brighton, Harvester.

Hebdige, D. (1979) *Subculture: The Meaning of Style*, London, Methuen.

Hebron, S. and Wykes, M. (1990) 'Gender inequality in mining communities' in Cross, M. and Payne, G. (1991) *Work and the Enterprise Culture*, London, Falmer.

Heidensohn, F. (1985) *Women and Crime*, London, Macmillan.

Herman, E. and Chomsky, N. (1988) *Manufacturing Consent*, New York, Pantheon.

Hite, S. (1981) *The Hite Report on Male Sexuality*, London, McDonald.

HMSO (1999) *Race and the Criminal Justice System*, Home Office Publication under section 95 of the Criminal Justice Act 1991.

Hoggart, R. (1958) *The Uses of Literacy*, London, Penguin.

Holland, P. (1998) 'The politics of the smile: "Soft news" and the sexualisation of the popular press' in Carter, C., Branston, G. and Allan, S. eds, *News, Gender and Power*, London, Routledge.

Hollingsworth, M. (1986) *The Press and Political Dissent*, London, Pluto Press.

Holway, W. (1989) *Subjectivity and Method in Psychology: Gender, Meaning and Science*, London, Sage.

Howitt, D. and Cumberbatch, G. (1975) *Mass Media Violence and Society*, London, Elek.

Husband, C. ed. (1975) *White Media and Black Britain*, London, Arrow.

Husband, C. (1978) 'Social identity and the language of race relations' in Giles, H. and Jacques, M., *Language and Ethnic Relations*, London, Macmillan.

Husband, C. (1984) *Social Identity and Race*, E3542: 5–6, Milton Keynes, Open University Press.

Hutter, B. and Williams, G. (1981) *Controlling Women. The Normal and the Deviant*, London, Croom Helm.

Inglis, F. (1990) *Media Theory. An Introduction*, Oxford, Blackwell.

Jameson, F. (1984) 'Post modernism or the cultural logic of late capitalism' in *New Left Review*, 146.

Jefferson, T. (1992) 'Wheelin' and Stealing' in *Achilles Heel*, Summer.

Jenkins, C. and Sherman, B. (1981) *The Leisure Shock*, London, Methuen.

Jones, A. (1991) *Women Who Kill*, London, Gollancz.

Jones, K. (1991) 'The limits of protest: media coverage of the Orgreave picket during the miners strike', 1984 Coal and Community Conference, Sheffield City Polytechnic.

Kaplan, A. (1978) *Women in Film Noir*, London, BFI.

Keane, J. (1991) *The Media and Democracy*, Cambridge, Polity.

Kennedy, H. (1992) *Eve Was Framed*, London, Chatto & Windus.

Kettle, M. and Hodge, R. (1982) *Uprising*, London, Pan Books.

Kidd-Hewitt, D. (1995) 'Crime and the media: a criminological perspective' in Kidd-Hewitt, D. and Osborne, R. eds, *Crime and the Media*, London, Pluto Press.

Kidd-Hewitt, D. and Osborne, R. eds (1995) *Crime and the Media*, London, Pluto Press.

Kress, G. and Hodge, B. (1979) *Language as Ideology*, London, Routledge and Kegan Paul.

Kress, G. and Van Leeuwen T. (1998) 'Front pages: the (critical) analysis of newspaper layout' in Bell, A. and Garrett, P. eds, *Approaches to Media Discourse*, Oxford, Blackwell.

Kristeva, J. (1980) *Desire in Language: A Semiotic Approach to Literature and Art*, Oxford, Blackwell.

Kristeva, J. (1988) 'Women's time' in Belsey, C. and Moore, J. eds (1989) *The Feminist Reader*, London, Macmillan.

Lacan, J. (1976) *The Language of Self* (trans. Anthony Willden 1953) Baltimore MD, Johns Hopkins University Press.

Lacan, J. (1977) *Ecrits*, London, Tavistock.

Lakoff, R. (1975) *Language and Women's Place*, New York, Harper & Row.

Lakoff, R. and Johnson, M. (1980) *Metaphors We Live By*, London, University of Chicago Press.

Lea, J. and Young, J. (1982) 'The riots in Britain 1981: urban violence and political marginalisation' in Cowell, D., Jones, T. and Young, J., *Policing the Riots*, London, Junction Books.

Lea, J. and Young, J. (1984) *What Is To Be Done About Law and Order?*, Harmondsworth, Penguin Books in association with the Socialist Society.

Leech, G. (1981) *Semantics: The Study of Meaning*, Harmondsworth, Penguin.

Lees, S. (1989) 'Naggers, whores and libbers: driving men to violence', paper presented at BSA Plymouth 1989.

Lees, S. (1993) *Sugar and Spice: Sexuality and Adolescent Girls*, London, Penguin.

Lees, S. (1995) 'Media reporting of rape: the British date rape controversy' in Kidd-Hewitt, D. and Osborne, R. eds, *Crime and the Media*, London, Pluto Press.

Levi-Strauss, C. (1958) *Structural Anthropology* (1972 edition), Harmondsworth, Penguin.

Lippman, W. (1922) *Public Opinion*, New York, Free Press.

Lombroso, C. and Ferrero, W. (1895) *The Female Offender*, New York, Appleton.

Lukes, S. (1986) *Power*, Oxford, Blackwell.

Lukes, S. (19.4.99) *Using the Homelessness Legislation* at <http://www.ris.org.uk/useleg.htm>.

McCoombs, M.E. (1981) 'Setting the agenda for agenda setting research' in Wilhoit, G. and de Bock, H. eds, *Mass Communication Review Yearbook*, 2, London, Sage.

McCoombs, M.E. and Shaw, D.L (1972) 'The agenda setting function of the mass media' in *Public Opinion Quarterly*, 36.

McGuigan, J. (1992) *Cultural Populism*, London, Routledge.

McGuigan, J. (1996) *Culture and the Public Sphere*, London, Routledge.

McGuigan, J. ed. (1997) *Cultural Methodologies*, London, Routledge.

McIntosh, M. (1988) 'Introduction to an issue: family secrets as public drama' in *Feminist Review*, 28, January.

McKenna, J. (1982) Reporting the Brixton riots' BACS Occasional Papers 1, Sheffield City Polytechnic.

Macleod, E. (1982) *Women Working: Prostitution Now*, London, Croom Helm.

McLuhan, M. (1964) *Understanding Media*, London, Routledge and Kegan Paul.

McNair, B. (1994) *News and Journalism in the UK*, London, Routledge.

McNair, B. (1996) *Mediated Sex: Pornography and Postmodern Culture*, London, Edward Arnold.

McNair, B. (1998) *The Sociology of Journalism*, London, Edward Arnold.

McRobbie, A. (1982) '"Jackie": an ideology of adolescent femininity' in Waites, B., Bennett, T. and Martin, G., *Popular Culture: Past and Present*, London, Croom Helm.

McRobbie, A. (1991) *Feminism and Youth Culture: From 'Jackie' to 'Just Seventeen'*, London, Macmillan.

McRobbie, A. (1993) 'Feminism, post modernism and the real me' in *Theory, Culture and Society*, 10.

McRobbie, A. (1997) '*More!* New sexualities in girls and women's magazines' in McRobbie, A. ed., *Back to Reality: Social Experience and Cultural Studies*, Manchester, Manchester University Press.

McRobbie, A. and Nava, M. eds (1984) *Gender and Generation*, Basingstoke, Macmillan.

Malcolmson, Robert W. (1973) *Popular Recreations in English Society, 1700–1850*, London, Cambridge University Press.

Marsh, P. (1978) *The Rules of Disorder*, London, Routledge and Kegan Paul.

Marx, K. (1970) *The German Ideology*, London, Lawrence and Wishart.

Middleton, R. and Muncie, J. (1982) *Counter Culture*, Open University Unit 18, 19, 20 Buckingham, Open University Press.

Moi, T. (1989) 'Feminist, female, feminine' in Belsey, C. and Moore, J. eds, *The Feminist Reader*, London, Macmillan.

Morley, D. (1980) *The Nationwide Audience*, London, BFI.

Morley, D. (1986) *Family Television, Cultural Power and Domestic Leisure*, London, Comedia.

Morley, D. (1990) 'The construction of everyday life' in Swanson, D. and Nimmo, D. eds, *New Directions in Political Communication*, London, Sage.

Morris, A. and Gelsthorpe, L. eds (1981) *Women and Crime*, Cambridge, Cambridge University Press.

Mulvey, L. (1975) 'Visual pleasure and narrative cinema' in Easthope, A. and McGowan, K. eds (1992) *A Critical and Cultural Studies Reader*, Buckingham, Open University Press.

Murdock, G. (1973) 'Political deviance: the press presentation of a militant demonstration' in Cohen, S. and Young, J. eds (1981) *The Manufacture of News: Deviance, Social Problems and the Mass Media*, London, Constable.

Murdock, G. (1997) 'Thin descriptions: questions of method in cultural analysis' in McGuigan, J. ed., *Cultural Methodologies*, London, Routledge.

Murdock, G. and Golding P. (1977) 'Capitalism, communication and class relations' in Gurevitch, M. and Woollacott, J. eds, *Mass Communication and Society*, London, Open University Press.

Nava, M. ed. (1997) *Buy This Book: Studies in Advertising and Consumption*, London, Routledge.

Nicholson, J. ed. (1990) *Feminism/Post Modernism*, London, Routledge.

Nietzsche, F. (1887) *On the Genealogy of Mortality*, Cambridge, Cambridge University Press.

O'Donnell, C. and Craney, J. (1982) *Family Violence in Australia*, Cheshire, Longman.

Osborne, R. (1995) 'Crime and the media: from media studies to post-modernism' in Kidd-Hewitt, D. and Osborne, R. eds, *Crime and the Media*, London, Pluto Press.

O'Sullivan, T., Dutton, B. and Rayner, P. (1994, 1998) *Studying the Media*, London, Edward Arnold.

Pateman, T. (1984) *Linguistics as a Branch of Critical Theory*, Norwich, University of East Anglia Press.

Pearson, G. (1983) *Hooligan: A History of Respectable Fears*, London, Macmillan.

Pearson, G. (1985) 'Lawlessness, modernity and social change: a historical appraisal' in *Theory, Culture and Society*, 2 (3).

Perkins R. (1991) *Working Girls*, Canberra, Australian Institute of Criminology.

Petley, J. (1997) 'Us and them' in Barker, M. and Petley, J. eds, *Ill Effects*, London, Routledge.

Pitts, J. (1986) 'Black young people and juvenile crime' in Matthews, R. and Young, J. eds *Confronting Crime*, London, Sage.

Pollak, O. (1950) *The Criminality of Women*, Philadelphia, University of Pennsylvania Press.

Poster, M. (1984) *Foucault, Marxism and History: Mode of Production v. Mode of Informat*, Cambridge, Polity.

Propp, V. (1968) *Morphology of a Folk Tale* (trans. L. Scott) Bloomington, Indiana University Press.

Rabinow, P. ed. (1984) *The Foucault Reader*, London, Penguin.

Radford, J. (1987) 'Women and policing: contradictions old and new' in Hanmer, J., Radford, J. and Stanko, E. eds, *Women, Policing and Male Violence*, London, Routledge.

Reicher, P. (1984) *The St Paul's Riots*, Chichester, Wiley.

Ricoeur, P. (1978) *The Rule of Metaphor: Multi Disciplinary Studies in the Creation of Meaning in Language*, London, Routledge and Kegan Paul.

Roberts, K. (1981) *Leisure*, London, Longman.

Rowe, D. (1992) 'Modes of Sports Writing' in Dahlgren, K. and Sparks, C. eds, *Journalism and Popular Culture*, London, Sage.

Saussure, F. (1974) *Course of General Linguistics* (trans. of *Cours de linguistiques general* 1915) London, Fontana.

Scraton, P. (1985) *The State of the Police*, London, Pluto Press.

Segal, L. (1990) *Slow Motion: Changing Masculinities, Changing Men*, London, Virago.

Segal, L. (1994) *Straight Sex: The Politics of Pleasure*, London, Virago.

Seidler, V.J. (1989) *Rediscovering Masculinity: Reason, Language and Sexuality*, London, Routledge.

Seidman, S. (1992) *Embattled Eros: Sexual Politics and Ethics in Contemporary America*, New York, Routledge.

Seldon, A. (1997) *Major: A Political Life*, London, Weidenfeld and Nicolson.

Shapland, J. and Vagg, J. (1988) *Policing by Communities*, London, Routledge.

Shelter (1996) *Homelessness: The Costs*, Leeds, Shelter.

Smart, C. (1976) *Women, Crime and Criminology*, London, Routledge and Kegan Paul.

Smart, C. (1979) 'The new female criminal: reality or myth', *British Journal of Criminology*, 19, January.

Smart, C. (1989) *Feminism and the Power of Law*, London, Routledge and Kegan Paul.

Smelser, N. (1962) *Theory of Collective Behaviour*, London, Routledge and Kegan Paul.

Sounes, H. (1995) *Fred and Rose*, London, Warner Books.

Stanko, E. (1985) *Intimate Intrusions: Women's Experience of Men's Violence*, London, Routledge and Kegan Paul.

Stanko, E. (1990) *Everyday Violence*, London, Pandora.

Stephenson, H. and Bromley, M. (1998) *Sex, Lies and Democracy: The Press and the Public*, London, Longman.

Stevenson, N. (1995) *Understanding Media Cultures*, London, Sage.

Stevenson, N. (1997) 'Media ethics and morality' in McGuigan, J. ed., *Cultural Methodologies*, London, Routledge.

Storey, J. ed. (1994) *Cultural Theory and Popular Culture*, Hemel Hempstead, Harvester Wheatsheaf.

Tajfel, H. and Fraser, C. eds (1978) *Introducing Social Psychology*, Harmondsworth, Penguin.

Tarde, G. (1907) *Les Lois de l'imitation* (5th edition), Paris, Alcan.

Taylor, A.J.P. (1970) *English History, 1914–1945*, Harmondsworth, Penguin.

Taylor, I. (1971) 'Soccer consciousness and soccer hooliganism' in S. Cohen ed., *Images of Deviance*, Harmondsworth, Penguin.

Taylor, I. (1982) 'On the sports violence question: soccer hooliganism revisited' in Hargreaves, J., *Sports, Culture and Ideology*, London, Routledge and Kegan Paul.

Taylor, I.R., Walton, P. and Young, J. (1973) *The New Criminology: For a Social Theory of Deviance*, London, Routledge.

Thatcher, M. (1995) *The Downing Street Years*, London, HarperCollins.

<theherald.co.London>(11.5.99) at
  <www.theherald.co.London/business/archive/16 10 98 23 4 15.html>

<The Scotsman.980.html> (4.5.99) at <www.yahoo.co.London/headlines/ 19990504/scotsman/scotsman980.html>

<thisisyork.co.London> (11.5.99) at
  <www.thisisyork.co.London/archive/03/york13.3.99/news2.html>

Thompson, E.P. (1970) *The Making of the English Working Class*, London, Penguin.

Thompson, J.B. (1984) *Studies in the Theory of Ideology*, Cambridge, Polity Press.

Tracy, M. and Morrison, D. (1979) *Whitehouse*, London, Macmillan.

Trew, T. (1979) 'Theory and ideology at work and linguistic variation and ideological difference: what the papers say' in Fowler, R., Hodge, B., Kress, G. and Trew, T. *Language and Control*, London, Routledge and Kegan Paul.

Tuchman, G. (1978) 'The symbolic annihilation of women by the mass media' in Cohen, S. and Young, J. eds (1982) *The Manufacture of News: Deviance, Social Problems and the Mass Media*, London, Constable.

Tudor, A. (1992) 'Them and us: story and stereotype in TV World Cup coverage' in *European Journal of Communication*, 7.

Tunstall, J. (1983) *The Media in Britain*, London, Constable.

Tunstall, J. (1996) *Newspaper Power*, Oxford, Clarendon Press.

van Dijk T. (1987) *Communicating Racism: Ethnic Prejudice in Thought and Talk*, London, Sage.

van Dijk, T. (1998) 'Opinions and ideologies in the press' in Bell, A. and Garrett, P. eds, *Approaches to Media Discourse*, Oxford, Blackwell.

Van Zoonen, L. (1994) *Feminist Media Studies*, London, Sage.

Van Zoonen, L. (1998) 'One of the girls: the changing gender of journalism' in Carter, C., Branston, G. and Allan, S. eds, *News, Gender and Power*, London, Routledge.

Volosinov, V.N. (1929) *Marxism and the Philosophy of Language* (trans. Matejka, L. and Titunik, I.R. 1973) New York and London, Seminar Press.

Waddington, D., Jones, K. and Critcher, C. (1989) *Flashpoints: Studies in Public Disorder*, London, Routledge.

Waddington, D. and Wykes, M. (1989) 'Voting with their feet' in *New Statesman and Society*, 6.1.89.

Waddington, D., Wykes, M. and Critcher, C. (1991) *Split at the Seams*, Milton Keynes, Open University Press.

Walvin, J. (1982) 'Black caricature: the roots of racism' in Husband, C. ed., *Race in Britain*, London, Hutchinson.

Watney, S. (1988) 'AIDS, moral panic theory and homophobia' in Aggleton, P. and Homans, H. eds, *Social Aspects of AIDS*, London, Falmer.

Watson, J. (1985) *What Is Communication Studies*, London, Edward Arnold.

Weedon, C. (1987) *Feminist Practice and Post Structural Theory*, Oxford, Blackwell.

Weedon, C. (1994) 'Feminism and the principles of post structuralism' in Storey, J. ed., *Cultural Theory and Popular Culture*, Hemel Hempstead, Harvester Wheatsheaf.

Weedon, C., Tolson, A. and Mort, F. (1980) 'Theories of language and subjectivity' in Hall, S. *et al.* eds, *Culture, Media, Language*, London, Hutchinson.

Weeks, J. (1981) *Sex, Politics and Society: The Regulation of Sexuality since 1800*, London, Longman.

Weeks, J. (1985) *Sexuality and Its Discontents*, London, Routledge,.

Welldon, E.V. (1988) *Mother, Madonna, Whore. The Idealisation and Denigration of Motherhood*, London, Free Association Books.

Whannel, G. (1979) 'Football crowd behaviour and the press' in *Media Culture and Society*, 1.

Wilczynski, A. (1991) 'Neonaticide', paper presented at the Perspectives on Female Violence Conference, St George's Hospital, London.

Wilczynski, A. (1995) 'Child killing by parents: social, legal and gender issues' in Dobash, R., Dobash, R. and Noaks, L. eds, *Gender and Crime*, Cardiff, University of Wales Press.

Williams, J. (1984) *Hooligans Abroad: The Behaviour and Control of English Fans in Continental Europe*, London, Routledge and Kegan Paul.

Williams, R. (1961) *The Long Revolution* (1984 reprint), Harmondsworth, Pelican.

Williams, R. (1977) *Marxism and Literature*, Oxford, Oxford University Press.

Williams, R. (1983) *Towards 2000*, London, Chatto & Windus.

Willis, P. (1977) *Learning to Labour: How Working Class Kids Get Working Class Jobs*, Farnborough, Saxon House.

Willis, P. (1978) *Profane Culture*, London, Routledge and Kegan Paul.

Wilson, D. (1969) *I Know It Was the Place's Fault*, London, Oliphants.

Wolf, N. (1991) *The Beauty Myth*, New York, Anchor Books.

Wollstonecraft, M. (1759–97) *A Vindication of the Rights of Women*, Cambridge, Cambridge University Press, 1995.

Worral, A. (1989) *Nondescript Women*, London, Routledge.

Worral, A. (1990) *Offending Women*, London, Routledge.

Wykes, M. (1991) 'Alternative reporting: how new was "News on Sunday" paper?' in *Culture Matters*, Sheffield Hallam University.

Wykes, M. (1995a) 'Accounting for Intimate Killing: The Press, Gender and Discourse', PhD thesis, University of Sheffield.

Wykes, M. (1995b) 'Passion, marriage and murder' in Dobash, R., Dobash, R. and Noaks, L. eds, *Gender and Crime*, Cardiff, University of Wales Press.

Wykes, M. (1998) 'A family affair: the British press, sex and the Wests' in Carter, C., Branston, G. and Allan, S. eds, *News, Gender and Power*, London, Routledge.

Wykes, M. (1999) 'The burrowers: news about tunnels, trees and green guerillas' in Allan, S., *Media Environment and Risk*, London, Routledge.

Wykes, M. and Cere, R. (1990) 'News and new technology' in Hartley, P. and Williams, N. eds, *The Technology of Human Communication*, London, Pinter.

Wykes, M. and Jones, K. (1994) 'Danger, desire and identity' in *Language and Discourse*, 2, September.

Wykes, M. and Woodcock, R. (1996) *Representations of Homelessness*, Leeds, TASC/Shelter.

Young, A. (1988) 'Wild women: the censure of the suffragette movement' in *International Journal of the Sociology of the Law*, 16.

Young, A. (1990) *Femininity In Dissent*, London, Routledge.

Young, A. (1991) *Feminism and the Body of Criminology*, BCC York plenary paper.

Young, A. (1996) *Imagining Crime*, London, Sage.

Young, J. (1971) 'The myth of drug-takers in the mass media' in Cohen, S. and Young, J. (1982) *The Manufacture of News: Deviance, Social Problems and the Mass Media*, London, Constable.

Index

Index compiled by Auriol Grffith-Jones